D0899271

Intergenerational Locative Play

Intergenerational Locative Play: Augmenting Family

MICHAEL SAKER
City, University of London, UK

LEIGHTON EVANS
Swansea University, Wales

United Kingdom – North America – Japan – India – Malaysia – China

Emerald Publishing Limited
Howard House, Wagon Lane, Bingley BD16 1WA, UK

First edition 2021

Reprints and permissions service
Contact: permissions@emeraldinsight.com

British Library Cataloguing in Publication Data
A catalogue record for this book is available from the British Library

ISBN: 978-1-83909-140-7 (Print)
ISBN: 978-1-83909-139-1 (Online)
ISBN: 978-1-83909-141-4 (Epub)

ISOQAR certified
Management System,
awarded to Emerald
for adherence to
Environmental
standard
ISO 14001:2004.

Certificate Number 1985
ISO 14001

INVESTOR IN PEOPLE

For Mark and Edgar

Table of Contents

About the Authors

Michael Saker is a Senior Lecturer in Media and Communications at City, University of London. His research focuses on digital media, with an emphasis on the application of mobile and locative media in daily life. More recently, his research has extended to the phenomenology of emerging augmented and virtual reality technologies. He is co-author of *Location-Based Social Media: Space, Time and Identity* (2017).

Leighton Evans is a Senior Lecturer in Media Theory at Swansea University, Wales. His research focus is on phenomenology and digital media, with interests in locative media, virtual and augmented reality, the experience of labour in data intensive environments and the subjective experience of technological implementation. He is the author of *Locative Social Media: Place in the Digital Age* (2015), *The Re-Emergence of Virtual Reality* (2018) and co-author of *Location-Based Social Media: Space, Time and Identity* (2017).

Abstract

Intergenerational Locative Play: Augmenting Family examines the social, spatial and physical impact of the hybrid reality games (HRGs) Pokémon Go on the relationship between parents and their children. The ubiquity of digital media correlates with a mounting body of work that considers the part digital technologies, such as video games, play in the lives of children. Consequently, commentators have deliberated the effects of rising levels of screen time and the association of this trend with antisocial behaviour, mental health–related problems and the interference of family life. Yet, recent studies have demonstrated that the intergenerational play of video games can, in fact, strengthen familial connections by facilitating communication between adults and children and allowing adolescents to experiment with a range of roles. Research on intergeneration play, however, has tended to focus on video games played within the domestic sphere. In contrast, locative games such as Pokémon Go involve players physically interacting and moving through their surroundings. Through an original study of Pokémon Go, then, this book extends developing research on intergenerational play to the field of locative games. In doing so, the book explores families who play locative games together through the following themes, spatial practices and mobilities, family life, social relationships and communities, and the digital economy and surveillance capitalism.

Acknowledgements

Mike. A colossal thanks go to Eryn Parker. You went above and beyond in all aspects of your role in this project. Your enthusiasm, knowledge and rigour have been pivotal to this publication. A mammoth thanks go to my friend and long-term collaborator, Leighton Evans. While the past few months have not been easy – to say the very least – I would not have known this looking at your productivity. As always, you are a force to be reckoned with. A sincere thanks go to all the participants and respondents who took the time to provide a window on their worlds. This access has been invaluable.

I would like to offer a big thanks to all of my colleagues at City, University of London. Were it not for the Pump Priming funding Leighton and I received, the research underpinning this book would not have been possible. Special thanks go to Dan Mercea, Johnny Ilan and Chris Rojek. Your comments, observations and suggestions are always appreciated. Other thanks go to Jen McCall and everyone at Emerald. I hope we get to work together again in the future. A gargantuan thanks go to my family and friends for their encouragement and support along the way. In particular, an unreserved thanks to my mum who has listened to me discuss various aspects of this book. You are endlessly appreciated.

Finally, a wholehearted thanks go to my amazing wife, Megan, and beautiful children, Una and Elliott, for providing a constant source of love, light and levity. A large chunk of this book was written during lockdown when our world suddenly became much smaller. As long as you three are in it that is all I need.

Leighton. Two people in particular deserve a huge and heartfelt acknowledgement from me for this book. Firstly, Eryn Parker for her incredible research work and diligence during the data collection and preparation for this book. It was a pleasure to work alongside Eryn and I know she will become a name to watch in this field. Secondly, the indomitable Mike Saker for taking the lead, keeping me focused and motivated and showing immense patience during the writing of this book. In a very difficult time for me personally, cheers mate barely begins to cover it.

Other thanks go to my colleagues William Merrin and Rhys Jones for their always excellent comments and suggestions, Sian Rees for all her support, Richard Thomas and Sarah Crowther for keeping an eye on me and all my colleagues at the department of Media and Communication at Swansea University. Also thanks to my parents and friends for helping me through a tough time when writing this book.

Chapter 1

Introduction: Locative Games and Intergenerational Play

This book explores how an assortment of families incorporate, integrate and utilise digital technologies on a daily basis, both within and outside of their homes. More precisely, it is a book that focuses on families who play locative games together: those games that are played in public spaces with the aid of smartphones and related applications. It considers the effect this practice might have on their mobilities, experiences of space and place and social relationships, alongside nested concerns about surveillance and the digital economy. It is, therefore, a book that examines the varied familial advantages, opportunities and threats that playing locative games might elicit for those families who do so. Importantly, it adopts the perspective of parents and the reflexive meanings they attribute to these locative interactions. To be clear, this book does not demonise digital technologies or condemn emergent forms of mobile media as eroding the sanctity of the public space. Similarly, the book does not make sweeping generalisations about the growing number of families that occupy the same physical space, while engaging in a range of digital activities explicitly disconnected from the physical setting. Instead, this book appreciates the effect of any given technology as being indicative of the assemblage within which it is configured (Latour, 2005). In other words, there is nothing intrinsic about any given media, however new or shiny it might appear, that guarantees a particular effect or outcome. Digital technologies, in this context, can lead to families spending quality time together, just as they can lead to families spending time apart.

Moving forward, then, the purpose of this introduction is to begin unpacking some of the central themes that this book engages with. First, the chapter will outline significant historical developments within the field of locative media, with questions concerning space and place dominating the agenda, and foreshadowing much of the literature surrounding locative games. Second, the chapter will examine the changing landscape of locative media from 2009 onwards and how these advancements eventually provided the necessary foundations for the next generation of locative games to emerge. Third, the chapter will provide an overview of the hybrid reality game (HRG), Pokémon Go, which exemplifies this next generation of pervasive play. At the same time, the chapter will consider the suitability of this game to intergenerational play, while underlining the need for

Intergenerational Locative Play, 1–22

Copyright © 2021 Michael Saker and Leighton Evans

Published under an exclusive licence by Emerald Publishing Limited

doi:10.1108/978-1-83909-139-120211004

research in this filed to move beyond traditional video games. Fourth, the chapter will introduce and describe the original research project that undergirds the various points, comments and observations made throughout this book. Finally, the chapter will outline an exegesis of the remainder of the book through a summary of the ensuing chapters.

1.1 Locative Media and the Centrality of Space and Place

During the early 2000s, discussions about mobile media were regularly marked by questions concerning location (Tuters & Varnelis, 2006), and for good reason. An array of digital artists and groups were frequently experimenting with the social and spatial possibilities of emergent locative media (Kabisch, 2010; Tanaka & Gemeinboeck, 2008; Wilken & Goggin, 2014), alongside their ability to 'reframe the relationship between people and spaces' (de Souza e Silva & Sheller, 2014, p. 3). Blast Theory is a key example of this trend, creating one of the first location-based games in their early work, *Can You See Me Now* (2001). In doing so, these experiments began to slowly normalise nascent locative assemblages.

At the same time, the mobile social network, Dodgeball, developed by Dennis Crowley in 2000, established that the affordances of mobile phones could create new forms of sociality in urban environments (Humphreys, 2007, 2010). Here, '[users] would post their location on Dodgeball's accompanying website and it would send out a series of SMS text messages to a defined list of friends' (Evans & Saker, 2017, pp. 4–5); producing ad hoc social interactions based on physical proximity. While Dodgeball was eventually taken over by Google in 2005, before being shut down in 2009, it nonetheless served as an important primer for the locative possibilities of more technologically advanced handsets that were on the cusp of being released.

The advancement of mobile phones around 2007, following the release of the iPhone 3GS, from devices that permitted phone calls and SMS text messages to smartphones that incorporated myriad technologies, such as global positioning system (GPS), meant these handsets could be located in concrete space (Frith, 2018). This bringing together of the physical and digital aspects of the city (Licoppe, 2016) through the mobile web (Saker & Evans, 2016) effectively allowed information technology to move beyond the desktop and into everyday urban life (McCullough, 2006), leading to what de Souza e Silva (2006) seminally describes as 'hybrid space'. As Frith (2018) explains, '[the] digital information people access in hybrid spaces is not exterior to the place; it becomes a part of that place for the user, just as a street sign or other physical informational becomes a part of a place' (p. 24).

By 2010, then, locative media had notably shifted from something artistic, obscure and specialised to something commercial, commonplace and ubiquitous (Wilken, 2012). For Wilken and Goggin (2014), '[as] mobile phones developed into fully fledged media devices, various affordances led to new kinds of sociotechnical marshalling of location' (Wilken & Goggin, 2014, p. 4). And this development can readily be observed with the advent and subsequent success of the location-based social network (LBSN), Foursquare.

Released in 2009, Foursquare permitted users to share their physical position with a defined group of 'friends' by manually 'checking in' at their current location. The affordances of this LBSN functioned in four broad ways. First, check-ins enabled users to coordinate social gatherings, as well as initiate unplanned social interactions *à la* Dodgeball – albeit in a more technologically advanced manner. Second, users were awarded points for their check-ins. Friends would, therefore, compete for the highest score at the end of the week. Likewise, users who had checked in to a site more than anyone else during a period of 60 days would become the 'mayor' of that venue. Mayorships often involved benefits that extended into the physical world, such as a free refill of coffee in participating coffee shops. Users could also receive a variety of badges if they checked in to a specified combination of locations. Third, users were able to leave reviews and 'tips' about the places that they frequented, which could be additionally furnished with images. Lastly, users' physical movements were archived by Foursquare, allowing this LBSN to function as an *aide-mémoire* (Saker & Evans, 2016).

From the time Foursquare was released, a substantial body of work has coalesced around the wider field of locative media (de Souza e Silva & Glover-Rijkse, 2020; Evans & Saker, 2017; Frith, 2018; Halegoua, 2020; Wilken, 2019). While explicit examples of locative media have changed, as we discuss later in the chapter, extant literature on earlier locative applications remains vital in signalling the kind of scholarly interests that foundationally support this field, and which continue to influence and direct related research on the next generation of locative games today (Evans & Saker, 2019; Saker & Evans, 2020). And while we do not intend on granularly unpacking the entirety of this work, as such an endeavour would surpass the scope of this chapter, it is still important to provide a more detailed overview of these interconnected areas of attention, as we will return to many of these themes in later chapters.

In the main, studies of locative media have typically considered the impact of this phenomenon on phenomenological understandings of space, place (Evans & Saker, 2017; Farman, 2016; Hamilton, 2009) and culture (Galloway & Ward, 2005; Speed, 2010) – and often from the perspective of everyday life (Hjorth, Pink, & Horst, 2018; Özkul, 2014; Saker & Evans, 2016). Research has shown that the embodied space of mobile media (Farman, 2013) can augment the urban environment (Townsend, 2008), craft new environmental experiences (Southern, 2012) and turn ordinary life 'into a game' (Frith, 2013). Likewise, location-based applications can reshape mobilities (de Lange, 2009; Lemos, 2010; McGarrigle, 2010), with pervasive play modifying the routes and pathways users take to traverse their surroundings (Saker & Evans, 2016), thus producing novel urban narratives (de Souza e Silva, 2013; Papangelis et al., 2017) and more personalised experiences of the municipal setting (Saker & Evans, 2020), which echo the Situationist's idea of the *dérive* (de Souza e Silva & Hjorth, 2009).

The digital sharing of one's location through locative media also implicates the social realm, as various studies readily corroborate (Frith, 2014; Sukto & de Souza e Silva, 2011). From this position, LBSNs can produce resourceful cultures predicated on mediated proximity (Licoppe & Inada, 2010), which facilitate serendipitous encounters (Saker & Evans, 2016), different approaches to coordinating communal interactions (Campbell & Kwak, 2011; Sutko & de Souza e Silva, 2011; Humphreys & Liao, 2013; Licoppe, 2013; Saker & Frith, 2018; Wilken, 2008) and distinctive ways of connecting with the local social situation (Frith & Saker, 2017), grounded on persistent forms co-presence (Licoppe, 2004; Ling & Horst, 2011; Rainie & Wellman, 2012) that can restructure the experience of concrete space (Campbell & Ling, 2009; Gordon, Baldwin-Philippi, & Balestra, 2013; Martin, 2014).

For other commentators, a critical aspect of locative media and its recursive archival functionality revolves around the political economy, which underpins LBSNs (Perng, Kitchin, & Evans, 2016), as well as recent HRGs like Pokémon Go. For these scholars, locative media raises pressing questions about the developing value of locative data (Evans, 2013) together with apprehensions over surveillance (Humphreys, 2011; Lemos, 2011; Santaella, 2011), and the extent to which related services have the potential to either create new forms of social control (Hemment, 2004), based on the digital reimagining of the panopticon (Zeffiro, 2006), or enact geoplaced tactics of resistance (Berry, 2008) that can disrupt top-down systems of command through collective action (Townsend, 2006).

In a similar vein, these assemblages have allowed new visual practices to emerge (Hjorth & Pink, 2014; Pink & Hjorth, 2012), as well as novel methods for getting users to reflect on the images they associate with their LBSN check-ins (Wilken & Humphreys, 2019). To this end, Hjorth & Pink's (2014) notion of the 'digital wayfarer' provides a helpful toolbox to comprehend the mobile media user who not only ambulates her environment following different pathways, but who does so while creating congruent visualities through the camera functionality of smartphones, signalling a shift from 'networked visuality to emplaced visuality and sociality' (Pink & Hjorth, 2012) that both shape, and are shaped by, 'intimate cartographies of place' (Hjorth, 2013).

To a lesser extent, locative media has been inspected from the viewpoint of identity construction (Schwartz & Halegoua, 2014) with the marking of one's whereabouts through LBSNs like Foursquare effectively empowering users to present their identity via the inscription of space (Saker, 2016). Consequently, territoriality has become a central concept in understanding LBSN usage (Papangelis et al., 2020), with locative applications allowing distinctive revealings of place to materialise (Evans, 2015; Saker, 2017). Equally, the documenting of mobilities through LBSN as an aide-mémoire (Saker & Evans, 2016) can disrupt the relationship between time and place (Speed, 2011, 2012) and permit users to algorithmically exchange archived mobilities for future locative suggestions (Evans & Saker, 2017).

In short, while locative media has evidently implicated a range of interests, issues and concerns, the most impactful and enduing area of circumspection remains notions of space and place, followed by sociality, and matters pertaining to the digital economy and the use of personal data in the context of surveillance. And these are the central themes that underpin much of this book. Yet, this brief literature review still does not account for the emergence of recent locative games like Pokémon Go. In the following section, then, we explore how the waning popularity of LBSNs and explicit locative applications towards the end of 2013 ultimately provided the necessary foundation for the next generation of locative games to surface.

1.2 The Evolution of Locative Media

By 2014, Foursquare was in the midst of a deep identity crisis. The company had decided to separate its social side – the side where users would share their location with friends by 'checking in' – from its locative side – the side where users would provide reviews about particular locations, such as restaurants or bars. The latter kept the original Foursquare name, while the former was rebranded, Swarm. As Frith and Wilken (2019) explain, this decision was 'in part because those [social] elements were difficult to monetise and because of shifting end-user interest in and engagement with features' (p. 144). To a certain extent, this rebranding was in vain. Swarm was riddled with technical issues and simply could not recreate the same social appeal that had made Foursquare the most popular commercial LBSN to date. In fact, the only thing swarming during this period was the growing number of analysts proclaiming the death of locative media and detailing the various companies whose legacy would soon revolve around a very short-lived period in the annals of digital culture (Walsh, 2020).

In reality, of course, the evolution and development of locative media is more complex, convoluted and enduring than this reductive narrative suggests (Evans & Saker, 2017). While applications such as 'Gowalla (bought by Facebook and then closed), SCVNGR, Loopt, Sonar and Rummble' (Evans & Saker, 2017, p. 2) seemingly vanished as quickly as they appeared, for the most part, we attribute this trajectory to the limited affordances of earlier locative services. Though the 'check-in' functionality, synonymous with the likes of Foursquare, and more broadly, LBSNs, was an important development in the context of smartphones and hybrid space (de Souza e Silva, 2006), its value soon dwindled as the novelty of this feature failed to find its 'killer app'. It would be wrong, however, to label locative media as being a 'failure' or resigning earlier applications to the realm of 'dead media'. '"Dead" would obviously imply no longer active but the evidence is that both the form and the data of LBSN continue to play important roles in the social and digital media environments' (Evans & Saker, 2017, p. 69).

Today, the digital marking of location is no longer something that stands out as particularly innovative or revolutionary but rather a well-established, and often backstage, feature of social media behemoths like Facebook, Twitter and Instagram, as well as a central element of surveillance capitalism (Zuboff, 2015). Indeed, '[every] day, tens of millions of mobile users navigate and way-find using mobile maps that pinpoint their location' (Wilken & Goggin, 2014, p. 1). As the following vignettes demonstrate:

> In Helsinki, a family plays *Angry Birds* together, as the app gathers information on their location via the smartphone and its location technologies and sensors … In rural United States, a child calls 911 emergency services for help, and the ambulance is dispatched using the location information available via their absent parents' phone. (Wilken & Goggin, 2014, p. 1)

Claims about the death of locative application, then, are not so much symptomatic of the disappearance of locative media *per se*, but counterintuitively the ubiquity of location as a recursive function of mobile media. In other words, the locative affordances of earlier locative media have been reabsorbed into the broader digital economy. As Evans & Saker (2017) put it, locative media has become an example of 'zombie' media. 'We now see that the form and function of LBSN, and the data residues of LBSN, are informing the development of other, new services and platforms' (Evans & Saker, 2017, p. 95). Consequently, these '[locative] features of digital media ... have changed from visible location-driven aspects of user interfaces, such as check-in features and location badges, toward more inconspicuous ways of relating to location through automated backend processes' (Erdal, Øie, Westlund, & Oppegaard, 2019, p. 166). Yet, it would be wrong to suggest *all* locative services have followed this fate. As Frith and Wilken's (2019) analysis of Yelp and Foursquare demonstrates, some companies have successfully adapted to this changing landscape.

Around the same time that Foursquare released the ill-fated Swarm, the organisation made a number of sagacious decisions that would eventually see the company amass over $100 million in revenue (Walsh, 2020). First, it moved its social aspect to Swarm and continued to function as a 'search and recommendations service' (Frith & Wilken, 2019, p. 134). Second, it began selling its vast data to countless groups and organisations, including 'brands, marketers, advertisers and data-hungry investors' (Walsh, 2020), while 'charging developers for the use of its location technology in their own apps (it has worked with more than 150,000 to date)' (Walsh, 2020). As Frith and Wilken (2019) explain, Foursquare's Pilgrim software and Places API are integral parts of 'tens of thousands of apps, sites and interfaces' (p. 141), including the likes of Twitter, Tinder and Uber. And let us not forget that Foursquare still gathers locative data on its users. Whereas this was once performed through manual 'check-ins', today this information is passively gathered, backstage, in accordance with users' privacy setting. Equally, foursquare continues to experiment with the possibilities of locative data. This can be readily be seen with its 'hypertrending' feature showcased to attendees during SXSW 2019 that provided users with a real-time heat map of Austin, Texas, when it transformed their handsets into anonymised blips on a live map (Walsh, 2020).

In short, Foursquare very much continues to impact experiences of space and place, much like it always did. Only now the impact of this reshaping is multiplied by the, '[many] apps [that] ... rely on Foursquare's location data' (Frith & Wilken, 2019, p. 144). As Frith and Wilken (2019) put it, 'spatial data are more valuable than ever before' (p. 134). While these two complementary understandings of the evolution of locative media as either 'zombie media' – with the mainstreaming of locative features into the broader media environment – or 'adaptive media' – with services like Yelp and Foursquare, successfully navigating 'the fluctuating demands of end-users within a complicated, competitive and continuously evolving geomedia ecosystem' (Frith & Wilken, 2019, p. 133) – are helpful in understanding how applications of locative media have changed, a more critical engagement with the advancement of pervasive play, and locative games is required at this juncture.

1.3 Locative Games and Intergenerational Play

The conceptual picture painted above would seem to imply that ludic interactions with locative media have dissipated as the social and playful function of this media has been surpassed by its monetary value in other areas. In reality, of course, the story of locative play does not end there. Just as Foursquare survived the mass extinction of earlier locative application, the logic of pervasive play similarly persists. Here, our understanding of 'zombie media' extends beyond the normalising effect of locative affordances within the 'geo media ecosystem' (Frith & Wilken, 2019), or the adaptability of certain services; more specifically, the legacy of seminal LBSNs created the necessary conditions for a new generation of locative games to eventually emerge that have – partially at least – overcome some of the problems associated of earlier applications. This new generation of locative games have – outwardly at least – created richer gamic experiences that forge more compelling bridges between the physical and digital aspects of contemporary life (Evans & Saker, 20198). We are, of course, talking about Pokémon Go.

Launched in July 2016, Pokémon Go has been downloaded more than one billion times (Fingas, 2019), and is still played by five million people across the world on a daily basis. In other words, it is a global phenomenon. 'In contrast to earlier HRGs like Mogi (2004), as well as LBSNs like, Pokémon Go is an augmented reality (AR) application' (Evans & Saker, 2019, p. 1). Nonetheless, following a similar logic to earlier locative games, Pokémon Go involves players traversing a game space that is both physical and digital. Through the GPS and the gyroscope built into contemporary smartphones, the physical and digital aspects of this gamic experience are visually merged. 'Players are presented with a digital representation of their immediate surroundings that has been augmented with the superimposition of Pokémon' (Evans & Saker, 2019), even if it is 'a bit crude in phenomenological terms' (Licoppe, 2017, p. 2).

Though later chapters will reveal the complexity of this game, on the surface at least, and for the purposes of this brief introduction, the aim of Pokémon Go is simple enough (Evans & Saker, 2019). Players must discover and then capture Pokémon by venturing out into the streets.

> These Pokémon can be found in locations throughout the world, and areas of interest in the game are mapped on to real locations of interest such as landmarks, historic buildings and public art displays. (Tran, 2018, p. 114)

Once a Pokémon has been discovered, the process of capturing it involves throwing a 'Poke ball' in its general direction through the AR functionality of the application. If the player is successful, the Pokémon will then be under their control. Beyond the central aim of this HRG, and its apparent simplicity, lies a number of important features that testify to the richer gamic experience on offer.

These features include (1) PokéStops, (2) Poké balls, (3) Gyms, (4) Community Days, (5) Field Research tasks and (6) Raids. PokéStops are the sites players can gather items, such as eggs, which can hatch valuable Pokémon, and Poke balls, which can be used to capture Pokémon. PokéStops are normally situated around noteworthy physical places, for example historical sites, monuments and art installations. In contrast, Gyms are the sites where players can improve the battling potential of their Pokémon as well as battle another players' Pokémon. Equally, players can trade collected Pokémon. Community Days take place every month on a designated day, when a particular Pokémon will appear more often than usual for an allotted three-hour period. Likewise, once a month

> …there are a number of Field Research tasks available, which are basically quests you obtain by spinning PokéStops. By completing enough of these tasks, [players] achieve a Research Breakthrough to encounter a legendary Pokémon. (Wilson, 2020)

Lastly, Raids are difficult battles with large Pokémon that occur at gyms, and commonly require a team of players in order to defeat the 'boss' Pokémon, with these Pokémon changing once a month.

Game features to one side, Pokémon Go has been the subject of many media stories since its release. Resonating with the dialectical commentary that customarily surrounds new technology (Humphreys, 2017; Marvin, 1988), alongside the spatial focus of locative media studies, the popular press has tended to either celebrate or critique the spatial impact of this HRG. Almost immediately after its release

> …[stories] circulated about players going to inappropriate places such as the Holocaust Museum or an old church that has been turned into a private home to capture Pokémon and play against others. (Humphreys, 2017, pp. 15–16)

Similarly, stories surfaced involving players unwittingly putting themselves in physical danger by focussing on the digitality of their smartphones at the expense of the materiality of their surrounding (Frank, 2016; Rosenberg, 2016). This trend eventually culminated in the first reported Pokémon Go death linked to player negligence (Soble, 2016). The implicit suggestion, then, has been that '[the] game had made [players] a menace both to themselves and to those around them' (Humphreys, 2017, p. 16). Nevertheless, these adverse stories have been somewhat tempered by reports of Pokémon Go producing genuine human-to-human interaction' (Wawro, 2016) as well as reinvigorating previously underused public spaces (Perry, 2016). As Mäyrä (2017) optimistically suggests, Pokémon Go

> …encourages people to play … out in the open, visiting public spaces in order to make use of their PokeStops, or to openly engage in Pokémon gym battles, in the city streets and squares. (p. 1)

Moving forward, two themes can be identified in the surrounding literature. First, the cultural significance of Pokémon Go seemingly revolves around the effect this HRG can have on daily life (de Souza e Silva, 2017). Second, Pokémon

Go superficially offers a new kind of experience that markedly differs from other digital games (Evans & Saker, 2019). While the first point seems self-evident, the second implication is more complicated (Licoppe, 2017). As our brief historical account of key developments within locative media demonstrates, '[for] at least 15 years, researchers and artists have experimented with the affordances of location-based technology to create playful experiences that take place across physical and digital (hybrid) spaces' (de Souza e Silva, 2017, p. 21). That is, the confluence of the physical and digital space underpinning Pokémon Go has a lengthy history (see de Souza e Silva & Frith, 2010; Evans, 2015; Evans & Saker, 2017; Wilken, 2012), with related studies examining the influence locative media has had on urban mobilities (de Souza e Silva & Sutko, 2008; Ling & Campbell, 2009; Gordon et al., 2013), sociability (Campbell & Kwak, 2011; Wilken, 2008) and experiences of place (Frith & Saker, 2017; Saker & Evans, 2016). As a corollary to this, themes pertaining to 'mobility, sociability and spatiality' (de Souza e Silva, 2017, p. 21) have dictated much of the literature on Pokémon Go (Mäyrä, 2017).

More relevant to this book, however, is research that has shed a light on the broader range of players that engage with this game (Evans & Saker, 2019), such as families of all ages. And the familial scope of Pokémon Go has not gone unnoticed by other scholars. Existing studies have explored this HRG in the familial context of physical activity (Lindqvist, Castelli, Hallberg, & Rutberg., 2018), health (Das, Zhu, McLaughlin, Bilgrami, & Milanaik, 2017), the parental challenges this experience might produce (Serino, Cordrey, McLaughlin, & Milanaik, 2016), as well as the perception parents have of the game itself (Sobel et al., 2017). While this body of work unquestionably expands knowledge about the social, spatial and physical effects of Pokémon Go, beyond a handful of studies (see Sobel et al., 2017) there is very little research that specifically examines this HRG through the lens of intergenerational play, or/and joint media engagement (JME), in relation to locative media, which forms the exigency of this book. Given the design of Pokémon Go and the extent to which the affordances of this HRG seemingly lend themselves to familial play, this gap is noteworthy.

To begin with, Pokémon Go is the technological development of a mid-1990s computer game that was – and continues to be – hugely popular throughout the world. Consequently, many parents – particularly younger parents – are very likely to have experienced Pokémon, in some form, digital or otherwise, at some point in their lives, and may, therefore, appreciate the prospect of playing Pokémon Go as providing the potential for nostalgia (Keogh, 2017). Second, the technological ability to engage with this HRG is predicated on users owning a smartphone. Though young children might not own a smartphone or have unsupervised access to the mobile web, they are likely to have heard about the game itself. For many children, then, the ability to play this HRG will be reliant upon their parents, with access typically involving some form of co-mobility, co-play and supervision (Evans & Saker, 2019). Third, the gamic experience of Pokémon Go explicitly offers a form of 'distributed imagination' (Giddings, 2017). At a phenomenological level, it encourages players 'to adopt an "as-if" structure of experience, moving through the environment "as if" it was game terrain or an urban playground' (Hjorth & Richardson, 2017, p. 5). From this position, physical space is intimately involved in the development of the game world (de Souza e Silva, 2006; Evans & Saker, 2017; Frith, 2013), which resonates with childhood and its proclivity for imaginative play. Fourth, because of the locative aspect of Pokémon Go, it outwardly avoids some of the negative connotations associated with rising levels of screen time. This knowledge might, therefore, prompt some parents to be more open to playing Pokémon Go with their children. Finally, as a consequence of the digital economy, Pokémon Go is free to download (Jin, 2017). In sum, then, Pokémon Go represents a relatively low-cost activity that involves physical exploration, and which can provide space for families to spend time together.

At the same time, and symptomatic of the points made above, Pokémon Go is equally significant to the field of intergenerational play. As Aarsand (2007) helpfully outlines, research suggests that children are gradually moving away from the streets (Zelizer, 1985) and turning towards their homes and bedrooms (Livingstone, 2002). Of course, a marked feature of the domestic sphere in today's world is the prevalence and prominence of digital technologies (Costa & Veloso, 2016, p. 43; see also Bunz, 2012; De Schutter, Brown, & Vanden Abeele, 2014). For our purposes, an important part of this development is the mounting presence of games consoles. While video games are played alone by countless young children, research also suggests a rising number of families now play these games together (Siyahhan & Gee, 2018). And this practice can have a number of benefits. For many academics and practitioners alike, gaming can facilitate social interactions between younger and older generations (Costa & Veloso, 2016; Siyahhan & Gee, 2018), which is important. As Siyahhan and Gee (2018) outline, the co-playing of video games can strengthen familial connections, reinforce shared bonds, allow adolescents to experiment with different roles and initiate conversations between different age groups that would not have otherwise happened. Equally, and more importantly for the purposes of this book, it is also apparent that the kind of games commonly explored through the lens of intergenerational play are normally played within the home. In contrast, and as detailed above, locative games, such as Pokémon Go, implicate a very different experience that explicitly involves players physically interacting and moving through their surroundings. It is, therefore, our contention that Pokémon Go might permit a different kind of intergenerational play that could extend familial relationships through emerging mobilities and developing socio-spatial relationships. In the following section, then, we introduce and describe the original research project that these claims are grounded on.

1.4 The Original Research Project behind This Book

The chief intention of this book is to draw together two important lines of research: studies on the physical, spatial and social impact of Pokémon Go, alongside studies on video games from the vantage point of those families that play them together. To reiterate, this kind of experience is very different to the kind of games commonly interrogated through the lens of intergenerational play. Not only does Pokémon Go facilitate, motivate and prompt co-playing between parents and children, it does so within the physical flows of public environments

(Evans & Saker, 2019). In doing so, this markedly under researched form of locative play can strengthen familial connections and reinforce shared bonds in a variety of ways (Sobel et al., 2017), while offering a counterpoint to the suggestion many adolescents have now moved out of the streets (Zelizer, 1994) and into their bedrooms (Livingstone, 2002). Likewise, it is equally our contention that the digital economy underpinning this form of gameplay (Jin, 2017), and with it the gathering of personal data, presents a new range of challenges for parents to work through that exceeds the kind of concerns commonly associated with video games that are situated within the domestic sphere.

By drawing on established approaches to locative media, alongside developed frameworks for approaching intergenerational play, then, this book offers an updated comprehension of a new generation of locative media that are marked by absorbing, compelling and durable experiences that extend the connection between digital devices, location and play. The following chapters will explore these themes in more detail through an original study of an assortment of parents who play Pokémon Go with their children. While this project was primarily conducted between August 2019 and November 2019, we have included two interviews that were conducted in 2017. In the context of the research conducted in 2019, this encompasses two distinct phases, as detailed below.

The first phase involved an online survey in Qualtrics that explored the impact of parents who play Pokémon Go with their children in the context of space, place, sociality and intergenerational play. Following ethical approval, respondents were recruited through relevant Facebook groups that revolved around Pokémon Go. The survey explored the following questions: What rules are established to govern the co-playing of Pokémon Go? Do your child/children ever ask you to play Pokémon Go at times when they cannot join in? What roles do you and your child/children adopt while playing Pokémon Go? What impact might this game have on the relationship with your child/children? What are the benefits of playing Pokémon Go with your child/children? What fears or concerns do you have about this kind of game? What knowledge is shared between you and your child/children?

The survey received 351 responses from parents across the world who played Pokémon Go with their children. 142 respondents were from the United States of America, 78 from the United Kingdom of Britain and Northern Ireland, 20 from Canada, 15 from Australia, 2 from Ireland, 1 from Malaysia, 1 from New Zealand, 1 from Uruguay. 106 were between 35 and 44, 84 were between 25 and 34, 46 were between 45 and 54, 15 were between 55 and 64, 9 were between 18 and 24, 3 were between 65 and 74 and 1 was 85 or older. 217 identified as female, 55 identified as male and 1 preferred not to say. 235 were white, 11 were Asian, 10 preferred to self-describe, 6 preferred not to say, 3 were American Indian or Alaska Native, 3 were Native Hawaiian or Pacific Islander, 2 were black or African American. Children per household ranged from 1 to 6.

The second phase involved 24 semi-structured interviews with parents who play Pokémon Go with their children. This second phase allowed us to gain rich qualitative information about key insights taken from our online survey. Here, we employed purposeful sampling to recruit a diverse range of participants. Again, participants were identified and recruited through relevant Facebook groups that revolve around Pokémon Go. 15 participants were from the United States, 7 from the United Kingdom and 2 from Canada. The age of participants ranged from 26 to 59. 16 identified as female and 9 identified as male. Children per household ranged from 1 to 5. In the main, interviews lasted for roughly one hour and were conducted over Skype. Initial interviews were used to further develop the questions underpinning this phase of the research. Interviews were transcribed as the project progressed.

Following the transcription of all interviews, alongside the ordering of open-ended survey responses, a period of post-research thematic analysis commenced. Throughout this period, we used the qualitative data analysis computer software package, NVivo. Once our data had been uploaded to NVivo, it was read and reread before meaningful sections of text were highlighted and nodes added in accord with the underlying interests of the study. We revisited these materials, while continuing to develop and refine our code. All coded material was organised into broader themes relating to different chapters of the book. Closed-end survey responses were analysed through Qualtrics' reporting tool.

The remainder of this chapter will be spent outlining the structure of the book.

1.5 Structure of the Book

Chapter 2 is concerned with examining the families that play Pokémon Go together within the context of spatial practices. The chapter begins by outlining the general approach to spatiality that we adopt throughout this book, which is predicated on the 'spatial turn' within the social sciences (Soja, 2008). Here, spatial practices are understood as being socially constructed (de Certeau, 1984; Lefebvre, 1974/1991) in day-to-day lives, as opposed to being something simply given. In other words, 'the *concept* of the city' and the 'urban *fact*' (de Certeau, 1984, p. 1, italics in original) are not one and the same thing. Instead, the phenomenology of space is moulded in the social realm as part of the *practice of everyday life*, which has consequences for HRGs like Pokémon Go. After delineating between 'space' and 'place' *à la* the 'mobilities turn' (Sheller, 2014), we shift our attention to embodied approaches to urban life. This begins with an examination of the art of the *flânerie* (Baudelaire, 1964/1863; Benjamin, 1983, 1999[1927]), which has been reimagined to account for the ubiquity of mobile media – i.e. Luke's (2005) 'phoneur' – and more recently, locative games – i.e. Saker and Evans' (2016) 'playeur'. A review of the literature surrounding locative games demonstrates that, for the most part, concerns about spatiality have not extended to the kind of intergenerational play that is the focus of this book. Drawing on our original study of Pokémon Go, as outlined above, then, the chapter is driven by the following research questions. First, to what extent does Pokémon Go lead to families spending more time outside, and how is this reshaping experienced. Second, what effect does this HRG have on the routes and pathways families choose to follow while traversing their physical setting, as well as the sites they frequent. Third, to what extent do families engage with the various elements of Pokémon Go, and what does this suggest about the evolution of locative play in the context of earlier LBSNs.

Chapter 3 is concerned with exploring the various ways in which Pokémon Go complements or challenges family life. The chapter begins by explicating the multisided concept of play and the myriad definitions that surround this term (Duncan, 2015; Eberle, 2014). Having established the various ways in which this phenomenon can improve the lives of those who engage in it – physically (Burdette & Whitaker, 2005; Hart, 2002), emotionally (Barros, Silver, & Stein, 2009), cognitively (Ginsburg, 2007) and socially (Blurton Jones, 1972) – we go on to consider how play has gradually shifted from public spaces and into designated playgrounds (Agate, Agate, Liechty, & Cochran, 2018; Chudacoff, 2007; Frost, 2010; Gray, 2009; Mintz, 2004), and how this trend corresponds with children concurrently moving away from the streets and into their bedrooms Livingstone, 2002). Following this, we explore the impact digital technologies are having on the practice of parenting (Takeuchi, 2011), paying particular attention to video games as a significant facet of youth culture (Aarsand, 2007; Siyahhan & Gee, 2018) that is often associated with a range of negative connotations (see Sobel et al., 2017). Yet, video games are not intrinsically bad. As we outline, research on intergenerational play and JME readily demonstrate the many benefits families can experience when these games are played together (Siyahhan & Gee, 2018). What is missing from this developing body of work is more research on the familial playing of locative games, and the extent to which this practice adds contours to our understanding of this field. The chapter is, therefore, driven by the following research questions. First, why and how do families play Pokémon Go? This includes the different roles that family members adopt, alongside motivations for families playing this game, how the playing of this game complements the rhythms of family life and the extent to which this HRG is suited to intergenerational play. Second, what impact does locative familial play have on families, collectively speaking, and regarding individual family members? Here, we are not just interested in whether this game allows families to bond and how this bonding process is experienced, but also whether the familial play of Pokémon Go provides families with any learning opportunities that might facilitate personal growth beyond the game. Third, what worries might parents have about the familial playing of Pokémon Go and to what extent does the locative aspect of this game reshape their apprehensions?

Chapter 4 is concerned with the social relationships and communities that families engage with while playing Pokémon Go. The chapter begins by considering the release of this HRG in the summer of 2016 (Wong, 2016), and the extent to which it seemingly lends itself to communities and the development of social relationships through play (Kaczmarek, Misiak, Behnke, Dziekan, & Guzik, 2017; Hjorth & Richardson, 2017). Following this, we demonstrate that while the evidence for Pokémon Go facilitating new relationships is apparent (Bonus, Peebles, Mares, & Sarmiento, 2018; Paasovaara, Jarusriboonchai, & Olsson, 2017; Vella et al., 2019), the *kind* of relationships in question are not explicitly explicated through extant literature. Accordingly, we develop the theoretical framework that undergirds the exigency of the chapter. This includes Granovetter's (1973) taxonomy of social ties among people in social networks – strong, weak and latent ties – and the suggested effect these categories have on the sharing of information. Having outlined the implication of this taxonomy for comprehending social relationships forged through Pokémon Go, we introduce Gerbaudo's (2012) 'liquid organising' to explore how weak ties have been enhanced through social media, which raises pertinent question in the context of familial locative play. Critically, then, this chapter looks to understand what kind of social ties can be formed when the playing of Pokémon Go is itself performed in the context of the family unit, using the theoretical frameworks outlined above. This chapter is driven by the following research questions. First, what kinds of social relationships have developed for the families that play Pokémon Go together? This includes whether intergenerational players have made new friends as well as strengthened current relationships. Second, has this HRG facilitated friendships for the children that play Pokémon Go? In other words, is a community of players still a salient feature of playing this HRG, in the same way that it was shortly after its release in the Summer 2016?

Chapter 5 is concerned with examining Pokémon Go in light of the digital economy and surveillance capitalism. The chapter begins by developing the theoretical framework underpinning this undertaking, which includes Bauman and Lyon (2013) 'liquid surveillance' and Zuboff's (2019) 'surveillance capitalism'. Following this, we outline the various implications involved in the playing of Pokémon Go, when the production of locative data is not framed as leisure but labour. While Pokémon Go might be suited to the machinations of surveillance capitalism (Zuboff, 2019), as we establish, little research has examined this topic from the position of familial locative play or JME. As a corollary to this, then, one of the aims of this chapter is to understand how issues of surveillance are perceived by the parents who play this HRG with their children. Consequently, the chapter is driven by the following research questions. First, are families cognisant of the data they produce by playing this HRG and how this data might be used? Second, do families think critically about the gamic mechanics of this HRG, such as the spawning locations of Pokémon, and the reasoning behind these decisions? Third, are participants concerned about the potential application of their gamic data, and if so, how are these concerns reconciled? Fourth, do participants use the familial playing of Pokémon Go as an opportunity to discuss the production of data and its multifaced uses with their children?

This chapter reiterates the conclusions drawn on Pokémon Go in the context of intergenerational play. We begin by reflecting on the exigency of this book, before summarising our key findings under the following headings: (1) spatial activity and cognisance, (2) familial rhythms and digital labour, (3) playful bonding and 'non-confrontational spaces', (4) personal development and cursory connections, (5) familial challenges and concerns, (6) surveillance and the game beneath the game. Importantly, these findings are discussed in a manner that extends beyond the specificity of Pokémon Go. That is to say, our findings are used to establish how the next generation of locative games differs from the previous generations. Here, we pay particular attention to the various ways this current generation is predicated on a more dynamic digital architecture than earlier locative games and LBSNs. Accordingly, this section is critical in terms of both surveying the area as it stands and positioning the current project in the canon of both locative media and intergenerational play. Moving forward, we reflect on how the experience of playing Pokémon Go has changed to accommodate the social restrictions put in place to help combat the COVID-19 global pandemic (Byford, 2020a, 2020b; Orland, 2020; Takahashi, 2020). In particular, this section highlights the adaptability of current HRGs such as Pokémon Go in the wider field of locative games. Finally, this section looks to the future by deliberating how Pokémon Go might continue to develop in a COVID-19 world, and what these developments might suggest about our approach to environments that increasingly feel at odds with the notion of play.

References

Aarsand, P. A. (2007). Computer and video games in family life: The digital divide as a resource in intergenerational interactions. *Childhood, 14*(2), 235–256.

Agate, J. R., Agate, S. T., Liechty, T., & Cochran, L. J. (2018). 'Roots and wings': An exploration of intergenerational play. *Journal of Intergenerational Relationships, 16*(4), 395–421.

Barros, R. M., Silver, E. J., & Stein, R. E. K. (2009). School recess and group classroom behavior. *Pediatrics, 123*, 431–436. doi:10.1542/peds.2007-2825

Bauman, Z., & Lyon, D. (2013). *Liquid surveillance: A conversation*. Hoboken, NJ: John Wiley & Sons.

Berry, M. (2008). Locative media: Geoplaced tactics of resistance. *International Journal of Performance Arts and Digital Media, 4*(2–3), 101–116.

Benjamin, W. (1983). In H. Zohn (Trans.), *Charles Baudelaire: A lyric poet in the era of high capitalism*. London: Verso.

Benjamin, W. (1999[1927]). In H. Eiland & K. McLaughlin (Trans.), The arcades project. Cambridge, MA; London: Harvard University Press.

Blurton Jones, N. (1972). Categories of child-child interaction. *Ethological studies of child behavior*, 97–127.

Bonus, J. A., Peebles, A., Mares, M. L., & Sarmiento, I. G. (2018). Look on the bright side (of media effects): Pokémon Go as a catalyst for positive life experiences. *Media Psychology, 21*(2), 263–287.

Bunz, U. (2012). Revisited: Communication media use in the grandparent/grandchild relationship. *Journal of Community Informatics, 8*(1).

Burdette, H. L., & Whitaker, R. C. (2005). A national study of neighborhood safety, outdoor play, television viewing, and obesity in preschool children. *Pediatrics, 116*, 657–662. doi:10.1542/peds.2004-2443

Byford, S. (2020a). Pokémon Go adds remote raids so you don't have to go outside. *The Verge*. Retrieved from https://www.theverge.com/2020/4/15/21221659/pokemon-go-remote-raid-passes-coronavirus. Accessed on June 24, 2020.

Byford, S. (2020b). Tickets for the online-only Pokémon Go Fest 2020 go on sale today. *The Verge*. Retrieved from https://www.theverge.com/2020/6/15/21291244/pokemon-go-fest-2020-events-details-ticket-price. Accessed on June 24, 2020.

Campbell, S., & Kwak, N. (2011). Mobile communication and civil society: Linking patterns and places of use to engagement with others in public. *Human Communication Research, 37*, 207–222.

Campbell, S. W., & Ling, R. (2009). Effects of mobile communication. In M. B. Oliver, A. A. Raney, & J. Bryant (Eds.), *Media effects: Advances in theory and research* (pp. 592–606), New York, NY: Routledge.

de Certeau, M. (1984). *In S. Rendell (Trans.), The practice of everyday life*. Berkeley; Los Angeles, CA: University of California Press.

Chudacoff, H. P. (2007). *Children at play: An American history*. New York, NY: NYU Press.

Costa, L., & Veloso, A. (2016). Being (grand) players: Review of digital games and their potential to enhance intergenerational interactions. *Journal of Intergenerational Relationships, 14*(1), 43–59.

Das, P., Zhu, M. O., McLaughlin, L., Bilgrami, Z., & Milanaik, R. L. (2017). Augmented reality video games: New possibilities and implications for children and adolescents. *Multimodal Technologies and Interaction, 1*(2), 8.

De Schutter, B., Brown, J. A., & Vanden Abeele, V. (2015). The domestication of digital games in the lives of older adults. *New Media & Society, 17*(7), 1170–1186.

Duncan, P. A. (2015). Pigs, plans, and Play-Doh: Children's perspectives on play as revealed through their drawings. *American Journal of Play, 8*(1), 50–73.

Eberle, S. (2014). The elements of play: Toward a philosophy and a definition of play. *American Journal of Play, 6*(2), 214–233.

Erdal, I. J., Øie, K. V., Westlund, O., & Oppegaard, B. (2019). Invisible locative media: Key considerations at the nexus of place and digital journalism. *Media and Communication, 7*(1), 166–178.

Evans, L. (2013). How to build a map for nothing: Immaterial labour and location-based social networking. In G. Lovink, & M. Rasch (Eds.), *Unlike us reader: Social media monopolies and their alternatives (pp. 189–199). (Unlike Us)*. Amsterdam: Institute of Network Cultures.

Evans, L. (2015). *Locative social media: Place in the digital age*. Basingstoke: Springer.

Evans, L., & Saker, M. (2017). *Location-based social media: Space, time and identity*. Cham: Springer.

Evans, L., & Saker, M. (2019). The playeur and Pokémon Go: Examining the effects of locative play on spatiality and sociability. *Mobile Media & Communication, 7*(2), 232–247.

Farman, J. (2013). Mobile interface theory: Embodied space and locative media. *Abingdon: Routledge*.

Farman, J. (2016). Location-based media. In A. de Souza e Silva (Eds.), *Dialogues on mobile communication* (pp. 161–177). Abingdon: Routledge.

Fingas, J. (2019) 'Pokémon Go' introduces remote raids to encourage staying at home'. *Engagement*. Retrieved from https://www.engadget.com/pokemon-go-remote-raids-142038163.html?guccounter=1&guce_referrer=aHR0cHM6Ly93d3cuZ29vZ2xlLmNvbS8&guce_referrer_sig=AQAAABzP2td0eHnDlrmBxB-4UiH-kl_AootPHc0LiNGrZ2oq2lPSA-9XBqkSunDVyJrlslMf79YY5Se0VxhrbfRGX5IfSRsg1ZSWSW_p75rGWyG9KGMAaczBAPMUlxL06Omjojs4d35jLocGB0XQtO3-esCvZL-EW6d29ZpCOZlyrPXgV

Frank, A. (2016). Six Pokémon GO tips for the ultimate beginner. Retrieved from https://www.polygon.com/2016/7/9/12136310/Pokémon-go-tips-how-to-play-beginners

Frith, J. (2013). Turning life into a game: Foursquare, gamification, and personal mobility. *Mobile Media & Communication, 1*(2), 248–262.

Frith, J. (2014). Communicating through location: The understood meaning of the Foursquare check-in. *Journal of Computer-Mediated Communication*, Advance online publication, *19*(4), 890–905. Accessed on February 17, 2015. doi:10.1111/jcc4.12087

Frith, J. (2018). *Smartphones as locative media*. New York, NY: John Wiley & Sons.

Frith, J., & Saker, M. (2017). Understanding Yik Yak: Location-based sociability and the communication of place. *First Monday*, *22*(10).

Frith, J., & Wilken, R. (2019). Social shaping of mobile geomedia services: An analysis of Yelp and Foursquare. *Communication and the Public*, *4*(2), 133–149.

Frost, J. L. (2010). *A history of children's play and play environments: Toward a contemporary child-saving movement*. New York, NY: Routledge.

Galloway, A., & Ward, M. (2005). Locative media as socialising and spatialising practices: Learning from archaeology (DRAFT). *Leonardo electronic almanac*.

Gerbaudo, P. (2012). *Tweets and the streets: Social media and contemporary activism*. Lodon: Pluto Press.

Giddings, S. (2017). Pokémon GO as distributed imagination. *Mobile Media & Communication*, *5*(1), 59–62.

Ginsburg, K. R. (2007). The importance of play in promoting healthy childhood development and maintaining strong parent-child bonds. *Pediatrics*, *119*, 182–191. doi:10.1542/peds.2006-2697

Gordon, E., Baldwin-Philippi, J., & Balestra, M. (2013). Why we engage: How theories of human behavior contribute to our understanding of civic engagement in a digital era. *Berkman Center Research Publication*, *21*, 29.

Granovetter, M. S. (1973). The strength of weak ties. *American Journal of Sociology*, *78*(6), 1360–1380.

Gray, P. (2009). Play as a foundation for hunter-gatherer social existence. *American Journal of Play*, *1*, 476–522.

Halegoua, G. R. (2020). *The digital city: Media and the social production of place (Vol. 4)*. New York, NY: NYU Press.

Hamilton, J. (2009). Ourplace: The convergence of locative media and online participatory culture. In M. Foth, J. Kjeldskov, & J. Paay (Eds.), *Proceedings of the 21st Annual Conference of the Australian Computer-Human Interaction Special Interest Group: Design: Open 24/7* (pp. 393–396), New York, NY: Association for Computing Machinery.

Hart, R. (2002). Containing children: Some lessons on planning for play from New York city. *Environment and Urbanization*, *14*(2), 135–148.

Hemment, D. (2004). The locative dystopia. *nettime. org*. Retrieved from https://eprints.lancs.ac.uk/id/eprint/30831/1/Locative_Dystopia_2.pdf

Hjorth, L. (2013). Relocating the mobile: A case study of locative media in Seoul, South Korea. *Convergence*, *19*(2), 237–249.

Hjorth, L., & Pink, S. (2014). New visualities and the digital wayfarer: Reconceptualizing camera phone photography and locative media. *Mobile Media & Communication*, *2*(1), 40–57.

Hjorth, L., Pink, S., & Horst, H. (2018). Being at home with privacy: Privacy and mundane intimacy through same-sex locative media practices. *International Journal of Communication*, *12*, 1209–1227.

Hjorth, L., & Richardson, I. (2017). Pokémon GO: Mobile media play, place-making, and the digital wayfarer. *Mobile Media and Communication, 5*(1), 3–14. doi: 10.1177/2050157916680015

Humphreys, L. (2007). Mobile social networks and social practice: A case study of Dodgeball. *Journal of Computer-Mediated Communication, 13*(1), 341–360.

Humphreys, L. (2010). Mobile social networks and urban public space. *New Media & Society, 12*(5), 763–778.

Humphreys, L. (2011). Who's watching whom? A study of interactive technology and surveillance. *Journal of Communication, 61*(4), 575–595.

Humphreys, L. (2017). Involvement shield or social catalyst: Thoughts on sociospatial practice of Pokémon GO. *Mobile Media & Communication, 5*(1), 15–19. doi: 10.1177/2050157916677864

Humphreys, L., & Liao, T. (2013). Foursquare and the parochialization of public space. *First Monday, 18*(11).

Jin, D. Y. (2017). Critical interpretation of the Pokémon GO phenomenon: The intensification of new capitalism and free labor. *Mobile Media & Communication, 5*(1), 55–58.

Kabisch, E. (2010). Mobile after-media: Trajectories and points of departure. *Digital Creativity, 21*(1), 46–54.

Kaczmarek, L. D., Misiak, M., Behnke, M., Dziekan, M., & Guzik, P. (2017). The Pikachu effect: Social and health gaming motivations lead to greater benefits of Pokémon GO use. *Computers in Human Behavior, 75*, 356–363.

Keogh, B. (2017). Pokémon Go, the novelty of nostalgia, and the ubiquity of the smartphone. *Mobile Media & Communication, 5*(1), 38–41.

de Lange, M. (2009). From always on to always there: Locative media as Playful Technologies. In A. de Souza e Silva & D. M. Sutko (Eds.), *Digital cityscapes: Merging digital and urban playspaces* (pp. 55–70). New York, NY: Peter Lang.

Latour, B. (2005). *Reassembling the social: An introduction to actor-network-theory.* Oxford: Oxford University Press.

Lefebvre, H. (1991[1974]). *The production of space. In D. Nicholson-Smith (Trans.).* Oxford: Blackwell.

Lemos, A. (2010). Post—mass media functions, locative media, and informational territories: New ways of thinking about territory, place, and mobility in contemporary society. *Space and Culture, 13*(4), 403–420.

Lemos, A. (2011). *Locative media and surveillance at the boundaries of informational territories.* In R. J. Firmino, F. Duarte, & C. Ultramari (Eds.), *ICTs for mobile and ubiquitous urban infrastructures: Surveillance, locative media and global networks* (pp. 129–149). New York: IGI Global.

Licoppe, C. (2004). 'Connected' presence: The emergence of a new repertoire for managing social relationships in a changing communication technoscape. *Environment and Planning D: Society and Space, 22*(1), 135–156.

Licoppe, C. (2013). Merging mobile communication studies and urban research: Mobile locative media, "onscreen encounters" and the reshaping of the interaction order in public places. *Mobile Media & Communication, 1*(1), 122–128.

Licoppe, C. (2016). Mobilities and urban encounters in public places in the age of locative media. Seams, folds, and encounters with 'pseudonymous strangers'. *Mobilities, 11*(1), 99–116.

Licoppe, C. (2017). From Mogi to Pokémon GO: Continuities and change in location-aware collection games. *Mobile Media & Communication, 5*(1), 24–29.

Licoppe, C., & Inada, Y. (2010). Locative media and cultures of mediated proximity: The case of the Mogi game location-aware community. *Environment and Planning D: Society and Space, 28*(4), 691–709.

Lindqvist, A. K., Castelli, D., Hallberg, J., & Rutberg, S. (2018). The praise and price of Pokémon GO: A qualitative study of children's and parents' experiences. *JMIR Serious Games, 6*(1), e1.

Ling, R., & Campbell, S. W. (2009). Effects of mobile communication. *Media Effects: Advances in Theory and Research*, 592–606.

Ling, R., & Horst, H. A. (2011). Mobile communication in the global south. *New Media & Society, 13*(3), 363–374.

Livingstone, S. M. (2002). *Young people and new media: Childhood and the changing media environment*. London: SAGE Publications.

Luke, R. (2005). The phoneur: Mobile commerce and the digital pedagogies of the wireless web. In P. P. Trifonas (Ed.), *Communities of difference* (pp. 185–204). New York, NY: Palgrave Macmillan.

Martin, J. A. (2014). Mobile media and political participation: Defining and developing an emerging field. *Mobile Media and Communication, 2*, 173–195.

Marvin, C. (1988). *When old technologies were new: Thinking about electric communication in the late nineteenth century*. New York, NY: Oxford University Press.

Mäyrä, F. (2017). Pokémon GO: Entering the ludic society. *Mobile Media & Communication, 5*(1), 47–50.

McCullough, M. (2006). On the urbanism of locative media. *Places Journal, 18*(2), 26–29.

McGarrigle, C. (2010). The construction of locative situations: Locative media and the Situationist International, recuperation or redux?. *Digital Creativity, 21*(1), 55–62.

Mintz, S. (2004). *Huck's raft: A history of American childhood*. Cambridge, MA: Harvard University Press.

Orland, K. (2020). How to play Pokémon Go when everyone's stuck inside. *Arstechnica*. Retrieved from https://arstechnica.com/gaming/2020/03/pokemon-go-adjusts-to-the-quarantine-era/. Accessed on June 24, 2020.

Özkul, D. (2014). Location as a sense of place: Everyday life, mobile, and spatial practices in urban spaces. In M. Sheller & A. de Souza e Silva (Eds.), *Mobility and Locative Media* (pp. 121–136). Abingdon: Routledge.

Paasovaara, S., Jarusriboonchai, P., & Olsson, T. (2017, November). Understanding collocated social interaction between Pokémon GO players. In *Proceedings of the 16th International Conference on Mobile and Ubiquitous Multimedia* (pp. 151–163). New York, NY: ACM.

Papangelis, K., Chamberlain, A., Lykourentzou, I., Khan, V. J., Saker, M., Liang, H. N.,. . . & Cao, T. (2020). Performing the digital self: Understanding location-based social networking, territory, space, and identity in the city. *ACM Transactions on Computer-Human Interaction (TOCHI), 27*(1), 1–26.

Papangelis, K., Metzger, M., Sheng, Y., Liang, H. N., Chamberlain, A., & Khan, V. J. (2017). *"Get Off My Lawn!" Starting to Understand Territoriality in Location Based Mobile Games*. In G. Mark & S. Fussell (Eds.), *Proceedings of the 2017 CHI Conference Extended Abstracts on Human Factors in Computing Systems* (pp. 1955–1961). New York, NY: Association for Computing Machinery.

Perng, S. Y., Kitchin, R., & Evans, L. (2016). Locative media and data-driven computing experiments. *Big Data & Society, 3*(1), 2053951716652161.

Perry, F. (2016, July 22). Urban gamification: Can Pokémon GO transform our public spaces? The Guardian. Retrieved from https://www.theguardian.com/cities/2016/jul/22/urban-gamification -Pokémon-go-transform-public-spaces

Pink, S., & Hjorth, L. (2012). Emplaced cartographies: Reconceptualising camera phone practices in an age of locative media. *Media International Australia, 145*(1), 145–155.

Rainie, H., & Wellman, B. (2012). *Networked: The new social operating system* (Vol. 419). Cambridge, MA: MIT Press.

Rosenberg, E. (2016). In a safeguard for children, some civil liberties groups see concerns. *The New York Times*, p. 14.

Saker, M. (2016). Foursquare and identity: Checking-in and presenting the self through location. *New Media & Society, 19*(6), 934–949. doi:10.1177/1461444815625936

Saker, M. (2017). Foursquare and identity: Checking-in and presenting the self through location. *New Media & Society, 19*(6), 934–949.

Saker, M., & Evans, L. (2016). Everyday life and locative play: An exploration of foursquare and playful engagements with space and place. *Media, Culture & Society, 38*(8), 1169–1183. doi:10.1177/0163443716643149

Saker, M., & Evans, L. (2020). Personalising the urban: A critical account of locative media and the digital inscription of place. In N. D. Odeleye & L. P. Rajendran (Eds.), *Mediated identities in the futures of place: Emerging practices and spatial cultures* (pp. 39–55). Cham: Springer.

Saker, M., & Frith, J. (2018). Locative media and sociability: Using location-based social networks to coordinate everyday life. *Architecture_MPS, 14*(1), 1–21.

Santaella, L. (2011). Mobile and locative media: In between Thanatos and Eros. In R. J. Firmino, F. Duarte, & C. Ultramari (Eds.), *ICTs for mobile and ubiquitous urban infrastructures: Surveillance, locative media and global networks* (pp. 294–311). Hershey, PA: IGI Global.

Schwartz, R., & Halegoua, G. R. (2014). The spatial self: Location-based identity performance on social media. *New Media & Society, 17*(10), 1643–1660. doi:10.1177/1461444814531364

Serino, M., Cordrey, K., McLaughlin, L., & Milanaik, R. L. (2016). Pokémon Go and augmented virtual reality games: A cautionary commentary for parents and pediatricians. *Current Opinion in Pediatrics, 28*(5), 673–677.

Sheller, M. (2014). Sociology after the mobilities turn. *The Routledge handbook of mobilities*, 45–54.

Siyahhan, S., & Gee, E. (2018). *Families at play: Connecting and learning through video games*. Cambridge, MA: MIT Press.

Soble, J. (2016, August 25). Driver in Japan playing Pokémon GO kills pedestrian. The New York Times, p. 2.

Sobel, K., Bhattacharya, A., Hiniker, A., Lee, J. H., Kientz, J. A., & Yip, J. C. (2017, May). It wasn't really about the PokéMon: Parents' perspectives on a location-based mobile game. In *Proceedings of the 2017 CHI Conference on Human Factors in Computing Systems* (pp. 1483–1496).

Soja, E. W. (2008). Taking space personally. In B. Warf & S. Arias (Eds.), *The spatial turn* (pp. 27–51). London & New York, NY: Routledge.

Southern, J. (2012). Comobility: How proximity and distance travel together in locative media. *Canadian Journal of Communication, 37*(1), 75–91.

de Souza e Silva, A. (2006). From cyber to hybrid. *Space and Culture, 9*(3), 261–278.

de Souza e Silva, A. (2013). Location-aware mobile technologies: Historical, social and spatial approaches. *Mobile Media & Communication, 1*(1), 116–121.

de Souza e Silva, A.. (2017). Pokémon Go as an HRG: Mobility, sociability, and surveillance in hybrid spaces. *Mobile Media & Communication, 5*(1), 20–23.

de Souza e Silva, A., & Frith, J. (2010). Locative mobile social networks: Mapping communication and location in urban spaces. *Mobilities, 5*(4), 485–505.

de Souza e Silva, A., & Glover-Rijkse, R. (Eds.). (2020). *Hybrid play: Crossing boundaries in game design, players identities and play spaces.* Abingdon: Routledge.

de Souza e Silva, A., & Hjorth, L. (2009). Playful urban spaces: A historical approach to mobile games. *Simulation & Gaming, 40*(5), 602–625.

de Souza e Silva, A., & Sheller, M. (Eds.). (2014). *Mobility and locative media: Mobile communication in hybrid spaces.* Abingdon: Routledge.

de Souza e Silva, A., & Sutko, D. M. (2008). Playing life and living play: How hybrid reality games reframe space, play, and the ordinary. *Critical Studies in Media Communication, 25*(5), 447–465.

Speed, C. (2010). Developing a sense of place with locative media: An "Underview Effect". *Leonardo, 43*(2), 169–174.

Speed, C. (2011). Kissing and making up: Time, space and locative media. *Digital Creativity, 22*(4), 235–246.

Speed, C. (2012). Walking through time: Use of locative media to explore historical maps. In L. Roberts (Ed.), *Mapping Cultures* (pp. 160–180). London: Palgrave Macmillan.

Sutko, D. M., & de Souza e Silva, A. (2011). Location-aware mobile media and urban sociability. *New Media & Society, 13*(5), 807–823.

Takahashi, D. (2020). Niantic is updating Pokémon Go and other games as coronavirus keeps us inside. *Venturebeat.* Retrieved, from https://venturebeat.com/2020/03/30/niantic-is-updating-pokemon-go-and-other-games-as-coronavirus-keeps-us-inside/. Accessed on June 24, 2020.

Takeuchi, L. (2011). *Families matter: Designing media for a digital age.* New York, NY: The Joan Ganz Cooney Center at Sesame Workshop.

Tanaka, A., & Gemeinboeck, P. (2008). *Net_Dérive: Conceiving and producing a locative media artwork. Mobile Technologies: From Telecommunications to Media.* Abingdon: Routledge.

Townsend, A. (2006). Locative-media artists in the contested-aware city. *Leonardo, 39*(4), 345–347.

Townsend, A. (2008). Augmenting public space and authoring public art: The role of locative media. *Artnodes, 8*, 1–5.

Tran, K. M. (2018). Families, resources, and learning around Pokémon Go. *E-learning and Digital Media, 15*(3), 113–127.

Tuters, M., & Varnelis, K. (2006). Beyond locative media: Giving shape to the internet of things. *Leonardo, 39*(4), 357–363.

Vella, K., Johnson, D., Cheng, V. W. S., Davenport, T., Mitchell, J., Klarkowski, M., & Phillips, C. (2019). A sense of belonging: Pokemon GO and Social Connectedness. *Games and Culture, 14*(6), 583–603.

Walsh, J. D. (2020). Ten years on, Foursquare is now checking in to you. *Intelligencer* Retrieved from https://nymag.com/intelligencer/2019/08/ten-years-on-foursquare-is-now-checking-in-to-you.htm

Wawro, A. (2016). How did Pokémon GO conquer the planet in less than a week. Retrieved from http://www.gamasutra.com/view/news/276955/How_did_Pokémon_Go_conquer_the_planet_in_less_than_a_week.php

Wilken, R. (2008). Mobilizing place: Mobile media, peripatetics, and the renegotiation of urban places. *Journal of Urban Technology*, *15*(3), 39–55.

Wilken, R. (2012). Locative media: From specialized preoccupation to mainstream fascination. *Convergence*, *18*(3), 243–247. doi:10.1177/1354856512444375

Wilken, R. (2019). *Cultural economies of locative media*. New York, NY: Oxford University Press.

Wilken, R., & Goggin, G. (Eds.). (2014). *Locative media*. London: Routledge.

Wilken, R., & Humphreys, L. (2019). Constructing the check-in: Reflections on photo-taking among Foursquare users. *Communication and the Public*, *4*(2), 100–117.

Wilson, I. (2020) Pokemon Go Guide: Everything you need to become a master trainer and catch 'em all. *Gameradar*. Retrieved from https://www.gamesradar.com/uk/pokemon-go-guide/

Wong, J. C. (2016) The world's largest Pokémon Go gathering hits the streets of San Francisco. The Guardian. Retrieved from https://www.theguardian.com/technology/2016/jul/21/pokemon-go-gathering-san-francisco. Accessed on July 21, 2016.

Zeffiro, A. (2006). The persistence of surveillance: The panoptic potential of locative media. *Wi: Journal of the Mobile Digital Commons Network*, *1*(1), 3.

Zelizer, V. A. (1985). *Pricing the priceless child: The changing social value of children*. New York, NY: Basic Books.

Zelizer, V. A. (1994). *Pricing the priceless child: The changing social value of children*. Princeton, NJ: Princeton University Press.

Zuboff, S. (2015). Big other: Surveillance capitalism and the prospects of an information civilization. *Journal of Information Technology*, *30*(1), 75–89.

Zuboff, S. (2019). *The age of surveillance capitalism*. New York, NY: Profile.

Chapter 2

Familial Locative Play: Spatial Practices and Mobilities

2.1 The Spatial Turn, Emerging Mobilities and the Complexity of Place

The approach to spatiality that we adopt throughout this book is congruently centred on an established scholarly shift in the humanities and social sciences that challenge the hegemony of time (Foucault, 1980). As Frith (2018) explains, '[space] and place began to see a resurgence in academic thought in the 1970s and 1980s with the "spatial turn"' (p. 34). For the most part, this 'spatial turn' can be attributed to scholars like Lefebvre 1991[1974] and de Certeau (1984), who prioritised such discussions. To this end, Lefebvre 1991[1974] was committed to 'developing the conceptual tools for an active theory of space that sees space as a process' (Freys & Meier, 2016, p. 15). Equally, Lefebvre's insistence on the importance of 'social space', as he referred to it, was also a clear reaction to the Kantian comprehension that space was merely an 'empty background for perceptions' (Mandoki, 1998, p. 73). In other words, '[space] was treated as dead' (Foucault, 1980, p. 70). As Lefebvre 1991[1974] notes, 'space, albeit relative, albeit a tool of knowledge, a means of classifying phenomena, was yet quite clearly separated (along with time) from the empirical sphere' (p. 2). Circuitously, then, 'Lefebvre's 1991[1974] seminal work *The Production of Space* can … be understood as an attempt to overcome the Cartesian divide between mental space and real or lived space' (Evans & Saker, 2017, p. 10).

In reality, 'people do not live in a framework of geometric relationships but in a world of meaning' (Hubbard & Kitchin, 2010, p. 6). The socially constructed nature of spatial practices (de Certeau, 1984; Lefebvre, 1991[1974] endlessly exceeds geometry. A useful way of explicating this surplus is through de Certeau's (1984) seminal text, *The Practice of Everyday Life*, and his view from the 110th floor of the World Trade Center, as he looked out at Manhattan. This vista, as captivating as it no doubt would have been, was markedly different to the *lived* reality of the people wandering the streets 'down below'. More precisely, this refraction was indicative of a fundamental disparity between two different views of the city: 'the *concept* of the city' and the 'urban *fact*' (de Certeau, 1984, p. 11, italics in original), with the former unable to translate 'the countless paths, stories and

Intergenerational Locative Play, 23–53

Copyright © 2021 Michael Saker and Leighton Evans

Published under an exclusive licence by Emerald Publishing Limited

doi:10.1108/978-1-83909-139-120211012

perspectives that are traced by the pedestrians that inhabited these spaces, forged at the street level' (Evans & Saker, 2017, p. 11). For de Certeau, then, and much like Lefebvre, space is not an inert vessel or 'empty background' but rather an active component in the *practice of everyday life*. In a similar vein, our interest in locative media and location-based play is not about cartography *per se*, or the abstract lines and measurements that can be employed to interpret any given milieu, but the *lived* experiences of those bodies that produce 'social space'. Our concern, then, is the process by which space becomes place and how this practice might be reshaped by the inclusion of digital technologies.

Place, of course, is a term that is commonly used. And for good reason. 'Place structures much of individuals' thought and memory, yet … 'place is clearly a complicated concept' (Cresswell, 2014, p. 50)' (Frith, 2018, p. 31). Following Lefebvre 1991[1974], space can be understood as being '"made up" through a three-way dialectic between perceived, conceived and lived space' (Hubbard & Kitchen, 2010, p. 6), with place emerging as 'a distinctive (and more or less bounded) type of space which is defined by (and constructed in terms of) the lived experience of people' (Hubbard & Kitchen, 2010). Developing this idea further, Tuan (1979) posits that the practice of place involves a confluence of public symbols and what he refers to as 'fields of care'. 'Public symbols have high manageability; that is, they are well known externally, beyond the place itself' (Baer, 2002, p. 24). Examples of public symbols include monuments, holy sites and noteworthy buildings. In contrast, fields of care 'are places that become meaningful as emotionally charged relationships between people find an anchorage at a particular site through repetition and familiarity' (Baldwin, 2004, p. 142). Importantly, then, 'place [is] more than a site upon which people act. Place instead plays a role in shaping action and identity' (Frith, 2018, p. 36). At the same time, this process connotes something provocative about movement and its effect on social space (Frith, 2018), which is important given the extent to which contemporary life is marked by ambulation.

As Sheller and Urry (2006) accurately observe, '[all] the world seems to be on the move' (p. 207). This includes the physical movement of myriad people and groups, such as asylum seekers, businesspeople, commuters, backpackers, holi-day makers, young professionals, to name but a few. These movements involve airplanes, ships, cars, buses and trains. And '[new] forms of "virtual" and "imaginative" travel are [also] emerging, and being combined in unexpected ways with physical travel' (Sheller & Urry, 2006). Mobile media, for example, allows users to communicate with physically distant others while in transit, construct 'telecocoons' in public environments (Habuchi, 2005) predicated on 'absent presence' (Gergen, 2002), and, in the setting of mobile virtual reality (MVR), inhabit 'dislocated spaces' that are phenomenologically distinct from the physical locations that ground them (Saker & Frith, 2019). For other scholars, however, a marked symptom of this development is not the imbuing of space with new meanings, but rather the homogenisation of space, leading to sense of 'placelessness' (Relph, 1976). To this end, Augé's (1995) phrase 'non-places', those 'everyday sites such as supermarkets, chain hotels, airports and motor-ways, in which faceless, contractual obligations replace human interaction'

(Moran, 2005, p. 94), is a prominent example of this. And '[there] is a definite moral message here. Being rooted in "authentic" places is meaningful and good' (Baldwin, 2004, p. 142), while space is effectively rendered meaningless through mobilities.

Thankfully, 'the idea that places can be "authentic" or that movement (whether virtual or physical) harms a sense of place has been questioned by other scholars' (Frith, 2018, p. 38), under the auspices of a 'mobilities turn' in the social sciences (Sheller, 2017; Sheller & Urry, 2006) that began around the 1990s, and which builds on the 'spatial turn'. In part, at least, this inclusion of mobilities is thanks to Massey's (1994) appeal for 'a rethinking of the concept of place' (p. 120) to incorporate a 'politics of mobility' (Massey, 1993, p. 63). As Frith (2018) helpfully explains:

> Understanding place as open rather than closed, as dynamic rather than static, allows for the analysis of how the social construction of place happens from both the inside and outside. Notably, a 'progressive sense of place' also recognizes the importance of movement, which is key to understanding the ways in which people use mobile media to shape their experience of place. (p. 39)

With this in mind, the next section will outline a more embodied, peripatetic and playful approach to engaging with the urban environment that emerged in Paris at the turn of the nineteenth century in the form of *flânerie* (Baudelaire, 1863; Benjamin, 1983, 1999[1927]), which implicitly challenged the suggested divide between ordinary life and play made by early game scholars. Perhaps, the most famous example of this is Huizinga's (1992/1938) proposition that play occurs within a 'magic circle' (1992/1938) that is spatially and temporally distinct from ordinary life. Following this, we, then, explore how this practice has subsequently been updated in light of mobile media (Luke, 2005), and more recently still, location-based games (Evans & Saker, 2017, 2019; Saker & Evans, 2016a).

2.2 Embodied Approaches to Urban Life

The *flâneur* 'is generally depicted as a well-dressed male idler, leisurely stroller and privileged observer of nineteenth century urban experience' (Berard, 2018, p. 100), whose unhurried stride is a direct challenge to the quickening pace of urban life developing at that time. As Tester (1994) explains,

> ...the activity of strolling and looking which is carried out by the *flâneur* is a recurring motif in the literature, sociology and art of urban, and most especially of the metropolitan, existence. (p. 1)

And it is through these wanderings that 'he merges the "serious" space of the city ... with the ludic activity of casual walk, thus eliminating the boundaries that separate a distinct and separate playful space from ordinary spaces' (de Souza e Silva & Sukto, 2009, p. 7). While this practice has been written about by a number of scholars, it is best eulogised in the work of both Baudelaire (1863) and Benjamin (1983, 1999[1927]).

Beginning with Baudelaire (1964[1863]), then, the *flâneur* is an artist who 'strolls the city streets with a keen eye to observe and comment on urban life' (Berard, 2018, p. 100); he resides 'in the ebb and flow, the bustle, the fleeting and the infinite' (Baudelaire, 1972, p. 399) and can 'reap aesthetic meaning and an individual kind of existential security from the spectacle of the teeming crowd' (Tester, 1994, p. 2). Consequently, '[the] crowd is his domain, just as the air is the bird's, and water that of the fish. His passion and his profession is to merge with the crowd' (Baudelaire, 1972, p. 399). In stark contrast to this rather romantic depiction of urban mobility and freedom, Benjamin's (1983, 1999 [1927]) version of *flânerie* emerges under the shadow of consumer capitalism, commodity culture and alienation, with the *flâneur* 'living and dying on the streets of Paris' (Tester, 1994, p. 13). Here, *flânerie* is very much a product of urban life, marked by 'the construction of glass-covered arcades' (Saker & Evans, 2016a, p. 4).

> Flânerie could hardly have assumed the importance it did without the arcades … the arcades provide him with an unfailing remedy for the kind of boredom that easily arises under the baleful eye of a sated reactionary regime. (Benjamin, 2006, p. 68)

For Benjamin (1983),

> [the] *flâneur* only seems to break through this "unfeeling isolation of each in his private interest" by filling this hollow space created in him by such isolation, with the borrowed – and fictitious – isolations of stranger. (p. 58, cited in Tester, 1994, p. 13)

Yet, '[the] *flâneur*, strolling the streets of nineteenth-century Paris with cool but curious eye, is for Benjamin, a threatened species whom history is about to overtake' (Rignall, 2004, pp. 17–25, p. 17). As Tester (1994) puts it,

> Benjamin's argument is that the rationality of capitalism and, especially, commodification and the circulation of commodities, itself defined the meaning of existence in the city so that there remained no mystery for the *flâneur* to observe. (p. 13)

Consequently, '[the] *flâneur* is a passive spectator who is as duped by the spectacle of the public as the consumer is duped by the glittering promise of consumerism' (p. 14), and things do not necessarily improve with the advent of digital technologies.

In the context of the contemporary urban life, the *flâneur* no longer moves through a space that is solely physical but is equally embroiled in countless digital networks. To account for the progression of mobile media, Luke (2005) reimagines the *flâneur* as the 'phoneur': a figure enmeshed in the digital architecture that co-constitutes her experience of the city, and which interminably disrupts her wanderings. Accordingly, 'the "phoneur" is structured by the information city's ambience, whereby modes such as haptic and aural override the dominance of visual' (De Souza e Silva & Hjorth, 2009, p. 608). Consequently, the spatiality of the phoneur is effectively folded between the physical and digital; '[the] phoneur is the mobile tele-talker, stalked by corporate hunters (Luke, 2005, p. 188), and assimilated in the "flows of commodity and desire"' (Luke, 2005). In other words, the phoneur is endlessly surveyed by a succession of faceless organisations seeking to gather, collect and interpret patterns of consumption via omnipresent smart phones and wearable technologies, under the looming shadow of 'surveillance capitalism' (Zuboff, 2019). Just as Benjamin's *flâneur* was duped by the veracity of the spectacle, then, Luke's phoneur is deceived by the mobile phone as 'desiring machine' (Luke, 2005), rendering her gaze complicit in the cultural logic underpinning the commodity form.

Certainly, the phoneur is enframed as an individualised spectacle in her own right, by the informational city's desire to know all. The phoneur is not *of* the crowd, or even *in* it, but rather abstracted from the swarm through the tracking of her movements, with unification only feelingly materialising through the ubiquity of the capitalistic principle, and the extent to which the informational city quietly extends into the lives of the majority of people within 'hybrid space' (de Souza e Silva, 2006). In Foucauldian terms, then, the mobile phone assumes the role of a 'panoptic mechanism' (Foucault, 1997[1975], p. 365), with the phoneur wilfully submitting to the 'panoptic surveillance of activities within the wired and wireless networks, as well as the desire to possess the technology of mobile commerce and communication' (Luke, 2005, p. 189). Congruently,

> [within] the logic of m-commerce, the phoneur is attached to a machine (the cell phone) which is in turn attached to other machines (the networked data structure) in a machinic arrangement that produces social relations based on commodity production and consumption. (Luke, 2005)

As a corollary to this, then, mobile media is akin to a Trojan horse, superficially suggesting freedom, but in reality, ushering in a more granular regime of control. While a critique of the political economy is hugely important, and it is a topic we return to in later chapters, it is not the only way of conceptualising these advancements. Instead, our interest is in the effect more playful forms of spatial mediation might have on understandings of place, and, more pertinently, the disruptive impact this kind of playful engagement might have on the meanings associated with the mobilities of pervasive play (Huizinga, 1992/1938).

Drawing on both the *flâneur* (Baudelaire, 1863; Benjamin, 1983, 1999[1927]) and phoneur (Luke, 2005), and with a particular focus on location-based social networks (LBSNs), like Foursquare – pre-2014 – Saker & Evans (2016a) propose the 'playeur' as a conceptual lens to comprehend the spatial impact of locative media and location-based play.

> The concept of the 'playeur' makes explicit the temporal-contingent possibilities of locative play with spatial media and offers that affordance an identity that is congruent with other accounts of understanding place and social ties with LBSNs. (Saker & Evans, 2016a, p. 12)

In the realm of spatial relationships and related mobilities, the playeur is analogous to the phoneur. Only in this instance, the reshaping of mobilities arrives 'under the auspices of location-based play' (Saker & Evans, 2016a). At the same time, the playeur's experience of the urban environment – entangled in the same networks of the phoneur (Luke, 2005) – is overrulingly co-constituted through the playful interactions supported through LBSN. Fittingly, the development of place for the playeur is not just a sedentary site of alienated consumerism, but equally – and importantly – a form of symbolic disruption. That is, the apparent meaning of mobilities in the context of locative play extends beyond the logic of the commodity form, by configuring ludic experiences of place that exceeds commercial utility. This figure, then, challenges traditional suggestions about the division between ordinary life and play (Huizinga, 1992/1938; Saker & Evans, 2016a). Through the game mechanics of earlier LBSNs, characterised by the now passé 'check-in', the playeur ambulates space using modified routes, while strengthening local connections and developing deeper place-based relationships.

More fitting to the direction of this book, Evans and Saker (2019) utilise the playeur as a lens to explore the impact of the hybrid reality game (HRG), Pokémon Go, which is central to this book. Drawing on findings from an online survey conducted between May 2017 and July 2017 that involved 375 Pokémon Go players, they argue the following.

> First, players will often use new routes and break established, habitual routes of movement to improve their performance in the game and to play the game to a higher level. Second, thanks in part to this need to change established wayfinding, players are more likely to encounter new places in their everyday playing of the game, and are in some cases more inclined to visit new places or go to places they normally would have no need or no desire to visit because of their playing. Third, the playing of Pokémon Go has subsidiary social benefits that go beyond changes in mobility but are the result of this modification. (Evans & Saker, 2019, pp. 13–14)

While the spatial impact of Pokémon Go, then, is comparable to the spatial impact of Foursquare (Saker & Evans, 2016a), the locative tendencies of this practice are nonetheless amplified. The desire to spend time ambulating the urban environment is more pronounced, just as the affordances of this game mean that the search for Pokémon can lead players to playing this HRG in locations that really are off the 'beaten path'. Lastly, and more significantly to this book, 'for some playeurs, the gamic experience of Pokémon Go serves as a platform that allows players to spatially and temporally strengthen their familial connections' (Saker & Evans, 2016a, p. 14). While this is a point we will develop further in subsequent chapters, our chief focus here is considering the tendencies of the *playeur* in the context of families who play this HRG together.

To reiterate, the familial impact of Pokémon Go has not gone unnoticed by a growing number of scholars (Lindqvist, Castelli, Hallberg, & Rutberg, 2018; Sobel et al., 2017; Tran, 2018). Indeed, this HRG been explored as it pertains to learning and educational merit (Tran, 2018), familial bonding (Sobel et al., 2017), physical exercise and gamic design (Lindqvist et al., 2018), as well as familial motivations behind playing this game (Evans & Saker, 2019). Nonetheless, few studies have contextualised familial locative play within the wider field of locative media and locative games, nor have these studies considered the extent to which Pokémon Go has managed to move beyond the gamic limitations associated with earlier LBSNs. Moving forward, then, this particular chapter is driven by the following concerns. First, to what extent does Pokémon Go lead to families spending more time outside, and how is this reshaping experienced. Second, what effect does this HRG have on the routes and pathways families choose to follow while traversing their physical setting, as well as the sites they frequent. Third, to what extent do families engage with the various elements of Pokémon Go, as outlined above, and what does this suggest about the evolution of locative play in the context of earlier LBSN. After presenting our findings, we conclude this chapter by reflecting on the wider significance of this thematic strand of our research in the context of contemporary understandings of locative games, and more broadly, locative media.

2.3 Ordinary Life and Locative Play

When asked, 'has Pokémon Go made you more physically active as a family?', the majority of our respondents reported that it did. More precisely, 94 (55%) respondents reported, 'it definitely has'. This was followed by 49 (29%) respondents who reported, 'it probably has'. The lowest scoring category was 'it definitely has not' with no responses. In a similar vein, and in line with previous research on Foursquare (Saker & Evans, 2016a) and Pokémon Go (Evans & Saker, 2019; Sobel et al., 2017), the majority of participants interviewed suggested that this HRG had a notable effect on the physical activity within their households.

> We were walking to the lake a lot even before Pokémon Go, but it's probably like, tripled our walking around the lake. (Stephanie, 42, female, Orlando, Florida, US)

> We've really just started walking more. (Christine, 27, female, Denver, Colorado, US)

> Well we probably definitely go to the park a lot more. (Amelia, 45, female, Boise, Idaho, US)

For many participants, an important component of Pokémon Go is that it facilitates a positive increase in their daily movement. This can quite clearly be seen in the following extracts, with both Troy and Stephanie, positioning the game as an 'excuse' for 'a walk' and a reason 'to get out of the house'.

> So, it's kind of nice to have an excuse to go for a walk or, like I might occasionally go out for an hour or so that I wouldn't have normally done just because it's an excuse to go for a walk. (Troy, 29, male, Norwich/East Anglia, UK)
>
> Pokémon Go is a good excuse to get out of the house and walk around the neighbourhood. (Stephanie, 42, female, Orlando, Florida, US)
>
> It is getting us all out of the house instead of just sitting and being sedentary. (Carol, 34, female, San Antonio, Texas, US)
>
> It is just another facet that gets us out and doing something. (Alan, 50, male, Plymouth, Michigan, US)

At the same time, and perhaps building upon the likes of Foursquare – which prompted users to go out more, but was not their primary reason for engaging with this LBSN (Saker & Evans, 2016a) – part of the motivation to begin playing Pokémon Go for some participants was not the effect this HRG might have on their own ambulation *per se*, although this was welcomed, but rather the positive impact this game might have on the physical activity of their children. Equally, this motivation was increased by the knowledge the game would be played together, as a family.

> My boyfriend and I started playing together three years ago and my daughter was only three then. So, at that point it was just a way to get out of the house and get her walking... It was just a really cute way to get out and walk around the apartment complex mostly. (Mia, 39, female, Sonoma, California, US)
>
> I mean it definitely gets us moving together. (Liza, 42, female, Indianapolis, Indiana, US)
>
> It gives us an extra reason to get outside and to hang together and play together. (Stephanie, 42, female, Orlando, Florida, US)

For other participants, the inclusion of Pokémon Go effectively meant that they were able to persuade their children to do something that they might not be swayed to do were it not for this game.

> It gives them an incentive to get out of the house. (Ceri, 45, female, Essex, UK)

> She wants to catch everything and then she wants to walk around and see if she can find anything else. (Liv, 27, female, Boise, Idaho, US)

> So, we're kind of like, the kids don't like walking at all. They're like it's so boring. But you know, if we let them have our phones for Pokewalks, yeah. They absolutely love it and have fun. (Qui, 38, female, Plymouth, Michigan, US)

The value of this 'incentive' should not be underestimated. For these families, it functioned as an extremely important tool.

> She complains and does not want to go out on a walk-through nature with me. She finds trees boring. But if it's going to be a Pokémon walk, she's totally willing to go. (Mia, 39, female, Sonoma, California, US)

> We wouldn't be able to get him to walk for an hour otherwise. (Joe, 37, male, Southend-on-Sea, UK)

> So, it's an excuse to get him out of the house to play versus, like, you know at home he's begging to play video games on the TV. (Stephanie, 42, female, Orlando, Florida, US)

Stephanie touches on an interesting point – one we will return to in later chapters. WhilePokémon Go is a computer game and is mediated through screens – albeit mobile screens – it is also a qualitatively different experience to the kind of screen time commonly associated with, say, more traditional games played on more traditional game consoles. Of course, the disparity between locative games and console games is symptomatic of the affordances of this HRG, and more broadly locative media (Wilken & Goggin, 2014). Unlike traditional video games that are most likely mediated through a fixed television screen and played within the home by sedentary players, Pokémon Go, and the progression of this game, is markedly predicated on mobile media and mobility (Salen Tekinbaş, 2018). As Ceri elucidates:

> They play a lot of computer games, Xbox, PlayStation. So, it's an excuse for us to take a break. We've got a dog as well so we can take the dog with us, go outside, get a bit of fresh air. Even though they're still on a device, they're out and about and we can involve it with going to the park and things. Yeah, it's a nice little thing we do. (Ceri, 45, female, Essex, UK)

From this position, Pokémon Go seemingly strikes a workable balance between the desire of children to play digital games and the desire of parents to simultaneously limit their children's screen time, while increasing the time they spend outdoors exercising (Sobel et al., 2017).

Equally, it is our contention that the richer gamic mechanics of Pokémon Go amplify mobility patterns in a manner that exceeds earlier locative media (Evans & Saker, 2019). While LBSNs like Foursquare involved points, badges and mayorships, revolving around manual 'check-ins', rewards were not specifically based on the distance users travelled *per se*. More specifically, users were able to check-in at locations that did not in fact correspond with their physical location. Pokémon Go is different. The process of hatching an egg – a recursive feature of the game – is a good case in point. The speed with which an egg hatches directly relates to how far players have moved. For some participants, knowledge of this serves as not only a reason to go outside but also a motive to keep moving.

> It's really easy to just not, because I don't want to. But I do want to hatch that egg. I do want to see what's in there. I'm a little bit too curious about what's in those eggs. So, I do get out more. (Jane, 28, female, Tacoma, Washington, US)

> I'm just walking a lot more than, because we're trying to hatch eggs and there's bonuses if you get a certain number of kilometres in a week. So, like, I was trying to get the fifty this week, so we were like up in the morning trying to walk to get some extra kilometres in. (Stephanie, 42, female, Orlando, Florida, US)

While there are spoofing applications that enable users to virtually change their geographical coordinates (Zhao & Chen, 2017), as well as simulate travel between two concrete locations at a set speed in order to trick the game into thinking a person is walking, for our participants, the value of this HRG is directly commensurate with the exercise it provides. In other words, 'gaming the system' is not something that participants understood as offering any benefits.

As a corollary to the points above, the playing of Pokémon Go blurs the boundaries between play and daily life in a manner that resonates with extant literature on earlier locative media (Frith, 2013; Saker & Evans, 2016a), while similarly challenging tractional approaches to play that comprehend this phenomenon as being necessarily demarcated from ordinary life (Huizinga, 1992/1938). This can be seen in the following extracts.

> Me and my wife both are trying to be more active with our daughter because with her having asthma, it is a bit difficult to keep up from time to time. And with me gaining quite a bit after high school, it's um, kind of stuck somewhat. So, I am trying to get down to an amount of weight that I want to be at. (Victor, 26, male, Muncie, Indiana, US)

> I have a messed-up knee. I ruptured it one time. And walking is really important and I'm diabetic, so walking is really important. So, I like the fact that it gives me something to do when I'm out

pounding the pavement every day. I try to walk at least three miles a day so if I can play something while I'm at it, it makes it a little more enjoyable. (Wendy, 59, female, Orlando, Florida, US)

I have a leg injury. Sometimes it's a reason for me to get out of the house to go walking. Maybe sometimes when I'm in pain, I don't want to walk, but then if I'm like everyone's going to go do Pokémon Go then I'll go too. I don't feel like doing it, but I'll do it anyway. (Chloe, 27, female, Newfoundland, Canada)

Two years ago, I was diagnosed with stage four cancer on my fiftieth birthday. Yay. Happy birthday. And one of the things that, you know, they're like keep moving, keep staying active and some of the things I used to do I can't really do. But walking, I can walk all day long. So, my motivation became, you know, self-preservation, I guess. And it gave me something to do. Something to distract me. Gave me a reason, you know (Maureen, 51, female, Lansing, Michigan, US)

In this vein, then, the physical benefits of Pokémon Go surpasses the gamic environment. And these benefits are not just physical. As Rhonda and Christine explain:

Because I went through a divorce and we used to hike with my ex-husband. And it was a major life change. So, I think that was important. It got me kind of out of the house and walking and you know, having a thing to do. (Rhonda, 39, female, San Jose, California, US)

When my ex and I separated, and I was doing Pokémon Go as like my self-care kind of routine thing. (Christine, 27, female, Denver, Colorado, US)

Here, Pokémon Go does more than just nudge families to spend additional time outside. The playfulness of this practice readily melds with the daily lives of participants. As a corollary to this, an advancement in the gamic world corresponds with an advancement in the physical world. For some participants, this means an improvement in their physical well-being; for others, this means the opportunity for 'self-care'. In contrast to traditional understandings of the separation between ordinary life and play (Huizinga, 1992/1938), then, the digitality of this HRG and the physical realm framing this experience are not as distinct as it might seem.

Interestingly, for some families, this merging of the physical and digital did not just increase familial movement or provide the necessary lure to get children to spend time with their parents outside, it also affected how they experienced space and place. This can be seen in our survey, with the majority of respondents agreeing that this HRG changes how they feel about their environment. More precisely, when asked, 'has Pokémon Go changed how you feel about your environment?', 54 (32%) respondents answered, 'it definitely has', followed by 44 (26%) respondents who answered, 'it probably has'. The lowest scoring category was 'it definitely has not', with 10 (6%) respondents answering accordingly. The following extracts with Stephanie and Gavin help explain this process:

> You know, I think of it more. I didn't think of it as a Pokémon place before we started playing. You know I had heard about it, so yeah, we think about that a little different. (Stephanie, 42, female, Orlando, Florida, US)

> So, there is something quite nice about the way that the virtual Pokéstops and the gyms are overlaid on the real world. It feels like there's a permanent connection. It feels like you're putting on the magic glasses and you're seeing something that is actually there but isn't normally visible. And then when you see other people playing it and you might be battling at a gym and you can see somebody else there battling at the gym. We've had that before. And that feels nice because it's a real-world connection. (Gavin, male, Southampton, UK)

For Arthur, the prominence of the digital aspect of Pokémon Go actually led him to provide physical directions based on the digital architecture of the game. As he describes:

> The first year that it was out when we were playing it very heavily, I could have been guilty of giving people driving directions based on if you go to that gym and turn left at the Pokéstops. (Arthur, 38, male, Birmingham, UK)

Ceri touches on a similar point.

> Now we look at places and we go oh yeah that's where the Poke Gym is, or you know where so and so is, that's the Poke Gym. It's like a landmark now but then I say, it's that gym that's on the corner over there and they'll go like oh yes. (Ceri, 45, female, Essex, UK)

From this position, it is not so much that the physical and digital are commensurate, or that the imagined boundary between play and ordinary life has blurred; rather, for these participants, the digitality of the game has momentarily overtaken the physical space that frames it. As Liza puts it:

> It starts to feel that way when you play for so long, I think, right? …
> The virtual kind of ends up overlapping the real world. (Liza, 42, female, Indianapolis, Indiana, US)

At the same time, this is not to dismiss the physical aspect and the strengthening of this aspect through the digital layer. Indeed, some participants found that the relationship between this dialectic in fact strengthened their understanding of their physical surroundings.

> So just from playing Pokémon Go, I've found stuff out about the city that I didn't know before. Like a memorial to something becomes a Pokéstops because you go to the Pokéstops and when you spin it you see a picture of it, and you think 'oh what is that' and then you find out it's a memorial to the firefighters on the Titanic or something. (Gavin, male, Southampton, UK)

> looking at the Pokémon map is quite a good way to get a sense of the things that are valued to look at in the area you're in in the real world. (Arthur, 38, male, Birmingham, UK)

> Different memorials and statues or historic buildings. They're all marked as stops. And like, some of the, some of the ones marked as historic buildings downtown are, it just looks like an old house and that. And you're like, oh, this is actually like where the nurses' union was founded or something like that. (Mick, 26, male, Newfoundland, Canada)

> We get to see things. You know, we get to read, you know things about parks where the Pokéstops are that maybe we wouldn't get to read. Or maybe we wouldn't even realize was there. Or we get to walk trails that we didn't know were there. (Christine, 27, female, Denver, Colorado, US)

In sum, then, the impact of Pokémon Go on the ordinary life of the parents interviewed can be partially explained through the locative tendencies of the playeur (Evans & Saker, 2019). In line with this conceptual lens, the families who play Pokémon Go together experience an increase in their physical activities, just as they appreciate that this practice has value in a variety of areas beyond the game itself. In the main, this value revolves around the lure of familial ambulation and the fact this practice necessarily implicates their children. While, '[the] benefits of this kind of play do not simply revolve around the physical benefits of spending more time outside, but equally involve a genuine pleasure in the game itself' (Evans & Saker, 2019, p. 14), the digital architecture of this HRG is notably amplified. For some participants, Pokémon Go does more than just reshape their physical activity; it provides a qualitatively different revealing of place (Evans, 2013), which suggests a nuanced shift in the balance between the physical and digital aspects of the urban environment. For these participants, and in contrast to earlier LBSNs, it is not so much that the physical frames the digital, rather through the rich gamic structure of Pokémon Go the ludic takes precedence, with the 'virtual … overlapping the real world'. At the same time, and as detailed above, this is not to reduce the physical aspect. For many families, it is precisely through the gamic structure that they became more cognisant of their surroundings.

2.4 Mobilities, Pathways and Places

Our research found that Pokémon Go had a notable effect on familial mobilities, with participants subsequently choosing to take different daily routes and pathways as they moved through their environment, echoing extant research on LBSNs (Evans & Saker, 2017; Saker & Evans, 2016a). And this influence can clearly be observed in our survey data, with the majority of respondents, 57 (34%), agreeing that Pokémon Go 'definitely has' affected how they move through their environment. This was followed by 49 (29%) respondents answering, 'it probably has', and then 42 (24%) respondents suggesting, 'it may or may not have'. The lowest scoring category was 'it definitely has not', with only 3 (2%) responses. For some participants, the effect on their movements was understood as being relatively minor.

> Sometimes, you know, when we're going to a store and we're driving, I'll be like this road has more Pokéstops along the way. So, I'll go drive that way so the kids can spin the Pokéstops. (Qui, 38, female, Plymouth, Michigan, US)

> Every time we get in the car he says, 'can I do Pokémon Go?' Every time. So, if I'm not in a rush then I might drive an alternate route and stop so he can get all the Pokémon. (Beth, female, Brighton, UK)

> See where we live there's not really much with Pokémon Go in it. So, we may take a slightly different route every now and then if I haven't done a Pokéstops or something for the day. Or I might walk a slightly different way just to get a Pokéstops or something. (Troy, 29, male, Norwich/East Anglia, UK)

For Troy, the rather narrow impact on his movements is possibly symptomatic of the limited game-based opportunities surrounding him. Developing this point further, for other participants, the playing of Pokémon Go not only led to them using routes and pathways outside of normal ambulation but they would also incorporate longer routes if they deemed the gamic reward worthwhile.

> So, if there is, you know, a Pokémon that we need or what, then we might just go out of our way to get it. (Joe, 37, male, Southend-on-Sea, UK)

> Every once in a while, when we're driving somewhere, if we have like extra time, then we'll go out of our way to go someplace where we know there are Pokéstops and we'll stop for a minute and like spend that extra fifteen minutes we have doing a gym or flipping Pokéstops or something. So sometimes it does impact the route that we take. (Mia, 39, female, Sonoma, California, US)

The suggestion of increasing journey time, of course, appears counterintuitive to the implicit idea of much locative media. Certainly, GPS navigation systems, like Waze, for instance, provide physical directions that explicitly prioritise the quickest route from point A to B. Resonating with existing literature on Pokémon Go (Evans & Saker, 2019), as well as the physical tendencies of the playeur (Saker & Evans, 2016a), for some participants, the spatial inclinations of this HRG balk against pragmatism. Instead, locative decisions are frequently made in response to the gamic layer, as opposed to the physical aspect. Accordingly, outside of these assemblages and their internal logic, familial mobilities might appear rather strange. As Rhonda points out:

> So, if you traced our driving, instead of being straightforward from location A to location, it's a little bit weird. (Rhonda, 39, female, San Jose, California, US)

Equally, the suggestion that this HRG has reshaped familial spatial practices implies that there is a fixed destination in the first place. Such an assumption, however, overlooks the marked influence of this game. While Foursquare was often played in the context of an ordinary life that would occur with or without this LBSN, that is, users might check in at their local train station on the way to work, and then at their office when they arrive (Evans & Saker, 2017), Pokémon Go is different – or rather it has the potential to be. This application is not just much about turning daily life 'into a game' (Frith, 2013) *per se*, but more significantly, it is about allowing the gamic world to fleetingly supersede the conventional space of everyday life. For many participants, then, the richer game-based experience of this HRG means it can be approached as a viable activity in its own right, rather than simply a playful appendage to the familiar. As Stephanie deftly puts in:

> You know, normally it's like we're on a Pokémon walk so you know, we might go a different way. Like, 'oh, there's this Pokémon over this way,' so we'll go a different way to catch it. But it's not like we're on our way somewhere else. Like the Pokémon walk is the destination, you know what I mean? (Stephanie, 42, female, Orlando, Florida, US)

By nudging players to go out or move through their environment using different routes, participants frequently spent time in new environments. This impact can clearly be observed in our survey data. When asked, 'has Pokémon Go led to you spending time in new environment?', the majority of respondents, 107 (63%), answered, 'it definitely has'. This was followed by 47 (28%) respondents suggesting, 'it probably has', and then by 10 (6%) respondents who answered, 'it may or may not have'. The lowest scoring category was 'it definitely has not', with 1 (1%) response. The following extracts provide some interesting examples of this practice.

> We found that place, but we didn't know what it was for. It was just behind the water treatment center. Okay, it's probably just a boat club. But no, it's a rental place. Because it's a stop and it tells you that you can rent kayaks and stuff! It's like, oh that's cool! (Chloe, 27, female, Newfoundland, Canada)

Yes. I remember when the game first came out, there was certain Pokémon only available at nests in London. We travelled to London for the day purely to just play Pokémon. We've done the tour of the River Thames, like on the Pokémon tour boat. (Bill, 28, male, Southend-on-Sea, UK)

I'm not a big fan of peopling. It's not my favourite activity. I'm a little awkward socially. But if we know that there's something that Franklin really wants to catch or that we've never seen before or that our friends are going to this new school or this new park and it's not very far from the house, then we do go. (Jane, 28, female, Tacoma, Washington, US)

So, say on the summer holidays we needed to go out for the day. I would sometimes look and find places that I know that's got gyms or, you know, certain amount of Pokéstops and things. So, country parks and places like that. And that gives me the sort of lure to say to them, oh come on we're going to go here, it's got loads of Pokéstops and things like that. And then they'll be like oh okay, okay. (Ceri, 45, female, Essex, UK)

Eight months ago, there was some challenge that was going on and we had to hit like fifteen new Pokéstops. Well if you're always going on the same roads, obviously you can't do that. So, whenever that would happen, yes, it would change it because we'd be like oh, we haven't hit that area of town. (Amelia, 45, female, Boise, Idaho, US)

Being somewhere out of the ordinary certainly for me, my wife and the oldest girls is certainly an impetus to go see what sort of Pokémon are in this area. And potentially go, oh it's worth going down there, it looks like there's loads of stuff. (Arthur, 38, male, Birmingham, UK)

He likes going to new places now so say, when we went to Bournemouth, we explored Bournemouth because it's somewhere different. When you do actually see new Pokémon like this, because we were down by the beach, it might be a different biome, you might get different types of things down there. (Gavin, male, Southampton, UK)

From this position, Pokémon Go seemingly amplifies the locative tendencies associated with earlier LBSNs like Foursquare, where players would find themselves discovering new places as a symptom of the game (Saker & Evans, 2016a). Yet, there are also notable differences between these applications that should be mentioned. In the context of Foursquare, this kind of response was chiefly associated with people who were still in the 'early days' of using this particular LBSN. Consequently, the process of checking in was still novel. Second, gamic features like the mayorship mechanism necessarily involved users repeatedly going back to the same location in order to protect their status (Saker & Evans, 2016a). In contrast, while Pokémon Go might prompt players to return to certain pokéstops and gyms, there are also a range of additional features that can influence users to visit new locations. This can be observed in the following extracts:

> Eight months ago, there was some challenge that was going on and we had to hit like fifteen new Pokéstops. Well if you're always going on the same roads, obviously you can't do that. So, whenever that would happen, yes, it would change it because we'd be like oh, we haven't hit that area of town. (Amelia, 45, female, Boise, Idaho, US)

> Being somewhere out of the ordinary certainly for me, my wife and the oldest girls is certainly an impetus to go see what sort of Pokémon are in this area. And potentially go, oh it's worth going down there, it looks like there's loads of stuff. (Arthur, 38, male, Birmingham, UK)

> He likes going to new places now so say, when we went to Bournemouth, we explored Bournemouth because it's somewhere different. When you do actually see new Pokémon like this, because we were down by the beach, it might be a different biome, you might get different types of things down there. (Gavin, male, Southampton, UK)

Regarding Foursquare, while new environments opened up a suite of different check-in possibilities, the value of these check-ins was usually grounded on the ordinary life of players; beyond the inscription of place to demonstrate that a user was, say, on holiday, it is unlikely said user would drive to the other side of town just to check in at a location that they had not been to before (Saker, 2017). As detailed above, Pokémon Go presents more game-based reasons for participants to frequent new environment. For these participants, then, the reason for visiting new places was a by-product of available challenges, as well as the desire to experience different species of Pokémon, both demonstrating the richer gamic experience of Pokémon Go and the fact location matters in a way it perhaps did not with earlier LBSNs. At the same time, to be clear, these new environments were not solely valued for the gamic opportunities they opened up. As our survey attests, when asked, 'has the playing of Pokémon Go led to you visiting shops that you would not have done were it not for this game?', 53 (32%) respondents answered, 'it definitely has', followed by 32 (19%) respondents answering, 'it may or may not have', followed by 31 (19%) respondents answering, 'it probably has not'. The lowest scoring category was 'it definitely has not', with 22 (13%) respondents answering accordingly. This outcome was similarly discussed by several participants.

Here and there we'll find new locations that we've never been to or find a restaurant that we've never seen before. If we have the money and extra time, we'll check it out, take a look at it, stop maybe have a bite and what not. Sometimes it turns out to be a great idea. (Victor, 26, male, Muncie, Indiana, US)

I've gone, you know, like we'll be out wandering around, and it would start to rain so we'd hop into a store. I mean I found a really cool Father's Day present for my husband at a store I never would have gone to. It was raining and so I hopped in to get out of the rain a little bit because in Florida the rain, the systems go by really fast. I mean one minute it's perfectly sunny the next. So, I wandered in the store, it had a bunch of cool stuff. I ended up buying something. I find all sorts of cool little things. (Wendy, 59, female, Orlando, Florida, US)

Moving forward, while many participants evidently planned Pokémon Go–based excursions, this is not to suggest that all familial movements motivated by this HRG were necessarily planned for. Just as Pokémon Go has the power to nudge families to alter the routes chosen on a day-to-day basis, in a manner that mirrors the spatial practice of the *flâneur* (Benjamin, 1983, 1999[1927]), this HRG similarly has the power to nudge participants into spontaneous trips. As Beth explains:

Yes, so I had an all-time low. I checked my phone; I saw that there was a Pokémon nearby that I didn't have, and I jumped in the car and went and caught it. I drove to where it was. (Beth, female, Brighton, UK)

Joviality aside, the power of this lure should not be underestimated, as the following extracts indicate:

I've left the house at two o'clock in the morning to catch something before. Like I was awake, and I saw it and because my missus was on Facebook. She was like when most people hear their other half leave their house at two o'clock, they'd be concerned but I know it's Pokémon. And it has happened a few times when I've been sitting, I've had my dad around and other family and stuff and something happens because I live five minutes from town. And I'm looking at the radar and something's in town and I've never seen it before, so I picked up all three phones and just ran out the door and no one cared. Everyone knew where I was going. (Bill, 28, male, Southend-on-Sea, UK)

Every once in a while, the kids might turn it on and see something happening in the, because we live two blocks away, I can see about nine or, I don't know. I can see a lot of gyms from our house. And there was one I wanted for over a year and, I don't know, in the last week or so, my oldest son ran into me and said meet us at this gym in five minutes. We're all going over on our bikes. And I was already in my pyjamas. So, I threw on his Birkenstocks and my jacket and ran out the door in my car and there they all were waiting for me. (Liza, 42, female, Indianapolis, Indiana, US)

For other participants, the power of this lure moved beyond spontaneous mobilities to include more impactful decisions about potential job locations and holiday destinations.

There was a time a couple years ago, I had two potential job interviews. You're going to think this is hilarious. But they were both virtually equivalent software engineering positions. I was interviewing to do some freelance work actually, in addition to my normal job. And one of them was in a boring place, I can't even remember. And the other one was in Florida and I chose the interview in Florida because I wanted to catch Heracross and the regional Pokémon there are only available below a certain latitude. And Florida is the only United States state other than Hawaii that you can get that latitude. So, I chose the job interview in Florida and Fort Lauderdale just so that I could catch Heracross and I caught five of them. (Faizan, 49, male, Denver, Colorado, US)

We tend to go somewhere where there's a concentration of Pokémon available or a concentration of Pokéstops so we can maximize our play. If we're going on a vacation for the summer, I will admit that we chose our camping spots based on whether or not we would have WIFI and phone access. Because we went camping at one spot and there were no Pokémon and it was not as fun for my boyfriend and my child. And so, we went camping and had WIFI access and then we actually went out while we were camping and actually went on Pokémon walks. (Mia, 39, female, Sonoma, California, US)

In contrast to the digital lure of earlier LBSNs, then, that did lead to users reshaping their mobilities, as well as making occasional ad hoc trips (Saker & Evans, 2016a), we would suggest for some participants, the gamic value of Pokémon Go is notably more intense. And this can be readily seen in the examples above. Yet, this is not to suggest that all participants would simply follow the gamic layer wherever it took them, as many participants were very cognisant of the spaces that they chose to frequent.

In previous study of Pokémon Go, Evans and Saker (2019) found that the gamic structure of this HRG often led to users inhabiting environments that really were off the beaten track. Importantly, this differed from the likes of Foursquare which – owing to the check-in functionality – was commonly played in public spaces that involved significant congregations of people, such as bars, restaurants and cinemas. Of course, the affordances of Pokémon Go are different. Pokémon can spawn anywhere (Humphreys, 2017). Consequently, players might find themselves coming across Pokémon in all manner of dwellings and not always within sites conducive to play or playfulness (Frank, 2016; Rosenberg, 2016). In contrast to this, our survey found families were less likely to play in spaces they considered 'strange'. When asked, 'have you ever played Pokémon Go led in an environment that felt strange', 122 (74%) respondents answered, 'no', with only 43 (26%) answering 'yes'. Jane and Troy provide some reasoning as to why this might be the case:

> There are some parks that have trails that you can still find like Pokéstops at. We try not to do those when it's just me and Franklin. Safety. Because we get so absorbed in the game, we try not to be in places that if we called for help, it wouldn't be available. (Jane, 28, female, Tacoma, Washington, US)

> If it sounded sketchy or dodgy then we'd avoid it and we wouldn't go there because of him. Where we play, we don't sort of go around dodgy areas or anything, I wouldn't even consider going to a dodgy area or something with him. (Troy, 29, male, Norwich/ East Anglia, UK)

In a similar vein, many families specifically chose to play this game in parks, precisely because these spaces were more suited to familial locative play. And our survey supports this suggestion. When asked, 'has the playing of Pokémon Go led to you visiting any public sites (e.g. a square, a park or a library) that you would not have done were it not for this game?', the majority of respondents, 128 (78%) answered, 'it definitely has', followed by 17 (10%) respondents answering, 'it probably has', followed by 12 (7%) respondents answering, 'it may or may not have'. The lowest scoring category was 'it definitely has not', with 3 (2%) responses. As the following extracts concur:

> It's normally a park of some sort. Or yeah, anywhere that there's just lots of foot traffic. (Jane, 28, female, Tacoma, Washington, US)

> I would say mostly they're parks or other green locations. The urban locations are harder for me because I usually have my kids with me and it's just, it's just too hard to keep, it's too hard to play and keep the kids safe at the same time generally. (Liv, 27, female, Boise, Idaho, US)

> Yeah that would be that Pokémon park because it's safe, you know. Um, there are no places for kids to run off and hide. It's a big open field. And if we want a break, we can stop at the playground for the kids to just put down their phones and just go play. (Qui, 38, female, Plymouth, Michigan, US)

In sum, then, for many of our participants, Pokémon Go had a marked effect on their daily mobilities, with some families choosing longer journeys than were necessary in order to extend play. At the same time, while the likes of Foursquare was frequently played in the context of ordinary life (Saker & Evans, 2016a), Pokémon Go is more of a game in its own rights. For many families, they were outside precisely because they were playing this game. The potency of this lure should not be underestimated, as demonstrated by the examples of impromptu trips detailed above. Again, we would suggest this is indicative of the richer gamic experience that Pokémon Go offers. To be clear, however, this does not mean that families simply followed the game wherever it took them. Though previous research on Pokémon Go has demonstrated that some players found themselves playing this game in spaces that appeared either dangerous or ill-suited to play (Evans & Saker, 2019), familial locative play is different. For many of our participants, the familial playing of this HRG was predicated on the suitability of this physical setting. Providing families were happy with their environment, the digital layer could then supersede the physical aspect.

2.5 The Next Generation of Locative Games

In this final section, we want to briefly turn our attention towards the richer gamic experience that Pokémon Go seemingly offers, which we have been alluding to throughout the previous two sections – particularly in relation to earlier locative games and LBSNs. While these applications did, of course, involve numerous updates, for the most part, these updates were either incremental or more geared toward improving the digital architecture behind the experience. In other words, and again, broadly speaking, the affordances remained, for the most, very similar. Pokémon Go – as you might have guessed – is different. In contrast to earlier LBSN, like the aforementioned, Foursquare, and perhaps following a logic similar to the hugely successful game Fortnite – known for its 'blistering pace of updates' (Thier, 2019) – Pokémon Go is regularly updated in a variety of ways that continue to reshape the gamic experience. For many participants, these updates are explicitly understood as being an important element of the game.

> I think the game has evolved. There's a lot more sort of gain and you know, you're always trying to get things, a Shiny or gold gyms and things. So, there's a lot more to achieve within the game itself. And then you're naturally competitive with other people, aren't you? So especially boys and husbands. They're all like oh I've got this one, I've got this one. (Ceri, 45, female, Essex, UK)

> Oh yeah. It's definitely, I mean I think it becomes an addiction. Um, you know, I fully see what they do and how they do it and why they do it in order to keep you turning on the game every day. (Liza, 42, female, Indianapolis, Indiana, US)

> You know, what we, I don't know if we just kind of got bored with
> it and then we were talking to some friends, and they're like, 'ah,
> it's got all new kinds of Pokémon and there's new stuff!' And so,
> we logged back in and there was, really there was a lot of different
> things they didn't have before and it got fun again. I think we had
> just gotten kind of bored with it because we had caught all, or a lot
> of the Pokémon. (Stephanie, 42, female, Orlando, Florida, US)

For Stephanie, then, the ongoing introduction of new generations of
Pokémon serves as a necessary pull to keep her and her family playing. Likewise,
other participants equally found the addition of new Pokémon kept them
interested.

> Whenever like a 'new gen' is released, it always kind of, it always
> ramps up you know, the game plays a little bit. (Joe, 37, male,
> Southend-on-Sea, UK)

> So, the whole point is catching different creatures really. So, if they
> already have it, they're not interested. But when a new generation
> come out... (Qui, 38, female, Plymouth, Michigan, US)

> But, like whey they release a new generation then suddenly there
> are lots of Pokémon you've never seen before, then it's way more of
> a hype, you know? And then you want to catch a certain amount of
> them so you can evolve them. So, I think during those times it's a
> bit more like, it's a bit different. We do go to places just to catch
> this or that Pokémon. But then, you know, we've caught them
> all, we've evolved them all, and it kind of like dies down. This
> time period is not very long. (Rhonda, 39, female, San Jose,
> California, US)

At the same time, it would not be unreasonable to question precisely how
different the game environment actually is following the introduction of new
Pokémon. Much like the recursive check-in mechanism endemic of earlier
LBSNs, it doesn't really matter, on the surface at least, which Pokémon a player is
attempting to catch. Varying levels of difficulty to one side, the process usually
follows a similar pattern. Yet, Pokémon Go updates move beyond the surface. In
June 2018, for example, a new trading system (Philips, 2018) was announced,
which allowed players to exchange Pokémon among themselves. Not only does
this development underline the evolving character of this HRG, for many participants, this feature reshaped their experience of the game in a variety of ways.
As the following extracts illuminate:

> I have not traded any with her, but her dad has traded her some and
> has helped her get some really good Pokémon she would not have
> necessarily gotten at that lower level. (Mia, 39, female, Sonoma,
> California, US)

So, I caught extra Pokémon so I could trade it with him when he came back. (Stephanie, 42, female, Orlando, Florida, US)

Like stuff that they don't have I'll trade with them. But my rules with them are that they're not allowed to trade with each other. (Qui, 38, female, Plymouth, Michigan, US)

Yeah. So, before that it was more, like, just you yourself walking around interacting with the environment, collecting Pokémon. But now it's something that, um, you can do with other people, not just like alongside of them. But you can trade, so you can collect Pokémon for somebody else. (Rhonda, 39, female, San Jose, California, US)

Like, they get to manage their own accounts and do different things, if they want to trade their Hundo or you know if they want to transfer something, or you know, whatever. It's all their decision. They have complete control over their own accounts. (Christine, 27, female, Denver, Colorado, US)

For both Mia – or rather Mia's partner – and Stephanie, the ability to trades means they can help their children collect Pokémon they might not be able to access on their own. In a similar vein, Qui employs this feature so she can give her children with Pokémon that they do not have – albeit in a manner framed by stricter rules. For Rhonda, trading means the sociality of the process is effectively amplified, whereas Christine sees this mechanism as presenting her children with the opportunity to take responsibility for their actions. Motivation to one side, then, what we want to underline here is the broader suite of gamic experiences Pokémon Go provides players under the auspices of locative play. Traditionally speaking, earlier LBSNs were predominantly grounded on competition. In the context of Foursquare, say, players would attempt to beat their 'friends' through amassing points, badges and mayorships (Saker & Evans, 2016a). In contrast, Pokémon Go facilitates a wider experience that provides the gamic space for families to assist one another, as well as experiment with different roles (Sobel et al., 2017), which is a point we will return to in the next chapter.

Moving forward, ongoing events are another way Pokémon Go effectively differs from conventual locative games. These events include, raids – difficult battles with large Pokémon that occur at gyms, and commonly require a team of players in order to defeat the 'boss' Pokémon – and community days – a designated day each month when a particular Pokémon appears more often than it usually would for an allotted three-hour period. The popularity of these events can be readily observed in our survey, with the majority of respondents, 145 (88%), noting that they do 'take part in Pokémon Go events?', and only 20 (12%) respondents suggesting that they did not. Likewise, the majority of respondents, 55 (38%), suggested that this is something that they do 'often', followed by 54 (37%) respondents who suggested this is something that they do 'very often'. As Qui puts it:

> The Pokémon game is all about the events. (Qui, 38, female, Plymouth, Michigan, US)

For many participants taking part in events is not only a regular part of the gamic experience but also equally demonstrates their commitment to the game.

> Before we figured out the park thing, there was a community day that had a raid element and boy that was ridiculous. We were like, there were, we latched onto this group of guys and they were jumping in their cars and then racing off to the next gym. So, we were doing this, and I said to my husband, what are we doing? This is nuts! So yeah, it's a lot nicer to go to a park and to just walk from one gym to another with a group of people. (Liza, 42, female, Indianapolis, Indiana, US)

> The best feature is probably the raiding where the community gets together to go get that Pokémon. I think it's just fun to see who is there. Because, as I mentioned before, you get to see the same people and you know, it's kind of hey, hi, you know, kind of interesting to see who still plays. (Qui, 38, female, Plymouth, Michigan, US)

As both Mia and Liza explain, these events are not completed quickly.

> On the weekend, if we were trying to catch a community day if it's possible. If there's one that's going, and her dad will be up in time. And so, we'll go out to the park and we can usually get about two hours of play on the weekend before her battery starts to die because she has an older phone. (Mia, 39, female, Sonoma, California, US)

> It's like two, two hours, I think. So, we plan on that block of two hours around our schedule. (Qui, 38, female, Plymouth, Michigan, US)

> If it's a community day coming up, which there was just one this past Sunday, you know we'll tell the kids hey, community day Sunday, we're playing eleven to two. So, we just kind of schedule our activities around if there's something special happening in the app. (Liza, 42, female, Indianapolis, Indiana, US)

At the same time, these events can comprise a substantial number of other players.

> There probably about a hundred to two hundred people here playing. (Wendy, 59, female, Orlando, Florida, US)

> We had a community day and it was amazing where there was a hundred of that certain Pokémon. And it was at the other end of the seafront and almost half of the people were at the other end. And they all came sprinting down and I just thought it was hilarious that, including us, running down the field. Other people that don't play must have been confused as anything. (Bill, 28, male, Southend-on-Sea, UK)

From this position, then, Pokémon Go is unquestionably a game in its own rights. While the earlier appeal of LBSNs was to turn ordinary 'into a game' (Frith, 2013), it is our contention that this particular HRG goes beyond this. Pokémon Go is not so much about blending play with ordinary space *per se*, but rather enacting something that is extraordinary – albeit fleetingly so. And this can quite clearly be observed in the examples detailed above. Families are engaged in activities that are both time consuming and implicate a considerable number of players. Simply put, these are events in every sense of the word. For these participants, then, part of their enjoyment in this HRG revolves around the digital layer temporarily taking precedence over the physical aspect of daily life.

2.6 Conclusion

The purpose of this chapter has been to contextualise the familial impact of playing HRGs with the dominant issues that have driven the surrounding field of locative media; namely, the effect of locative media on engagements with space and place. The chapter, therefore, began by providing a critical overview of extant literature that surrounds locative media, in order to advance a suitable understanding of 'place and place experience' (Wilken & Goggin, 2014, p. 59) from which to survey the spatial effect of locative media and, more fittingly, Pokémon Go. This literature review established the centrality of questions concerning space and place by reflecting on both the 'spatial turn' (Lefebvre, 1999) and the 'mobilities turn' (Sheller, 2017; Sheller & Urry, 2006) within the social sciences. In doing so, the chapter cast a light on the socially constructed nature of space as well as the importance of considering movement.

Developing this comprehension further, the chapter, then, examined the practice of *flânerie* (Benjamin, 2006) as indicating an approach to the urban environment that implicitly challenges the suggested division between the ordinary space of daily life and play (Huizinga, 1992/1938), a theme that runs through much of the early literature on locative media (Frith, 2013; Saker & Evans, 2016a). The chapter then updated this figure to account for emerging mobile media (Luke, 2005), as well as location-based play (Saker & Evans, 2016a). Importantly, these frameworks – the phoneur and *playeur*, respectively – underline 'that Internet-connected mobile technologies bring a digital layer to the construction of this urban playful space' (de Souza e Silva and Sutko, 2009, p. 8). Accordingly, the *playeur*

> ...makes explicit the temporal-contingent possibilities of locative play with spatial media and offers that affordance an identity that is congruent with other accounts of understanding place and social ties with LBSNs. (Saker & Evans, 2016a, p. 12)

While both the phoneur (Luke, 2005) and *playeur* (Saker & Evans, 2016a) traversed environments folded between the physical and digital, the latter's movements arrived 'under the auspices of location-based play' (Saker & Evans, 2016a). Consequently, the *playeur*'s physical experience and concomitant mobilities were co-constituted through locative media. In other words, the spatial practice of the *playeur* was more difficult to decipher outside of the gamic experience, which endlessly exceeded the physicality of any given concrete environment. At the same time, the *playeur* is very much a figure that relates to the earlier days of LBSNs, exemplified by the likes of Foursquare. More recently, of course, the prevalence of pervasive play has been supplanted by broader developments within the context of locative data.

In the context of this chapter, we examined what impact Pokémon Go is having on spatial practices of the families who play this HRG together along three interconnected lines. First, through the playing of this HRG, many of our participants experienced a marked increase in the physical activity within their households. Here, the lure of Pokémon Go became a fitting tool to persuade family members to go outside and exercise. As many participants suggested, were it not for this HRG, they would have struggled to convince their children to take part in such an activity. Likewise, the game mechanics of Pokémon Go – such as the process of hatching eggs – explicitly pushed participants to be more cognisant of how far they had moved. For many participants, and resonating with the effect of earlier locative Media (Saker & Evans, 2016a), the benefits of this HRG extended beyond the boundaries of play. As detailed above, Pokémon Go respectively functioned as an aid to physical recovery, as well as a form of 'self-care' for those who needed it. Nonetheless, Pokémon Go strikes s a different kind of balance between the physical and the digital aspects of the game. Many participants reported that their experience of certain physical sites became somewhat displaced by their concentration on game, with certain participants, then, providing directions pertaining to the digital layer. This is not to suggest, however, that the physical aspect was necessarily diminished because of this. More accurately, many participants found that they subsequently acquired new knowledge about their environment as a by-product of the game.

Second, many participants found that the routes and pathways they chose to move through their environments altered as a direct response to playing

Pokémon Go. In line with previous research on this HRG (Evans & Saker, 2019), participants often used routes that were longer (Evans & Saker, 2019). For other participants, and more significantly, their movements were solely motivated by the game. That is, Pokémon Go was the 'destination', as opposed to an appendage to the familiar. As a corollary to this, and again, commensurate with the spatial practices of earlier LBSNs (Saker & Evans, 2016a), Pokémon Go led to many participants frequenting new environments; a practice amplified by the game mechanics involved. Events, for instance – a recursive element of this HRG – explicitly nudged participants to venture into new spaces. And the experience of these spaces did not end with the game layer. Many participants would then explore these environments, by going into surrounding shops or restaurants. Similarly, not all game-based trips were necessarily planned for. Certainly, an assortment of participants would engage in unplanned for sessions of play, at times that were seemingly at odds with such a decision. This is not to suggest, however, that participants were not thinking about the environments that they played in. Contra previous studies of Pokémon Go, where players often found themselves playing in 'strange' spaces (Evans & Saker, 2019), our participants were more particular about the places they frequented. Many participants consciously chose to engage with this HRG in large open spaces such as parks (Perry, 2016), precisely because this meant they were in a better position to watch their children. In other words, while the digitality of this game had the power to supersede the physical aspect in certain situation, this did not mean that participants were not mindful of the environments they inhabited. As the chapter demonstrated, for many participants, the suitability of the physical environment was a prerequisite for them to engage in this form of play.

Finally, the richer gamic experience of Pokémon Go meant participants continued playing this game, beyond the point of novelty, which differs from earlier locative games (Saker & Evans, 2016a). For the majority of participants, ongoing updates, such as the introduction of new Pokémon, were an important aspect of their enjoyment in the game. And these updates extended beyond mere surface revisions. As detailed above, the trading system effectively provided an additional layer of sociality to familial mobilities and served as an additional lure to play. Equally, many participants regularly took part in events that involved large congregations of players and that lasted for extended periods of time. Again, these dynamics are demonstrative of the various ways in which this new generation of locative games has evolved beyond the limited affordance of earlier applications.

In sum, then, the impact of the mobilities and experience of place Pokémon Go has on families can be contextualised through extant literature on locative media (Evans, 2013; Evans & Saker, 2017; Frith, 2018). At the same time, this HRG notably differs from earlier locative games in a number of meaningful ways. While seminal LBSNs such as Foursquare reshaped the divide between ordinary life and play (Saker & Evans, 2016a) by effectively turning ordinary life 'into a game' (Frith, 2013), this was very much about the digital blending with the physical. In other words, there was a balance of sorts, ordinary life continued, only it became more playful. Consequently, this activity did not occur within a 'magic circle' (Huizinga, 1992/1938). Pokémon Go, however, is different or rather it has the potential to be. For many participants, their experience of this HRG specifically involved a particular environment – albeit an environment that moved with the game – for a demarcated period of time. The ensuing experience is, therefore, not so much about imbuing ordinary life with play *per se*, but rather temporarily replacing the familiar with something extraordinary.

In conclusion, while a particular version of locative media might have died (Frith & Wilken, 2019), the broader category of locative media did not. Instead, the legacy of earlier applications continues today (Evans & Saker, 2017). Not only did these media foreshadow the unprecedented prominence of location data, as well as the mainstreaming of this aspect into the broader media sphere, more germane to the chapter, these services eventually gave rise to the next generation of locative games – typified by Pokémon Go. Importantly, these games have managed to move beyond the shadow of novelty by creating compelling and dynamic experiences in their own right. In doing so, this generation of games have continued to add meaningful contours to the *playeur*'s ambulation. As we have previously stated, '[how] the "playeur" is remediated and remade by new media will [continue to] be a fruitful area for future research' (Saker & Evans, 2016a, p. 13). The same is true today.

References

Augé, M. (1995). *Non-places: Introduction to an anthropology of supermodernity*. London: Verso.

Baer, L. D. (2002). *Doctors in a strange land: The place of international medical graduates in rural America*. Lanham, MD: Lexington Books.

Baldwin, E. (Ed.). (2004). *Introducing cultural studies*. London: Pearson Education.

Baudelaire, C. (1964[1863]). *The painter of modern life and other essays*. New York, NY: Phaidon Press.

Baudelaire, C. (1972). The painter of modern life. In P.E. Charvet (Trans.), *Selected writings on art and artists* (pp. 390–435). Harmondsworth: Penguin.

Benjamin, W. (1983). In H. Zohn (Trans.), *Charles Baudelaire: A lyric poet in the era of high capitalism*. London: Verso.

Benjamin, W. (1999[1927]). In H. Eiland & K. McLaughlin (Trans.), *The arcades project*. Cambridge, MA; London: Harvard University Press.

Benjamin, W. (2006). *The writer of modern life: Essays on Charles Baudelaire*. Cambridge, MA: Harvard University Press.

Berard, M. F. (2018). Strolling along with Walter Benjamin's concept of the Flâneur and thinking of art encounters in the Museum. In R. L. Irwin & A. L. Cutcher (Eds.), *The Flâneur and education research* (pp. 89–108). Cham: Palgrave Pivot.

de Certeau, M. (1984). In S. Rendell (Trans.), *The practice of everyday life*. Berkeley; Los Angeles, CA: University of California Press.

Cresswell, T. (2014). *Place: A short introduction*. Malden, MA: Blackwell.

de Souza e Silva, A., & Frith, J. (2013). Re-narrating the city through the presentation of location. In J. Farman (Ed.), *The mobile story* (pp. 46–62). Abingdon: Routledge.

de Souza e Silva, A., & Hjorth, L. (2009). Playful urban spaces: A historical approach to mobile games. *Simulation & Gaming, 40*(5), 602–625.

de Souza e Silva, A. (2006). From cyber to hybrid: Mobile technologies as interfaces of hybrid spaces. *Space and Culture, 9*(3), 261–278.

Evans, L. (2013). How to build a map for nothing: Immaterial labour and location-based social networking. (Unlike Us). In G. Lovink & M. Rasch (Eds.), *Unlike us reader: Social media monopolies and their alternatives* (pp. 189–199). Amsterdam: Institute of Network Cultures.

Evans, L. & Saker, M. (2017). *Location-based social networking: Space, time and identity*. London: Palgrave Macmillan.

Evans, L., & Saker, M. (2019). The playeur and Pokémon Go: Examining the effects of locative play on spatiality and sociability. *Mobile Media & Communication, 7*(2), 232–247.

Foucault, M. (1997[1975]). *Discipline and punish: The birth of the prison*. London: Vintage.

Foucault, M. (1980). *Power/knowledge: Selected interviews and other writings, 1972–1977*. New York, NY: Vintage.

Frank, A. (2016). Six Pokémon go tips for the ultimate beginner. Retrieved from https://www.polygon.com/2016/7/9/12136310/Pokémon-go-tips-how-to-play-beginners

Freys, L., & Meier, L. (2016). *Encountering Urban Spaces: visual and material performances in the city*, London: Routledge.

Frith, J. (2013). Turning life into a game: Foursquare, gamification, and personal mobility. *Mobile Media & Communication, 1*(2), 248–262.

Frith, J. (2018). *Smartphones as locative media*. Hoboken, NJ: John Wiley & Sons.

Frith, J., & Wilken, R. (2019). Social shaping of mobile geomedia services: An analysis of Yelp and Foursquare. *Communication and the Public, 4*(2), 133–149.

Gergen, K. J. (2002). The challenge of absent presence. In J. E. Katz & M. Aakhus (Eds.), *Perpetual contact: Mobile communication, private talk, public performance* (pp. 227–241). Cambridge: Cambridge University Press.

Habuchi, I. (2005). Accelerating reflexivity. In M. Ito, D. Okabe, & M. Matsuda (Eds.), *Personal, portable, pedestrian: Mobile phones in Japanese life* (pp. 165–182). Cambridge, MA: The MIT Press.

Hubbard, P., & Kitchin, R. (2010). Why key thinkers?. In R. Kitchin & P. Hubbard (Eds.), *Key thinkers on space and place* (pp. 1–17). London: Sage.

Huizinga, J. H. (1992). *Homo ludens: A study of the play-element in culture*. Boston, MA: Beacon Press.

Humphreys, L. (2017). Involvement shield or social catalyst: Thoughts on sociospatial practice of Pokémon GO. *Mobile Media & Communication, 5*(1), 15–19.

Lefebvre, H. (1991[1974]). In D. Nicholson-Smith (Trans.), *The production of space*. Oxford: Blackwell.

Lindqvist, A. K., Castelli, D., Hallberg, J., & Rutberg, S. (2018). The praise and price of Pokémon GO: A qualitative study of children's and parents' experiences. *JMIR serious games, 6*(1), e1.

Luke, R. (2005). The phoneur: Mobile commerce and the digital pedagogies of the wireless web. In Trifonas, P. P. (Ed)., *Communities of difference*, pp. 185–204. New York, NY: Palgrave Macmillan.

Mandoki, K. (1998). Sites of symbolic density: A relativistic approach to experienced space. *Philosophies of Place*, 73–95.

Massey, D. (1993). Power-geometry and a progressive sense of place'. In J. Bird, B. Curtis, T. Putnam, G. Robertson, & L. Tickner (Eds.), *Mapping the futures: Local cultures, global change* (pp. 59–69). London: Routledge.

Massey, D. (1994). Double articulation. In A. Bammer (Ed.), *Displacements: Cultural identities in question* (pp. 110–122). Bloomington, IN: Indianapolis University Press.

Moran, J. (2005). *Reading the everyday*. Abingdon: Routledge.

Perry, F. (2016, July 22). Urban gamification: Can Pokémon GO transform our public spaces? *The Guardian*. Retrieved from https://www.theguardian.com/cities/2016/jul/22/urban-gamification -Pokémon-go-transform-public-spaces

Philips, T. (2018). Two years later, a Pokémon Go is finally getting a trading system. *Eurogamer*. Retrieved from https://www.eurogamer.net/articles/2018-06-18-Pokémon-go-is-finally-adding-trading-with-some-caveats

Relph, E. (1976). *Place and placelessness*. London: Pion.

Rignall, J. (2004). Benjamin's flâneur and the problem of realism. In C. Jenks (Ed.), *Urban culture: Critical concepts in literary and cultural studies*. (Vol. 2, pp. 17–25). New York: Taylor & Francis.

Rosenberg, E. (2016, August 22). In a safeguard for children, some civil liberties groups see concerns. *The New York Times*, p. 14.

Saker, M., & Evans, L. (2016a). Everyday life and locative play: An exploration of Foursquare and playful engagements with space and place. *Media, Culture & Society*, *38*(8), 1169–1183.

Saker, M. (2017). Foursquare and identity: Checking-in and presenting the self through location. *New Media & Society*, *19*(6), 934–949.

Saker, M., & Frith, J. (2018). Locative media and sociability: Using location-based social networks to coordinate everyday life. *Architecture_MPS*, *14*(1), 1–21.

Saker, M., & Frith, J. (2019). From hybrid space to dislocated space: Mobile virtual reality and a third stage of mobile media theory. *New Media & Society*, *21*(1), 214–228.

Salen Tekinbaş, K. (2017). Afraid to roam: The unlevel playing field of Pokémon Go. *Mobile Media & Communication*, *5*(1), 34–37. doi:10.1177/2050157916677865

Sheller, M., & Urry, J. (2006). The new mobilities paradigm. *Environment and Planning A*, *38*(2), 207–226.

Sheller, M. (2017). From spatial turn to mobilities turn. *Current Sociology*, *65*(4), 623–639. doi:10.1177/0011392117697463

Sobel, K., Bhattacharya, A., Hiniker, A., Lee, J. H., Kientz, J. A., & Yip, J. C. (2017). It wasn't really about the PokéMon: Parents' perspectives on a location-based mobile game. In *Proceedings of the 2017 CHI Conference on Human Factors in Computing Systems* (pp. 1483–1496).

de Souza e Silva, A. & Sutko, D.M . (Eds.). (2009). *Digital cityscapes: Merging digital and urban playspaces* (Vol. 57). London: Peter Lang.

Tester, K. (1994). *The Flaneur* (RLE Social Theory). London: Routledge.

Thier, D. (2019). Report reveals the dark side of the constant 'Fortnite' updates'. *Forbes*. Retrieved from https://www.forbes.com/sites/davidthier/2019/04/24/report-reveals-the-dark-side-of-the-constant-fortnite-updates/

Tran, K. M. (2018). Families, resources, and learning around Pokémon Go. *E-learning and Digital Media*, *15*(3), 113–127.

Tuan, Y. F. (1979). Space and place: Humanistic perspective. In G. Olsson & S. Gale (Eds.), *Philosophy in geography* (pp. 387–427). Dordrecht: Springer.

Wilken, R., & Goggin, G. (2014). *Locative media*. New York, NY: Routledge.

Zhao, B., & Chen, Q. (2017, July). Location spoofing in a location-based game: A case study of pokémon go. In M. P. Peterson (Ed.), *International Cartographic Conference* (pp. 21–32). Cham: Springer.

Zuboff, S. (2019). *The age of surveillance capitalism: The fight for a human future at the new frontier of power*. New York, NY: Profile Books.

Chapter 3

Familial Locative Play: Family Life

3.1 Play, Childhood and the Rise of Digital Technologies in the Home

Play is an 'elusive concept with many and varied definitions' (Duncan, 2015). As Eberle (2014) puts it, play is 'a roomy subject, broad in human experience, rich and various over time and place' (p. 214). And the numerous descriptions of this phenomenon not only attest to its indefinable character (Eberle, 2014; Gilmore, 1966; Power, 2000) but also its cultural significance. Certainly, '[throughout] time, play has been an important part of the human experience' (Agate, Agate, Liechty, & Cochran, 2018, p. 395), which may very well be 'one of the few aspects of life that is both universal and timeless'. A common approach to comprehending the meaning of play has, therefore, been to consider it in the context of attributes (see Burghardt, 2005; Henricks, 2006). Following this vein, Eberle (2014) distils play into five basic qualities: 'play is apparently purposeless, voluntary, outside of the ordinary, fun, and focused by rules' (p. 215). More precisely, and in the context of its suggested benefits, play can improve physical fitness (Burdette & Whitaker, 2005; Hart, 2002), heighten cognition (Barros, Silver, & Stein, 2009; Hart, 2002), advance emotional well-being (Ginsburg, 2007), increase psychological health (Kuo & Faber Taylor, 2004) and aid social development (Blurton Jones, 1972).

Moving forward, then, play has the capacity to offer 'a mix of physical, social, emotional, and intellectual rewards at all stages of life' (Eberle, 2014, p. 217; Sutton-Smith, 1997). Nonetheless, while 'research has suggested that play has benefits for health and well-being, social support, increased optimism, sense of identity, and can provide a valuable coping resource for age-related changes' (Agate et al., 2018, p. 397; see also; Hutchinson, Yarnal, Stafford-Son, & Kerstetter, 2008; Mitas, Qian, Yarnal, & Kerstetter, 2011; Son, Kerstetter, Yarnal, & Baker, 2007), it is more conventional for studies in the field to focus on children (Ginsburg, 2007; Gray, 2013; Kuo & Faber Taylor, 2004), or to frame the activities of youth through the lens of play (Corsaro, 1979; Garvey, 1984). Accordingly, play is generally understood as being 'fundamental to all domains of childhood and adolescent development – physical, intellectual, social and emotional' (Hart, 2002, p. 136; see also; Bruner, 1976; Sutton-Smith, 1997).

Intergenerational Locative Play, 55–92
Copyright © 2021 Michael Saker and Leighton Evans
Published under an exclusive licence by Emerald Publishing Limited
doi:10.1108/978-1-83909-139-120211013

Yet, commentators have long observed the gradual decline of opportunities for play in public spaces (Agate et al., 2018; Chudacoff, 2007; Frost, 2010; Gray, 2009; Mintz, 2004), which seemingly goes against conventional wisdom. As a result, educators (Jarrett & US Play Coalition, 2013); medical professionals (Ginsburg, 2007) and youth development scholars (Mainella, Agate, & Clark, 2011) alike have pondered the consequences of this drift. Tellingly, for Hart (2002), 'the value of play for creativity is ... little recognized by those who plan and design public settings' (p. 136). Consequently, the kind of free play children once enjoyed within their neighbourhoods and communities has slowly disappeared (Gray, 2011; Stegelin, Fite, & Wisneski, 2015). Correspondingly, play has gradually been moved to designated playgrounds, which form 'part of a wider trend in Europe and the USA since the nineteenth century to segregate children from the adult world and to stream them into age groups in all aspects of their life' (Hart, 2002, p. 138). Although the health and safety of children was a motivating force behind this movement, in reality, adults feared what might become of those children socialised in urban environments. Over time, of course, adolescents have also grown to be wary of their surroundings albeit for reasons that differ. As Bartlett (2002) explains, what specifically worries children 'is the extent to which they feel threatened by and excluded from their urban surroundings' (p. 7). Yet, these apprehensions are not without substance. There is mounting evidence about 'the dangers of urban living for children, including unsafe surroundings, traffic congestion, poor transport and in some areas lack of services and amenities' (Biggs & Carr, 2015, p. 102; see also; Clements, 2004). Perhaps partly because of this, children have gradually moved away from the streets (Zelizer, 1985, cited in; Aarsand, 2007) and turned towards their homes and bedrooms (Livingstone, 2002, cited in; Aarsand, 2007).

At the same time, it would be inaccurate to suggest these are the *only* reasons for the exodus of children from the avenues and neighbourhoods that typically characterise urban environments. Research also demonstrates that the passage from activities outside to activities indoors is consistent with the transition from childhood to adolescence (Crosnoe & Trinitapoli, 2008). In response to this temporal shift, '[family] relations undergo major transformations to accommodate the cognitive, behavioural, emotional, and social changes that children go through during adolescence (Eccles et al., 1993)' (Siyahhan, Barab, & Downton, 2010, p. 415). What makes this migration distinct from other times is the prevalence of digital technologies within the home (Lenhart, Madden, & Hitlin, 2005). Indeed, children in the Western world regularly experience digital media, such as video games and the Internet, on a daily basis (Livingstone, 2002). For Costa and Veloso (2016), '[the] last 2 decades have ... seen a growing trend toward the inclusion of emerging technologies in domestic spaces' (p. 43; see also Bunz, 2012; De Schutter, Brown, & Vanden Abeele, 2015). Consequently, digital technologies have become a dominant aspect of familial life (Takeuchi, 2011); and while these technologies are often referred to as being *new technology* or *new media* in surrounding discussions (Aarsand, 2007, p. 235; italics in original), as media scholars like Drotner (1999, cited in Aarsand, 2007) rightly point out, computers are not a new medium *per se*, but rather an established part of leisure time for children. What is novel, however, is 'the ways in which researchers (e.g., Gee, 2003; Prensky, 2001) and politicians talk about children's use of technology' (Aarsand, 2007, p. 235) and 'the *idea* that knowledge about computers is important for people living in western societies' (Aarsand, 2007, p. 236; italics in original). This knowledge, or digital literacy (Tyner, 1998) as it has also been referred together with the multifaceted practices surrounding this competence, can have a substantial and lasting impact on everyday familial life. More importantly to this chapter, the universality of digital devices equally correlates with a growing body of work that examines the role technologies, such as video games, might play in the lives of families (Aarsand, 2007; Siyahhan & Gee, 2018).

For Siyahhan and Gee (2018), 'the ubiquity of digital media technologies has sparked an interest among researchers from different fields in taking a closer look at how children and youth use these technologies' (p. 5). Curiosity here has commonly revolved around matters such as socializing, civic engagement, identity and self-experience, learning, and media production (Siyahhan & Gee, 2018, p. 5). At the same time, Sobel et al. (2017) suggest that academic considerations have also contemplated the undesirable effects that are frequently associated with rising levels of screen time (Kamenetz, 2018), which includes anti-social behaviour (Hiniker, Suh, Cao, & Kientz, 2016), addiction (Kardaras, 2016), obesity (Boone, Gordon-Larsen, Adair, & Popkin, 2007), mental health issues (Twenge, Joiner, Rogers, & Martin, 2018) and the disruption of family life and familial relationships (Steiner-Adair & Barker, 2013) to name but a few. And the 'growing trend towards the inclusion of emerging technologies in domestic spaces' (Costa & Veloso, 2016, p. 43) has only deepened this line of enquiry. For some commentators, the digital age is, therefore, marked by a propensity to replace embodied social interactions with the simulation of sociality through digitally mediated technologies (Turkle, 2017). Following in this vein, our increased reliance on screen-based media is a corporate snare effectively distancing us from what it means to be human. This dependence, so it goes, is not making us any happier; quite the opposite, in fact. For Turkle's (2017), the pervasiveness of digital media directly relates to rising levels of discontentment, despondency and depression, which has prompted some observers to suggest a viable solution to the problem is to simply switch off offending devices (Lanier, 2018).

Unplugging, however, comes at a cost. Digital media can enhance and enrich everyday life in a variety of ways that are perhaps as well-documented (Negroponte, 1996), as they are contested (Fuchs, 2014). Mobile media, for instance, can empower young people to fluidly coordinate social interactions, maintain contact with distant family members and effectively transform 'in-between' spaces, such as train stations, into something that feels more familiar and conducive to sociality (see Evans & Saker, 2017; Saker & Frith, 2018). While the impact of digital media continues to be disputed, what is more difficult to contest is the ongoing impression this age is having on family life. With this in mind, the next section attends to the impact digital technologies are having on parents and parenting, paying particular attention to the research on intergenerational play and the positive effect video games have been shown to have on the families that play them together. Yet, there is very limited research that considers these kinds of issues through the lens of locative play, which forms the main thrust of this chapter.

3.2 Parenting and Intergenerational Play

Digital media is inexorably changing the process and practice of parenting. As Clark (2013) notes, '[parents] recognize that young people are growing up in a world saturated by digital and mobile media' (p. x); a world that is typically very different from their own experiences of childhood.

> It is often argued that children, as regular users of new media, develop knowledge concerning how to use them, which is followed by the assumption that they handle and relate to digital technology in different ways from their parents. (Aarsand, 2007, p. 2)

For Siyahhan and Gee (2018), this mounting cognizance of a generational schism, and the array of issues it seemingly brings in its wake, has led to a hermeneutic shift of sorts, with studies now documenting 'family life in the twenty-first century from the view of parents, detailing the anxieties, tensions, challenges, and opportunities, families experience around children's use of digital media technologies' (p. 6). This broadening of the conversation about young people and digital media can readily be observed in the existing literature surrounding this topic (Lewis, 2014; Ribble, 2009; Santosa, 2015; Steyer, 2012). Equally, recent studies have also considered how parents comprehend the varied and wide-ranging digital technologies their children employ (Genc, 2014), the different parenting styles and approaches required to accommodate for these devices (Livingstone, Mascheroni, Dreier, Chaudron, & Lagae, 2015), as well as suggestions about how related technologies should be monitored and supervised (Funk, Brouwer, Curtiss, & McBroom, 2009). Related research has demonstrated the effect digital media technologies can have on the communicative practices of families (Aarsand, 2007; Siyahhan et al., 2010; Takeuchi, 2011), with projects highlighting that both parents and children can end up engaging in separate activities while sharing the same physical space. This is a point that we touched on in our opening chapter, but which bears repeating.

> Parents use cell phones and the Internet to facilitate communication with their children and to coordinate activities and daily life routines (Kennedy, Smith, Wells, & Wellman, 2008). Children, on the other hand, spend extensive time online, multitasking (e.g., chatting, downloading music, Internet surfing), and connecting with their friends. (Siyahhan et al., 2010, p. 416)

Perhaps more significantly, respective activities are not necessarily short-lived. Some studies, for instance, estimate that children between the ages of 8 and 18 years old can spend roughly eight hours each day in front of a screen (Rideout, Foehr, & Roberts, 2010).

On the surface at least, then, there are seemingly less opportunities for different generations to interact with one another, which is understand as being 'a significant concern' (Voida & Greenberg, 2012, p. 45). Developmentally speaking, the communication individuals experience with different age groups can have a hugely positive effect on their well-being (Voida & Greenberg, 2012). And this goes for both children and older adults alike. Intergenerational connections can provide young people with an important opportunity to 'expand the diversity of people with whom they interact' (Voida & Greenberg, 2012, p. 45), which can lessen depression (Ruiz & Silverstein, 2007). As Hausknecht, Neustaedter, & Kaufman (2017) note,

> [beyond] the benefit of simply interacting, they may be able to form new understandings through the coming together of differing perspectives … [which] could contribute to personal growth and a sense of lifelong learning. (p. 48)

Likewise, intergenerational relations can improve the life satisfaction of adults (Meshel & Mcglynn, 2004), as well as deepen their emotional well-being (Weintraub & Killian, 2007).

Interestingly, however, digital technologies are often implicitly framed as limiting intergenerational connections. In reality, of course, and as the above should clarify, this does not actually suggest anything inherently pernicious about digital media (Latour, 2005). More accurately digital technologies can when congruently configured improve communication between different age groups. To this end, surrounding research supportively suggests that related technologies can readily advance communicative channels between geographically dispersed families (see Holladay & Seipke, 2007; Marx, Cohen-Mansfield, Renaudat, Libin, & Thein, 2005), while forging a space for reciprocal learning (Kenner, Ruby, Jessel, Gregory, & Arju, 2007). At the same time, and importantly to the direction of this chapter, these benefits extend to the playing of video games (Takeuchi, 2011). Of course, games have existed long before the rise of digital technologies, just as they have afforded a platform for parents to bond with their children. Indeed, '[families] have been playing sports games (e.g., soccer, board games (e.g., backgammon), and card games (e.g., Go Fish) together for decades if not centuries' (Siyahhan & Gee, 2018, p. 19). Yet, video games are now providing the opportunity for a different kind of gamic experience to materialise within the domestic space of the home. And recent studies have sought to 'debunk some of the misconception's parents might have about video games' (Siyahhan & Gee, 2018, p. 6), such as the often repeated, misconception that they can logically fuel feelings of aggression (Scott, 1995). As a welcomed response to the many misunderstandings that surround this activity, scholars have highlighted the critical role video games now play in children's culture (Fromme, 2003), alongside the positive impact this pastime can have on learning (Thai, Lowenstein, Ching, & Rejeski, 2009), the development of knowledge (Ali, Aziz, & Maizub, 2011) and the promotion of creativity and imagination (Bredekamp & Copple, 1997). At the same time, gaming does not just benefit children; it can also have a positive impact on adults (Tran, 2018).

As a growing number of studies illuminate, video games can assist older people increase their cognition (Whitlock, McLaughlin, & Allaire, 2012), overcome social isolation (Khosravi, Rezvani, & Wiewiora, 2016), encourage physical exercise and limit falls (De Schutter & Vanden Abeele, 2008; Derboven, Van Gils, & De Grooff, 2012). More importantly for this chapter, video games can also provide the opportunity for different generations to play together. As Sobel et al. (2017) explain, '*joint media engagement* (JME) … refers to the experiences of people using media together, which include viewing playing, searching, reading, contributing, and creating with either digital or traditional media' (p. 1483, italics in original). In this vein, existing research demonstrates that the co-playing of video games can advance the connection felt between different generations (Al Mahmud, Mubin, Shahid, & Martens, 2010; Derboven et al., 2012), lessen intergroup anxiety (Chua, Jung, Lwin, & Theng, 2013), battle ageist attitudes (Harwood, 2007; Mesch, 2006), facilitate civic engagement that promotes a more inclusive society (Uhlenberg, 2000) and help families carve out a space to engage in quality time together (Siyahhan et al. 2010). Equally, the co-playing of video games can have a constructive effect on the different roles family members might adopt. Voida and Greenberg (2012), for example, found in their project encompassing four generations of video game players that console gaming afforded a more flexible suite of subject-based roles than 'more traditional … intergenerational activities' (p. 45), which were positively explored by constituent players. And far from hinder lines of communications, similar studies have shown that the generational gap between parents and children can be a fertile ground to facilitate longer in-game interactions (Aarsand, 2007). As Siyahhan and Gee (2018) concludingly observe, then, the co-playing of video games has the potential to strengthen familial connections, reinforce shared bonds, allow adolescents to experiment with different roles and initiate conversations that would not have otherwise happened.

At the same time, it is also apparent that the kind of games commonly explored within the context of intergenerational play and JME are normally situated within the private sphere (e.g., home). Because of this, there is only limited research that that examines the familial impact of locative games (see Sobel et al., 2017). Nonetheless, 'JME is not a static concept though, as the options for how families can co-engage with media as rapidly evolving' (Sobel et al., 2017, p. 1483). As previously detailed, locative games, such as Pokémon Go, implicate a very different gamic experience that is outwardly suited to being played by families. Not only does Pokémon Go facilitate, motivate and prompt co-playing between parent and children, as demonstrated in the previous chapter, it does so within the physical flows of public environments. Accordingly, it has been our undergirding contention that this markedly under researched form of locative play might strengthen familial connections, reinforce shared bonds, allow adolescents to experiment with different roles and initiate conversations that would not have otherwise happened (Siyahhan & Gee, 2018) within a physical setting that could develop these emergent properties in new and interesting ways perhaps offering a counterpoint to the suggestion many adolescents have now moved out of the streets (Zelizer, 1994) and into their bedrooms (Livingstone, 2002). This assertion is helpfully supported by Sobel et al.'s (2017) research on families who play Pokémon Go, and the impact they found the locative aspect of the game on the ensuing familial experience, which is something we will further develop in this chapter.

Moving forward, then, one of the chief aims of this chapter is to add much needed contours to this developing field by examining the various ways in which Pokémon Go either complements or challenges family life. Likewise, it is our intention to gain a more detailed comprehension as to the kind of bonding that occurs through this Hybrid Reality Games (HRG), while exploring whether parents choose to play this game alone and why. Accordingly, this chapter is driven by the following research questions. First, why and how do families play Pokémon Go? This includes the different roles that family members adopt, alongside motivations for families playing this game, how the playing of this game complements the rhythms of family life and the extent to which this HRG is suited to intergenerational play. Second, what impact does locative familial play have on families, collectively speaking, and regarding individual family members? Here we are not just interested in whether this game allows families to bond and how this bonding process is experienced, but also whether the familial play of Pokémon Go provides families with any learning opportunities that might facilitate personal growth beyond the game. Third, what worries might parents have about the familial playing of Pokémon Go and to what extent does the locative aspect of this game reshape their apprehensions? After presenting our findings, we conclude with some further thoughts on the wider significance of this research on contemporary understandings of intergenerational play.

3.3 Why and How Do Families Play Pokémon Go?

In line with other studies and the suggested motivations underpinning familial locative play (Evans & Saker, 2019), many of our participants began playing Pokémon Go soon after their children expressed an interest in doing so. This can be observed in the following extracts.

> Six months ago, she started asking to catch Pokémon. (Liv, 27, female, Boise, Idaho, US)

> Since the game was released in the UK, it was something that the kids were fairly hot about getting onto at the time. (Arthur, 38, male, Birmingham, UK)

> It came out in summer of 2016 I believe. And um, they were in camp with young adults of course - a day camp. And so, they came home and told us all about this game that they had been playing in the woods with their camp counsellors and that we needed to download it. So, we did. And we live in a village in the middle of Indianapolis, you know in a little village. And there are lots of Pokéstops and gyms. So, it was very easy for us to just walk out the door that evening and start playing. (Liza, 42, female, Indianapolis, Indiana, US)

While this desire to play the game could on the surface appear impulsive, children were often familiar with the Pokémon brand. Likewise, proposals were often made in the context of a particular location, with children suggesting that this HRG could complement the activity families were currently engaged in. As Amelia explains:

> So, my son at the time, I think he was nine years old. And we were on a trip to Oklahoma, so it was a three-day drive. And, honestly, like the last day of the drive, he said, 'man this would have been a really good chance to play Pokémon Go.' And he was talking to me about it in the car on the way there. I didn't really know, I had heard about it, but I wasn't really familiar at that point. I was not the kid that grew up with Pokémon being my big thing when I was a kid. I know a lot of people play the cards. I never showed any interest in them. And I was like well, okay, let's look at it. So, on the trip we went ahead and just downloaded it and he was just having a blast and just loving it. (Amelia, 45, female, Boise, Idaho, US)

The majority of children, of course, were either too young to play on their own or did not own a data-enabled smartphone. Because of this, and in a manner that perhaps differs from more traditional video games, parents were not just needed to provide the necessary hardware but were also required to physically play the game. At the same time, the initial motivation to play Pokémon Go did not always come from children. In certain instances, it was the parent or parents who downloaded the game of their own volition.

> So, like, you know, I downloaded the game and I fell in love with it and, you know, I was super active with it. (Christine, 27, female, Denver, Colorado, US)

> So, we started playing because of me. We did not start playing because of the children. We started playing because of me and they played because we all made it fun. Like going out and searching for Pokémon and stuff was just fun. (Faizan, 49, male, Denver, Colorado, US)

Irrespective of the initial reasons for locative play, many participants particularly younger parents found their pleasure extended beyond the game itself, as well the vicarious gratification of seeing their children's' enjoyment. More specifically, the playing of Pokémon Go could evoke a certain nostalgia in them (see Keogh, 2017), stemming from their own experiences with earlier Pokémon games when they were growing up. This point can readily be observed in the following extracts from Jane and Troy.

> Franklin brought it to us. He said hey, he was very interested in the different creatures. Yeah. So, he was wanting to know more about it and that opened up a lot of conversations about what we used to do when we were his age. (Jane, 28, female, Tacoma, Washington, US)

I had started playing when it first came out. Because I've been interested in Pokémon since I was a kid and stuff, collected all the cards, and all that stuff. (Troy, 29, male, Norwich/East Anglia, UK)

Accordingly, the familial playing of Pokémon Go provided these participants with the opportunity to relive a certain part of their youth only this time in tandem with their children.

So, then I got to kind of feel like I was six again and watch the series with him and the films. (Bill, 28, male, Southend-on-Sea, UK)

My husband was a big Pokémon player back when he was in elementary middle school. I don't even know what type of video game it was, but he used to play a video game. And, he used to know all the different characters. And now I find it amusing because it's like we've come full circle. Now our four, going on five-year-old is super excited. (Carol, 34, female, San Antonio, Texas, US)

Developing this point further, for other participants, the co-playing of Pokémon Go was not so much about reliving their youth *per se* although this might very well be an aspect of it but about continuing a family tradition of playing video games together.

We have a long history of playing video games together. When he was a little boy, he and I have always played video games together. (Wendy, 59, female, Orlando, Florida, US)

We used to play World of Warcraft together. (Maureen, 51, female, Lansing, Michigan, US)

Logistically speaking, while some parents would co-play this game using their own handset, a number of participants explained that their children would play on a secondary device tethered to their data-enabled smartphone (see Sobel et al., 2017). In these instances, secondary devices were able to access the mobile web a technical requirement of the game but could not make phone calls.

When we're out she tethers to my Wi-Fi and so we each have our own devices. (Amelia, 45, female, Boise, Idaho, US)

My husband and I have smartphones. And we got the hotspot. So basically, we just um, bought them like a cheap phone. Like an inexpensive phone for the kids to take along with us and we hotspot with them. Like you know, so they can access the internet because they don't have cell service. I don't let them have cell service. It is just like a tablet; like a small tablet. (Qui, 38, female, Plymouth, Michigan, US)

Echoing Sobel et al.'s (2017), a serendipitous advantage of this set up was that it meant children could not venture too far away from these parents. As Chloe and Rhonda explain:

> Because right now she's never out of sight from us. So, there's no real concern either. And I mean when it comes to the hotspot on our phones, she can't go too far without losing internet because her internet ability relies on being close to our phone. (Chloe, 27, female, Newfoundland, Canada)

> So even when we were playing together, you know, she had to stay close to me physically. (Rhonda, 39, female, San Jose, California, US)

In the context of these extracts, then, just as the physical and digital elements of the game co-constituted Chloe and Rhonda's experience, the intermingling of these aspects similarly facilitated a desirable form of co-play. And this assemblage was deemed as being valuable by both parties alike albeit for different reasons. For the children, it meant they had the freedom to access the gamic interface on their own. For the parents, it meant their children had to remain physically close to continue playing. Consequently and contra earlier Location-Based Social Networking Sites (LBSNS) it is our contention this grouping effectively establishes a familial 'magic circle' (Huizinga, 1992) of sorts that shifts as families ambulate their environment, with an extraordinary feature of this configuration being the establishment of a geofence that children *actually* want to remain within.

While familial locative play often involved multiple devices, the majority (54%) of our respondents (100 of 186) reported that decisions about how to play the game were made by the family as a whole. This was followed by 70 (38%) respondents who reported such decisions were made alone, and 10 (5%) respondents who suggested decisions were made by their children. Nevertheless, many participants noted that their children would often attempt to lead when familial locative play commenced.

> My oldest son wants to be the teacher or the leader. (Bill, 28, male, Southend-on-Sea, UK)

> She kind of like leads the way as to what we're doing. Like if she wants to go off and try and battle a gym or if we're walking and she sees a gym that she wants to battle in, she'll just sit down and start fighting in a gym. Like, oh okay, so this is what we're doing right now. (Mia, 39, female, Sonoma, California, US)

In the context of traditional video games, of course, studies have demonstrated that children are generally more comfortable using technology than their parents (Aarsand, 2007), which might explain why they often take charge. And Pokémon Go is no different (see Sobel et al., 2017). At the same time, the benefits of this dynamic transcended the game and seeped into other aspects of family life. As the following extracts describe:

> I think it just allows her to feel more comfortable and, and really at home with the game. And with me. I mean when she has control over something, whatever it is, it makes it easier to swallow the things she doesn't have control over. (Liv, 27, female, Boise, Idaho, US)

> You know, as a parent you're always the one telling your kids what to do and when to do it and how to do it. Playing the game gives him a little bit more of a leadership in the relationship. So, it evens things out a little bit, I think. (Wendy, 59, female, Orlando, Florida, US)

Yet, these positions were not set in stone. Echoing extant literature on the flexible suite of roles more traditional video games afford (Voida & Greenberg, 2012), our research found that some parents would gradually adopt more traditional roles (Tran, 2018).

> Because I knew nothing of it, right, when they first started. So, maybe they were more of a leader initially, right? Certainly, they had to teach me how to, they taught me how to play the game initially. But then I think I kind of, took over and surpassed them at that point. Ha! (Liza, 42, female, Indianapolis, Indiana, US)

> And then as I played more, then that's when it shifted a little bit back more to me being the teacher. (Amelia, 45, female, Boise, Idaho, US)

For these participants, then, as they became more informed, they were able to move beyond their initial learning-based role and in doing so reinstate their familial position as the teacher. It is our assertion here that this shift in dynamic is partially at least grounded on the locative affordances of the game. Although screen-based games commonly require a certain established dexterity usually involving fairly complicated game controllers Pokémon Go is markedly different. While this HRG might be more physical in nature, this physicality is, of course, not unusual, but instead a patent aspect of daily life. Accordingly, player progression is not granted through gamic deftness *per se á la* Fortnite but rather environmental access and knowledge, which parents can quite easily acquire. Likewise, another significance feature of this HRG is the dearth of official information provided by the interface (Tran, 2018). Because of this, 'Pokémon Go mostly leaves players to figure out how to play the game on their own' (Tran, 2018, p. 114). Consequently, learning how to play the game properly might involving speaking to members of wider community (see Lee, Windleharth, Yip, & Schmalz, 2017), which would very probably be done by parents. Again, this could provide another explanation as to why parents found themselves gradually adopting a leadership role.

Moving forward, a distinct finding from our study is the extent to which Pokémon Go complements family life. In accord with this suggestion, the majority (32%) of respondents (56 of 176) reported that the game 'definitely' complements the rhythms of family life, followed by 53 (30%) respondents who noted 'it probably does', and then 51 (29%) respondents who suggested 'it may or may not'. The lowest scoring category was 'it definitely does not', receiving only 6 (3%) responses. As a corollary to this, the familial playing of Pokémon Go was both spontaneous and planned for (see Sobel et al., 2017). In the context of spontaneous play, these gamic experiences regularly occurred during the working week and would take place alongside other activities. As Bill and Rhonda explain:

> We sometimes play it on the way to school. We'll sometimes leave twenty minutes earlier and walk kind of a longer route to school. And if there's like a raid that happens to be like ten minutes after school pick up, I'll pick Tommy up and say oh there's a raid, do you want to do it? And if he wants to, he doesn't always want to, if he wants to, we'll go do it from school. (Bill, 28, male, Southend-on-Sea, UK)

> let's say we're like on Thursdays, we go to class and then after class we go home. But often times, let's say, we'll go and do a little bit of play. And then I might say we need groceries. So, we'll do a little bit of play, you know, but then we'll also get groceries. And then we'll play around the area some more. So, like, it takes longer to complete things because now we have been playing on top of it. But I don't know, it's fun. (Rhonda, 39, female, San Jose, California, US)

In this vein, players did not carve out specific times to play the game but would instead play on an ad hoc basis that suited their current activities. Hence, the familial playing of Pokémon Go often resembled the kind of locative experience typically associated with earlier LBSNs, such as Foursquare, where the play of this application would effectively merge with daily routines (Evans & Saker, 2017; Saker & Evans, 2016) and hint at a different relationship between ordinary life and play (Frith, 2013). As the following extracts attests:

> We try to keep it really simple during the weekday. If I know I'm going to be running errands on like a lot of back roads and just be driving for a while, um, I will grab the tablet and I'll load Franklin's game up and I'll leave it running. Or have it on adventure sync so that he can get the walking distance and hatch all the little eggs. Um, after school we try to do maybe five minutes. Hit the Pokéstops on the way home so that he can hand his gifts out to his aunts. If we have extra time or if he's been really, really good at school then we'll take more time for that. But if he gets really aggressive, we shut it down and we pack up. (Jane, 28, female, Tacoma, Washington, US)

The boys don't play as much during the week although they will get their daily catch and I will try and get their daily PokeStops for them. It's mainly the weekends we play together as a family. Unless there's a special event on during the week. Then it's a bit different. (Ceri, 45, female, Essex, UK)

Symptomatic of this contextual blending, then, during weekdays the time spent playing Pokémon Go was often fairly short, with participants choosing to play, for instance, on their way to work or as they dropped their kids off at school.

As Ceri alludes to above, this practice was not always undertaken by the family as a whole but was often performed by parents on their own (Evans & Saker, 2019; Sobel et al., 2017). This is a point readily supported by our survey, with the majority (99%) of respondents (174 of 175) reporting that that there were times when they played the game alone. Tellingly, only 1 (1%) respondent suggested otherwise.

When it comes to a workday for the most part, what I'll just do is I'll check as I leave the house and see if there's anything interesting around. After that then I'll just head to work and do my job for the most part. (Justin, 26, male, Muncie, Indiana, US)

Most of the time if I'm playing alone it's mostly because I'm walking somewhere for a reason, not for Pokémon. Whenever I walk anywhere, I always play Pokémon Go. (Bill, 28, male, Southend-on-Sea, UK)

Right now, you know the kids are at school. My husband's at work. And I'm like, you know, if I'm doing laundry, I'm like okay I'll turn on my phone and just watch the screen to see what Pokémon pops up. (Qui, 38, female, Plymouth, Michigan, US)

It fits into my normal working routine. Because I commute in on the bus, so when I leave the house, I can put it on in my pocket and when I'm cycling, it will rack up a few kilometres or whatever, if I don't cycle too fast, which I rarely do. Then I get on the bus and then on the bus I can plug my phone into the charger on the nice new blue star buses now, so then I'll have it on in the bus and I can catch things if the bus goes slow enough. (Gavin, male, Southampton, UK)

Perhaps more significantly, the solo playing of Pokémon Go, was not necessarily a decision that participants made on their own (Evans & Saker, 2019). More precisely, the majority of participants did so because their children asked them to.

As soon as he comes out of school, the first thing he says to me is, 'What's happened on Pokémon Go? Have you hatched any eggs?' (Zoe, female, Brighton, UK)

I was actually raiding on his account as well because he asked me to. (Bill, 28, male, Southend-on-Sea, UK)

He was like, 'Mom, will you go do a couple raids for me.' It's like, 'okay, sure,' you know of course being the mom I am, I'm like, 'well, of course sweetie. No problem.' Yeah, then after a few months I was like wait a second, why am I doing his account? (Amelia, 45, female, Boise, Idaho, US)

As a by-product of the frequent setting of solo play i.e., on the way to work or on a lunchbreak these experiences were often fairly brief in duration and would involve the completion of specific goals. As Troy and Mia explain:

If I'm playing on my own it will be more sort of goal based. (Troy, 29, male, Norwich/East Anglia, UK)

It is a much more kind of hurried and passive experience. I'm just going to spin a couple of these, turn the game off, and keep going with whatever I was doing before. (Mia, 39, female, Sonoma, California, US)

While Pokémon Go is, of course, a game, and, therefore, predicated on play, for the most part the kind of play participants engaged with during the week was decidedly unplayful. Instead, the experience of playing this HRG alone seemed to mirror the environmental and temporal tone underpinning the competition of 'hurried' tasks. Put differently, just as this kind of play was frequently undertaken while in a work-based setting, participants similarly comprehended this practice as being a form of labour or 'maintenance' as some participants referred to it.

Well normally during the week, you can essentially just think of it as like maintenance'. So, getting at least one stop and one Pokémon. (Mick, 26, male, Newfoundland, Canada)

Typically, during the work week, Monday to Friday, we basically stop on the way home or go somewhere at lunch just so we can spin the stop and catch a Pokémon. (Chloe, 27, female, Newfoundland, Canada)

So, it means by the time I get to the weekend, I can have a couple hundred Poke balls and he gets to use it when we go out. Because where we live there aren't any Pokéstops. (Gavin, male, Southampton, UK)

For Gavin, then, the purpose of this 'maintenance' is to collect Poke balls that he can then use at the weekend when he plays with his son, which leads us on to the division between spontaneous and planned for periods of familial locative play.

Although locative play during the working week was ordinarily unprompted, short lived and could be performed alone, the familial playing of this HRG over the weekend presents a very different experience. As the following extracts describe:

> If it's a community day coming up, which there was just one this past Sunday, you know we'll tell the kids hey, community day Sunday, we're playing eleven to two. So, we just kind of schedule our activities around if there's something special happening in the app. (Liza, 42, female, Indianapolis, Indiana, US)

> The weekend, a community day only happens once a month on the weekend. So, you know, we plan for that. Um. It's like two, two hours, I think. So, we plan on that block of two hours around our schedule. (Qui, 38, female, Plymouth, Michigan, US)

> The only really, I guess, structured time would be on the weekends. Especially if it's a community day and then it's like oh my god, community day. Aaaaaaah! You know, we have to go out for like an hour and a half or two hours for that. (Maureen, 51, female, Lansing, Michigan, US)

> The only difference is when there are special events like the community day which usually happens on the weekend. And then we make plans and we go and often, like, meet other people and, you know, do the playing. (Rhonda, 39, female, San Jose, California, US)

As Rhonda points out, the weekend is the only real time she 'schedules' play, and this was a sentiment shared by other participants. For these families, then, the playing of Pokémon Go in the context of weekend is no longer about blending the game with the banal aspects of daily life. Instead, familial locative play revolves around scheduled events, such as raids and community days that can last for much lengthier periods of time, as well as implicate specific locations. And because of this, the experience of locative play is understood as being markedly different to the kind of locative play that occurs during the week.

> The intensity is definitely on the weekends. No question. (Amelia, 45, female, Boise, Idaho, US)

> During the weekend we'll probably do a little bit more serious play like looking for raid battles or going to a lot of different stops. (Mick, 26, male, Newfoundland, Canada)

In sum, then, and building upon the arguments made in the previous chapter, Pokémon Go meaningfully differs from older LBSNs and their implicit focus on challenging the suggested division between play and ordinary life

(Saker & Evans, 2016). While Foursquare and its limited mechanics did permeate daily life (Saker & Evans, 2016), and in doing so, did render ordinary life more playful, it was never able to go beyond this; it never *actually* turned 'ordinary life into a game' (Frith, 2013). Once the novelty of checking-in at this or that location wore off players were left with an experience that felt, well, fairly laborious and with good reason. The check-in mechanic was a form of labour (Evans, 2015). In reality, the leveraging of locative information was never really about the ludology of urban environments, as the continued success of Foursquare demonstrates. More precisely, these gamic elements provided a necessary lure for users to furtively develop granular understanding of space and place that could then be sold to other businesses (Frith & Wilken, 2019). Importantly for this chapter, though Pokémon Go does implicate a form of labour, it also implicates a form of play that is markedly different from the kind of play once associated with earlier LBSNs. That is, Pokémon does not simply blend with routine activities although it evidently can but also creates extraordinary experiences that are specifically predicated on their spatial and temporal separation from daily life. In other words, a notable feature of this new generation of locative games is not the blurring on the boundary between ordinary life and play *á la* Foursquare, but rather its reinstatement. In doing so, this HRG manages to create locative experiences that are compelling enough to become activities in their own right. As a corollary to this, many participants were willing to put in the working during the week to spend time with their children over the weekend. And as we will demonstrate in the next chapter, this 'quality' time is understood as having a number of positive benefits for both parents and children alike.

3.4 Pokémon Go and Family Life

For our participants, an important aspect of the playing of Pokémon Go is the opportunity it provides for spending time with their family (Evans & Saker, 2019; Sobel et al., 2017). This can be observed in the following extracts.

> It's always just been a fun bonding thing. (Jane, 28, female, Tacoma, Washington, US)

> It's something we can all do together. (Joe, 37, male, Southend-on-Sea, UK)

> I love seeing the excitement on their faces when they get new Pokémon or when there's new stuff out. I mean, you know, kids grow up so fast and, you know, when they get older, they really don't want to have anything to do with you. And I just want to savour the moment. You know. (Qui, 38, female, Plymouth, Michigan, US)

For these participants, playing Pokémon Go as a family is more than just spending time together. Of course, physical proximity does not guarantee a collective experience, as families can be physically together but cognitively else-where through digital technologies (Gergen, 2002). More importantly, this is deemed 'quality' time together. As Qui notes, playing Pokémon Go with her children lets her 'savour the moment'. Likewise, in much the same way that this HRG can nudge participants to spend more time outside, as outlined in the previous chapter, it can also nudge children to take part.

> I think it's like kind of the only reason we actually do play it as a family. (Mia, 39, female, Sonoma, California, US)

> It's another tool we use to spend some time together and interact with each other. (Troy, 29, male, Norwich/East Anglia, UK)

Consequently, an important outcome of this kind of familial locative play is the positive effect it has on participants' relationships with their children. In accord with this position, the majority (61%) of our respondents (114 of 187) reported that Pokémon Go 'definitely' strengthened the connections they had with their children. This was followed by 49 (26%) respondents who reported it 'probably' did and finally 3 (2%) respondents who reported it did not. Likewise, the strengthening of familial connections through locative play was a theme that also came up during interviews.

> It was definitely our thing as like mother and son. (Amelia, 45, female, Boise, Idaho, US)

> It's about one of the very few things I'm able to really interact with her in and connect close to her as a father daughter relationship. (Justin, 26, male, Muncie, Indiana, US)

For Amelia and Justin, then, a central feature of playing Pokémon Go with their children is the 'shared' connection it affords and the benefits this has for their relationships. At the same time, our research also found that this bonding opportunity was not just appreciated by parents vis-à-vis their children but could also extends to siblings. Here, the playing of Pokémon Go offers a space for brothers and sisters to be together in a manner that might not otherwise happen, as siblings particularly when they are different ages often struggle to find activities they both enjoy. As Jo puts it:

> I think it helps just get them out together and get them wanting to be with each other as brother and sister because they usually don't want to be together. (Jo, 50, female, Plymouth, Michigan, US)

Equally, and resonating with exiting studies examining traditional computer games and the propensity of children to adopt a lead role during play (Siyahhan & Gee, 2018), the locative bonding between sibling is accentuated by the opportunity Pokémon Go provides for older sisters or brother to adopt a supervisory role and help their younger sibling. In doing so, this HRG facilitates a form of play that successfully allows both younger and older relations to be together.

> And the oldest, you know, he's more than excited to teach his younger brother stuff in the new things. And you know, yeah, he can read. The oldest can read. He can look up information on the internet. But, you know, any information or stuff, we told him that he can ask us. And then he can relay that information to his brother so they can interact with each other too. (Qui, 38, female, Plymouth, Michigan, US)

> But it was more for her to do something with her brother that he enjoyed and he could, you know, give her pointers, you know, do this, do that, do this, do that, this is a good one, this is a bad one kind of thing. (Maureen, 51, female, Lansing, Michigan, US)

For both Qui and Maureen, then, a symptom of their children playing together was the pleasure their oldest child experienced by affirming their position as the big brother.

In contrast to this, many participants found the familial playing of this HRG did not so much affirm their parental role but enabled them to move beyond this.

> People get too serious, you know, especially in an environment where you know, parents are working fifty hours a week or sixty hours a week. They kind of forget that they have children and your only interactions with your children tend to be, you know, arguing about homework or eating their dinner or going to bed on time. That sort of thing. And when you can actually find time to have fun, I think that really makes a difference in the parent-child dynamic. (Wendy, 59, female, Orlando, Florida, US)

> I think that it's more bonding with them like I don't, I don't like to go out of my way to try to be like oh well I'm your mom I want you to do this you know like kind of thing. I want to build that relationship where I'm like yes, I'm your parent. You have to listen to me but at the same time it's I'm also your friend and you know, I'm here for you, you know? (Christine, 27, female, Denver, Colorado, US)

For Wendy and Christine, then, this transgression has a positive effect on their relationships with their children. Developing this point further, for Jane, the shifting of roles that Pokémon Go facilitates is in part at least predicated on its locative affordances. As she explains:

> I think we get stuck in our roles when we're in certain places. Even old schools that I used to go to, once I step in those buildings, it's

hard to shake off what I'm supposed to do or what I was used to doing in that space. So, if we're at home and usually it's, you know, a fight to do whatever chore you don't want to do, it's harder to open up. Because you're used to okay, this is home, we do boring things here. As opposed to going outside and we've got our devices out and oh okay, we're going to go out and have fun and we're going to do all the things. It changes your mindset. (Jane, 28, female, Tacoma, Washington, US)

Here, Jane touches on an interesting point. Environments play a role in identity (Saker, 2016). Just as, say, one's work-based identity is in part co-constituted through the locative aspect of the workplace, so too does the home underline the role of the parent. Accordingly, familial interactions within the domestic sphere arrive under the auspices of parental authority. Of course, the same is true of children, and this position equally carries its own baggage. By moving these gamic experiences outside, then, both parents and children are able to enjoy a certain flexibility in their roles, and this flexibility is deemed valuable in the context of strengthening familial bonds. As a corollary to this fluidity of roles, and through this 'shared' interest, children were happy talk to their parents about the game. As Joe explains:

Outside of, you know if I pick him up from school, I'll ask him how his day was, and I'll get absolutely nothing. You know, he'll just go 'good', or 'I can't remember'. Whereas if we were engaged in talking about Pokémon Go or something like that, he'll be interested to like, if I speak to him on the phone, he'll ask oh daddy did you get a shiny today? And I'll be like yes or no, and he'll be genuinely interested, and he'll want to talk about it himself. (Joe, 37, male, Southend-on-Sea, UK)

For Joe, then, by discussing Pokémon Go with his son, he was able to engage him in a livelier conversation than if he were to ask him about his day. In other words, this 'shared experience' creates the opportunity for dialogue to emerge that would not have otherwise happened. At the same time, and in line with Sobel et al. (2017), for other participants, an explicit aspect of the familial playing of Pokémon Go is that discourse would extend beyond the game.

[Pokémon Go] gives you sort of this non-confrontational time where you can talk and get into some deeper subjects while you're just playing. You know? You're not staring at each other eye to eye. And in having, you know, a deep conversation that way where it can get uncomfortable. But if you're just sort of walking around or playing with the video, you can chat about more important things that kind of sneak into the conversation to give you that opportunity. (Wendy, 59, female, Orlando, Florida, US)

Franklin is reluctant to tell us about his day. Partly because sometimes he gets in trouble and sometimes it's just boring. It's not something you want to relive with mom and dad. But if we can pull the phones up and say 'hey look, this is what I caught today' he opens up a little bit more. He's more willing to discuss. (Jane, 28, female, Tacoma, Washington, US)

When they start talking to you about that stuff, they can talk to you about other stuff too. They feel comfortable about. (Amelia, 45, female, Boise, Idaho, US)

For these participants, then, a marked benefit of the familial playing of this HRG is the provision of, what Wendy refers to as, 'non-confrontational time'. Symptomatic of the explicit ambulation involved in playing Pokémon Go and the fact that the attention of both parents and children necessarily includes their physical surrounding, deeper and 'more important' things were able to 'sneak' into the conversation. That is, by taking the focus away from the conversations occurring in tandem with the game, children became more 'comfortable' and this comfort allowed them to talk about aspects about their lives that they might not have spoken about in a different setting or while playing a different game.

Moving forward, just as Pokémon Go can provide families with a number of opportunities to bond, many participants also discussed the role this HRG plays in advancing the cognitive skills of their children. As the following extracts attest:

I think it provides an opportunity to teach them certain things as it relates to strategy. (Faizan, 49, male, Denver, Colorado, US)

We found this really old Pokémon book with all of the different Pokémon in it. So, he's taking the time to read that. And he's very careful about how he battles. (Jane, 28, female, Tacoma, Washington, US)

And then also just looking at different strategies when you're defeating certain bosses in the game, you know we take a minute before, or okay now which type of attack is strongest or weakest. So, you know, thinking like that is not, maybe it doesn't specifically have a direct live, you know, it doesn't directly change how you would live your life but just making a strategy before you go into a situation in general is a good skill to build. (Stephanie, 42, female, Orlando, Florida, US)

There are incredible memorization opportunities. My son can, I mean, I wish you could use some of this in school, honestly. But, you know, he knows everybody's evolution. He knows what type they are. And they're having to learn how to memorize that stuff. Um, understanding from a math standpoint, how much is something going to power up when I give it one berry. (Amelia, 45, female, Boise, Idaho, US)

It's just like they absorb the stuff and just can rifle the information off and talk about their attack powers, their defences, and how strong they are and how weak they are. And you know, what's best to use against the other in the fight. They just know this stuff. It's just kind of funny. (Alan, 50, male, Plymouth, Michigan, US)

Yet, it is not just the game that helps children advance. For many of our participants, an important aspect of the familial playing of this HRG is the ability to teach their children various life lessons. This suggestion resonates with our survey, as majority (85%) of our respondents (150 of 178) reported that this HRG has provided them with the space to impart a range of life lessons. Conversely, only 28 (16%) respondents suggesting otherwise. And this point is echoed by our participants.

There's a lot of great social opportunities where I was able to say, okay, this really isn't proper behaviour. (Amelia, 45, female, Boise, Idaho, US)

To understand that it is just a game and that sometimes things are going to run, you're not going to get something and it's okay to be like, other people will and you'll see that, which was a bit of a problem for my oldest when we first started playing. (Bill, 28, male, Southend-on-Sea, UK)

We've been teaching her, you know, how to deal with disappointment and sometimes you don't always get what you want or what you expect. But that there's always other opportunities if you just wait. (Mia, 39, female, Sonoma, California, US)

Just as the conversations that parents have with their children while playing this HRG exceed the game, the same is true of the life lessons parents impart. As the extracts with Bill and Mia above corroborate, learning to cope with disappoint is obviously not specific to Pokémon Go, but rather a recurring aspect of daily life. Consequently, the development of these skills is important in and of themselves. For Maureen, a significant outcome of this development is her daughter's mounting confidence in playing the game even though her character is not always ready to do so. As she explains:

It's like okay, you think we can take this gym? There's three of us and there's six monsters in there. Can we do it? Yeah, let's do it! You know, it helps build her self-confidence in some ways because she feels confident enough to go beat up other people's Pokémons. And she's always trying to get into raids like with a level hundred and fifty Pokémon. She's in there battling like fifty thousand health point Pokémon. But it's, and it teaches her persistence. (Maureen, 51, female, Lansing, Michigan, US)

Building upon this point, for other participants, children did not just become more confident in the game, they also became more confident communicating with adults.

> I think the main thing for my son is that he's way more confident in talking to other adults than I probably still am now. He'll go up and he will talk like, when we first started, you know, when you go and talk to people and you, he'd generally just stand by my leg and not do anything. Now, he'll talk their ears off all day. (Bill, 28, male, Southend-on-Sea, UK)

> She just walks up to anybody and says are you catching the Pokémon? What Pokémon are you catching? And most people respond pretty well and just show her their screens like yep, I'm catching another one. (Liv, 27, female, Boise, Idaho, US)

As we have detailed above, an aspect of intergenerational play in the context of traditional video games has been the effect this experience has on the communicative potential between different age groups, with adolescents often feeling more able to express themselves under the auspices of co-play (Al Mahmud et al., 2010; Chua et al., 2013; Derboven et al., 2012; Uhlenberg, 2000). In the same way that the game can take the focus away from communicative acts, it can also take the focus away from disparities associated with age. And this outcome is similarly observed through the lens of locative games. Yet, the locative affordances of Pokémon Go means this game provides a different kind of social experience. As Liza explains:

> What I like about Pokémon Go is that my job as a fundraiser is very soft-skill oriented and socializing and you know, as a generalization of millennials and younger folks who have just grown up with so much screen time that they lack those kinds of skills. And here is a game that is on that platform but that uses the environment in a way that I don't know of any other games doing. (Liza, 42, female, Indianapolis, Indiana, US)

For Liza, then, not only does Pokémon Go provide the space for 'younger folk' to develop their social skills, this game is implicitly positioned as being a viable antidote to the kind of 'screen time' children now experience growing up. In other words, Pokémon Go is comprehended as differing from traditional video games. Perhaps more importantly, an explicit part of this suggested remedy is the way in which this HRG uses the surrounding environment. In doing so, children are not just learning how to play the game *per se*. From Liza's position, the game is teaching them how to *be* within these environments and how to interact with other people both within and outside of the game.

At the same time, it is also apparent that the myriad benefits of the kind of locative play Pokémon Go offers families did not start and end with the children.

Many participants also discussed the various ways in which the playing of this HRG had helped aspects of their own lives as people not necessarily parents. As Mia and Liv explain:

> I have a hard time being around like a lot of people sometimes. But going to San Francisco to go catch a lot of Pokémon down by the water when there's like some sort of water event going on, it's kind of, it's more fun because it gives me something I'm focused on and I'm not doing anything with all those other people. (Mia, 39, female, Sonoma, California, US)

> Well I just, I, when I first started playing, my daughter was I think between six months and a year old. And I was struggling pretty hardcore with postpartum depression. And it gave me something to get me out of the house every day. So, whereas before I was choosing to be in the home and struggling with that, it gave me some, it gave me a reason and kind of a way to force myself out and get movement and go. And then of course once you get movement going, it tends to keep going. (Liv, 27, female, Boise, Idaho, US)

For Mia and Liv, then, the playing of Pokémon Go has not just improved the relationships they have with their children, it has also improved their mental health. And the power of this should not be underestimated, as the following comments from Christine attest.

> It's probably one of the things that kept me from sinking into a really dark depression. (Christine, 27, female, Denver, Colorado, US)

This finding is supported by other studies that have identified the positive influence this HRG can have on the lives of players with physical disabilities. As Evans and Saker (2019) point out, a favourable effect of this games is that 'physically disabled players experienced a … desire to be more active as part of the praxis of locative play' (p. 7). Yet, the benefits of this association are not simply physical. In the context of Foursquare, Saker and Evans (2016) also found that participants did not just enjoy being more active although this was part of the pleasure more precisely they enjoyed developing an identity that was able to move beyond the sedentariness of their physical condition. In a similar vein, we would also content that for some of our participants, an important aspect of playing this HRG is the imaginary distance it creates between themselves and their problems.

In sum, then, Pokémon Go has the potential to improve family life in a number of ways. Echoing other studies (see Sobel et al., 2017), this HRG provides participants with the necessary lure to entice children to spend extended periods of time with them as a family. And these periods of play can strengthen the familial bond between adults and children alike. Significantly, the strengthening of these bonds is directly associated with the locative aspects of the game. Symptomatic of having to ambulate space and place, parents and children are able to move beyond their commonplace roles *à la* the domestic sphere. Likewise, by focussing on the game as opposed to each, children are able to engage in deeper conversation that is outwardly protected by the cover of the game. Consequently, many participants found the game allowed their children to develop as people; becoming more confident in competing, less concerned about defeat and more able to speak to adults. Again, these developments are explicitly understood as stemming from locative aspects of the game, and the fact playing that this HRG involves being within physical space amidst various social flows. Lastly, for a number of participants, the playing of Pokémon Go did more than just strengthen their familial relationship, it also helped them overcome a range of issues that preceded the familial playing of this game.

3.5 Fears, Concerns and Compromises

For the most, our respondents did not express any major worries about playing Pokémon Go with their children, with 141 (86%) respondents reporting that they did not have any concerns about this familial pastime, and only 23 (14%) respondents reporting that they did. Nonetheless, when it came to interviews, participants were notably more vocal about the various apprehensions they have about playing this HRG as a family. In the main, these apprehensions revolve around the physical safety of their children. As Bill and Mia explain:

> The main actual issue is to keep looking at, like what's going on around them enough and not just staring at the phone. (Bill, 28, male, Southend-on-Sea, UK)

> Just about her being aware. Just about like traffic when we're in congested areas. Sometimes she'll forget that parking lots also count as the street and so she doesn't necessarily pay attention for the cars. (Mia, 39, female, Sonoma, California, US)

These particular fears, of course, directly relate to the locative affordances of the game, families do not play it in the comfort of their homes, but in public environments amidst other people. Correspondingly, such fears resonate with early research on mobile phones and the concerns commentators articulated about users injuring themselves because they were not paying enough attention to their physical surroundings (see Stavrinos, Byington, & Schwebel, 2011). At the same time, participants were not just worried about their children being focused on the game at the expense of concrete reality. For participants like Justin, another concern revolved around the possibility of other people continuing to play the game while they were driving, and the dangers this presents for other players.

> I think when it comes to actually the big updates that happen sometimes, more people tend to start playing it and then obviously you'll have those people who will tend to be not thinking too much. And as they're playing your game while driving as well either by themselves or with somebody else. They'll tend to not look at the road or if they are playing, they're not looking up all the time. And they'll end up getting in an accident like a lot of times that was happening early in the game. (Justin, 26, male, Muncie, Indiana, US)

This kind of worry which is both understandable and very much warranted (Revell, 2017) is demonstrative of the difference between Pokémon Go and earlier LBSNs (Evans & Saker, 2017). Although Foursquare users often incorporated this application into their daily flows (Saker & Evans, 2016a), this was usually done in the context of quotidian tasks. In other words, users were augmenting their ordinary lives rather than supplanting them with something extraordinary. Contra this, certain participants spoke of other Pokémon Go players using their cars during events, such as raids, so they could quickly traverse the gamic environment. Again, the reasoning for doing this is rooted in the gamic experience of this HRG. Regarding raids, these events last for a particular period of time. Accordingly, players are more likely to want to complete tasks quickly to maximise their opportunity for progress. Again, this underlines the advancement of pervasive play vis-à-vis the likes of Foursquare, which did not demarcate locative play from daily nor did it implicate such a large and diverse community (Evans & Saker, 2017).

As a corollary to the above, then, playing Pokémon Go presents numerous opportunities for players to meet and communicate with other people, which leads us on to another concern some participants brought up: the fear of strangers (Sobel et al., 2017). As Ceri explains:

> You know, just the usual stranger danger. That sort of thing. You do worry about, because you know, it could be someone could easily say oh yeah come and see my shiny Pokémon and then you know? (Ceri, 45, female, Essex, UK)

For participants like Qui, these concerns were specifically heightened during periods of planned locative play, such as raids and community days, which would commonly take place over the weekend.

> Because you know, because it's a community and you know, sometimes when we go to raids, we see familiar faces. It's like hi, I remember you. You know. We'll chat. And then Jett will try to chat too. I'm like Jett, please talk to other kids. Because I'm more comfortable with him talking to other kids than with grown-ups. (Qui, 38, female, Plymouth, Michigan, US)

To help combat these concerns about physical safety and the threat of strangers, many participants established rules for familial locative play. This is a point that can be observed in the findings from our survey. Here, the majority (56%) albeit a small majority of our respondents (108 of 193) reported that they established rules that governed the familial playing of Pokémon Go, followed by 85 (44%) respondents that reported they did not establish rules. However, generalisation about this narrow margin should not be made without delving further into the data. More precisely, there is a correlation between the application of rules and the age of the parents. While younger parents were likely to establish rules for locative play, older parents were not. And, of course, this makes sense, as older parents are more likely to have older children, who are less likely to require restrictions, and so on. Nonetheless, regarding the participants who did establish rules to govern locative play, the following guidelines were generally put in place: children must stay physically close to them during play, remain cognisant of their surroundings and refrain from talking to strangers on their own. These parameters can be observed in the following extracts.

> She is only allowed to play it with mummy. (Carol, 34, female, San Antonio, Texas, US)

> The rules are you are not allowed to be looking at the phone while you're crossing the street. That is pretty much the only rule because otherwise, yeah, she would be trying to catch something when she is crossing the street and that's not safe when we're downtown. (Mia, 39, female, Sonoma, California, US)

> Like, this is something we've talked about a lot. I'm like, 'you know when we're walking, put the phone down and let's look at what's going on.' And we always laugh because there's lots of animals around school, like 'see there's a real Pokémon!' You know, whether it's a squirrel, cats, turtles, whatever. So, I try to notice the real Pokémon too. (Stephanie, 42, female, Orlando, Florida, US)

> Yeah, so Nick and I discussed it and then we said hey Franklin, we're going to play this game. But here's the rules before we get started. Don't be crazy. Don't run out into space. Don't talk to strangers and we'll be fine. (Jane, 28, female, Tacoma, Washington, US)

In the context of fears surrounding strangers, participants would also keep a constant eye on their children's' 'friend list'. As Stephanie and Christine explain.

> I think it led to a conversation where I was telling him, 'hey I want to know who your friends are' and we've definitely been talking more lately about hey, you've got to be careful on social media and you can't, because he'd be like, 'why does it matter?' So, we've had that conversation with my husband, all three of us. About you

know, you have to be careful what you put out there, there's people that might try to harm you. (Stephanie, 42, female, Orlando, Florida, US)

I'm very into, you know, making sure that I know who's on their friends list and they're on my friends list and, you know, I can contact whoever. Or you know, it's, there's restrictions in place for safety and things like that, you know. (Christine, 27, female, Denver, Colorado, US)

While the establishment of rules did help participants feel better about playing this HRG with their children, we should also mention the role that the game, as well as the interface, play in pre-empting some of the fears outlined above. In the main, families seemingly play Pokémon Go in large open spaces (Mäyrä, 2017), away from the road, such as parks and fields (Perry, 2016). While the aesthetic benefits of these kinds of environment speak for themselves, it also makes it easier for families to remain close to their children and keep a constant eye on their movements. Equally, as detailed above, many families let their children play on a separate handset tethered to their data-enabled smartphone. This means children are implicitly nudged to stay reasonably close to their parents a point supported by other studies (see Sobel et al., 2017). Lastly, and as many participants pointed out, the gamic interface itself does not have a 'chat' features, which is a decision that was readily welcomed by the clearly majority of participants.

Moving forward, then, just as we have readily shown the various ways in which the familial playing of Pokémon Go can complement family life and provide a range of opportunities for families to strengthen their bond, this experience does not always come without a cost. As the following extracts highlight, the familial playing of Pokémon Go can be problematic if one member of the family does not want to play. This point can be observed in the following extracts.

She's quite happy for us to go off and play on set days. But if we're out doing something with the family and I get my phone out, she doesn't like that sometimes. And do a little moan or give a look. (Troy, 29, male, Norwich/East Anglia, UK)

I think that that one's kind of hard because my husband does not like Pokémon Go at all. He doesn't understand why we play. He really can't, like, if we get into a conversation in the car about something, he turns up the radio because he doesn't want to listen to it. That's kind of our cue to stop talking Pokémon. So, in terms of family rhythm, it, for us, for me and my kids it fits very well. But in terms of a whole family, not necessarily. (Amelia, 45, female, Boise, Idaho, US)

As Amelia points out, although Pokémon Go can suit the rhythms of family life for some family members, it might not be ideal for the family as a whole, which can then lead to familial friction. Consequently, participants who decided to continue playing the game against their children's wishes felt guilty for doing so. As Joe notes:

> We'll meet up with a group of other players. And loads of them have got kids as well. And they'll run around. But I think just because it's a six-year-old and a two-year-old, definitely more so with the two-year-old, they obviously just want to run off and do their own thing. And we're like walking past the playground she's like 'oh I want to go to the playground' and I'm like 'oh you can't', and that is asking a lot of her to like not to go in the playground. So, in that respect, you know, I'm under no illusions that sometimes, like when we play, our motivations are selfish. (Joe, 37, male, Southend-on-Sea, UK)

For other participants, and echoing extant literature (Sobel et al., 2017), they were not so much concerned about familial conflict *per se*, but the detrimental effect screen time might have on their children.

> Sometimes I feel guilty giving Franklin his own device to go do that with, you know. We're at this beautiful place and we're going to dink around on this machine. (Jane, 28, female, Tacoma, Washington, US)

> The parks we go to when we're trying to walk and get kilometres and also get some sort of like an environment, like nature, we want to go and do something wholesome kind of. But we are still looking at our screens which is ridiculous. (Mia, 39, female, Sonoma, California, US)

> At some point it became a hindrance. Because I wanted to be hiking and I wanted to be enjoying the nature but yet I was constantly like feeling the need to look at my phone. And that was frustrating that I couldn't, like, because I think that Pokémon Go is a little bit addictive and a little bit, you know, like what you have when you're gambling. I don't know what the word to use. Because you're like looking at it, what if I have something good? What if I have a good shiny? You know, it's like, I mean I'm not a gambler so I don't really know the slot machines or whatever, but I would imagine it's something similar. So, it can be really hard to regulate those urges. I have to think what actually I want to do right now. And I think that was also the reason why I would quit. But then I would come back to it again because it's interesting. It makes life a bit richer. (Rhonda, 39, female, San Jose, California, US)

Of course, concerns about screen time are commonplace (Graber, 2019). Yet, the worries participants experienced in this regard are also different, and this difference implicates the locative aspect of the game. Here, participants are not so much worried about locative play in the context of the kind of fears surrounding more traditional video games, but that the interface might take their attention away from the physical surroundings framing the gamic experience. As Mia puts it above, 'we are still looking at our screens'. Accordingly, for many participants, the playing of Pokémon Go was positioned as a compromise of sorts between the parental desire for families to be more physically active, while spending time together, and the want of children to play video games. This rationalisation can be observed in the following extracts.

> It's not just something you sit and play in the house. So, you can't just sit and play mindlessly for hours. (Liza, 42, female, Indianapolis, Indiana, US)

> Only the fact that I already hate how much they always want to be on a phone or a device. Like I think it's, it's kind of meeting in the middle. It's like they're on a device or a phone but they're outside with people. So at least there's a benefit to it. (Bill, 28, male, Southend-on-Sea, UK)

> He's quite happy to sit on a computer all day playing Minecraft, or he's got a Pokémon game on something called Roadblocks now, which is like an online thing. Um, so it was about getting him out of the house. And he would walk three- or four-miles playing Pokémon without blinking. (Gavin, male, Southampton, UK)

As Gavin explains, playing this HRG is still preferable to playing the likes of Minecraft, which does not offer the kind of trade-off that Bill notes. Nonetheless, this is not to suggest the familial playing of Pokémon Go is correlatively positioned as something commonplace. To further combat concerns about screen time, some participants would often use the playing of this HRG as a reward to be earned again, underlining it demarcation from ordinary life. As the following extracts attest:

> After school we try to do maybe five minutes. Hit the pokéstops on the way home so that he can hand his gifts out to his aunts. If we have extra time or if he's been really, really good at school then we'll take more time for that. But if he gets really aggressive, we shut it down and we pack up. (Jane, 28, female, Tacoma, Washington, US)

> If you clean up your room, we can go on a Pokémon walk. (Stephanie, 42, female, Orlando, Florida, US)

Here, the playing of Pokémon Go is grounded on children either behaving or completing tasks that parents have allocated to them. Conversely, just as Pokémon Go functions as a kind of reward system, the removal of play can also be employed as a punishment, with limited screen time being sanctioned because children either did not complete their tasks or do what they were asked to do. As Troy puts:

> If he's been particularly naughty one day then he doesn't get any
> screen time. (Troy, 29, male, Norwich/East Anglia, UK)

In sum, then, just as Pokémon Go can comfortably complement the rhythms of family life it can equally introduce a range of issues that need to be worked through (Sobel et al., 2017). To return to a point we made in the opening chapter, there is nothing intrinsic of a particular technology that guarantees this or that effect (Latour, 2005); just as media technologies can be used to pull families apart (Turkle, 2017), they can also be used to create new connections (Baym, 2015). Nonetheless, for the most part, the suite of concerns that Pokémon Go introduces coalesce around the status of this HRG as a legitimate game in its own right (Evans & Saker, 2019). In the context of earlier LBSNs, and as touched on above, players would incorporate these applications into their ordinary lives (Saker & Evans, 2016). Consequently, the gamic world rarely took precedence over the quotidian flows of day-to-day existence. In contrast, Pokémon Go offers a different kind of phenomenology. Here, families can take part in events that go on for specific periods of time, within certain spaces, amidst a much broader community of players. From this position, then, locative play is not so much about blending with ordinary life but supplanting it. At the same time, this shift equally leads to new concerns. In the context of familial locative play, parents would worry about the physical safety of their children, the opportunities the game presents for engaging with strangers, and the fact playing Pokémon Go is still a form of screen time albeit a form of screen time that is more preferable to conventional video games. Nonetheless, in line with other studies (Sobel et al., 2017), our participants were able to circumvent some of these fears and concerns by establishing rules that governed how their children should play the game. Equally, and again in line with extant literature (Turkle, 2017), children would often play on a secondary device tethered to their parents' data-enabled smartphone. Importantly, this provided another means to keeping children physically close to their parents. Similarly, many participants touched on the suitability of the Pokémon Go interface to the kind of familial locative play that underpins this book. More precisely, the absence of a 'chat' feature meant parents were able to let their children play on secondary devices without worrying about who they might be communicating with. In all these instances, then, these threats, as well as the compromises enacted, underline the various ways this HRG differs from traditional video games as a direct consequence of its locative status, a status which not only brings families together but is seen by some as offering an antidote to rising levels of screen time endemic of more traditional digital media.

3.6 Conclusion

The purpose of this chapter has been to explore how the hybrid reality game (HRG) Pokémon Go fits into the lives of families who play it together. In doing so, the chapter began by considering the importance of play for both children and adults alike (Eberle, 2014, p. 217; Sutton-Smith, 1997), and how free play in urban environments has gradually been moving away from the streets and towards designated playgrounds (Agate et al., 2018; Chudacoff, 2007; Frost, 2010; Gray, 2009; Mintz, 2004). At the same time, commentators have also observed the gradual movement of children from the streets into their homes and bedrooms (Livingstone, 2002). Tellingly, this shift correlates with the advancing role digital media technologies, such as video games, now play in the domestic sphere. While the relation between these trends can be debated, what is more difficult to contest is the effect technologies are having on parenting (Takeuchi, 2011) and not all parents feel this is for the better (Seo & Lee, 2017). Yet, a growing number of studies have demonstrated the positive effects families can experience when video games are played together (Siyahhan & Gee, 2018).

Indeed, intergenerational play, or JME as it is also referred, can provide a much needed space for different generations to be together, which can have a number of constructive consequences (Al Mahmud et al., 2010). For example, it can reduce intergroup anxiety (Chua et al., 2013), facilitate quality family time and enable younger players to experiment with a broader suite of roles than more traditional games (Voida & Greenberg, 2012). However, it is also apparent that the clear majority of extant studies revolve around video games that are played within the home through mounted television screens. Although the vast majority of computer games are played in this way, as we have demonstrated in previous chapters, computer games have also developed beyond the domestic sphere (Evans, 2015; Evans & Saker, 2017). More precisely, HRGs like Pokémon Go blend the gamic environment with physical space, and this blending presents a range of implications in the context of intergenerational play (Evans & Saker, 2019). Yet, only a limited number of studies have examined locative game through this scholarly lens (see Sobel et al., 2017). Addressing this gap has been the aim of this chapter.

First, we explored why and how families play Pokémon Go. For the most part, participants either began playing this game because their children expressed an interested in doing so, or because they were intrigued by the idea of an HRG. Perhaps more importantly, a chief finding from this research is the extent to which Pokémon Go complements the lives of the families that play this game together. During the week, families were able to incorporate this locative play into their daily lives in a manner the echoes earlier LBSNs (Saker & Evans, 2016), with participants playing this HRG while travelling to and from work. Of course, this would not be possible if they were playing a more traditional video game. Because of this blending, participants were also able to play this HRG on their own, and often at the request of their children. Here, solo play took on an interesting hue. While children were, of course, absent, this absence was more akin to a nuanced form of 'absent presence' (Gergen, 2002), with parents performing this 'maintenance' with their children firmly in mind if not in body. In other words, this practice revolved around asynchronous familial bonding. Significantly, these periods of solo play also meant that parents became more invested in the gamic experience, which then improved the familial play that would take place over the weekend, leading us on to another noteworthy finding. Although the co-playing of traditional video games might change at weekends, it is unlikely that this difference is mirrored in the game itself. In contrast, the familial playing of Pokémon Go at weekends implicates a very different experience, with the participants' ordinary lives being momentarily supplanted with special events, such as raids and community days, which last for lengthier durations and involve a wider community of players. Consequently, familial locative over the weekend provides a satisfying conclusion to the maintenance performed during the week that exhibits a sensitivity to time that is perhaps missing in the context of traditional video games.

Second, and directly building upon the previous point, we explored what impact the familial playing of this HRG has on the relationships between parents and children. In line with other studies (see Sobel et al., 2017), we found a marked benefit of the game was the fact it could be played as a family, and that the gamic mechanics were rich enough to entice children to spend protracted periods with their parents. Furthermore, for participants, this was not just perceived as time with their children, but more importantly it was perceived as being 'quality' time that provides a suite of familial benefits. For many participants, by engaging in a shared activity, they were able to form a stronger bond with their children. Because of this, parents then had a mutual talking point outside of the game. Yet, this discourse was not solely confined to the game itself. Some participants spoke of Pokémon Go providing a 'non-confrontational' space that allowed their children to open up about other aspects of their lives in a manner that would not be possible beyond the confines of the game. And this space was not only useful for deepening dialogue but also it allowed parents to surreptitiously impart a range of life lessons. In all instances, then, the various benefits families associate with the familial playing of this HRG revolve around its locative affordances. That is, the playing of Pokémon Go is not just about learning to play the game *per se*, but more meaningfully, it is about learning to navigate everyday life.

Third, our interest turned towards the various fears, concerns and compromises that surround the familial playing of Pokémon Go. Resonating with existing literature (Sobel et al., 2017), our participants were mainly fearful of physical danger and strangers, which, of course, speaks to the locative aspect of the game. In the context of events, such as raids and community days, the playing of this HRG involves specific sites for specific durations and can implicate a large community of players. Because of this, not only are children frequently more focused on their handsets than their physical surroundings, they are also in an environment that might lead to interactions with others particular in the context of raids, which are predicated on a certain number of players working together to complete certain tasks. To combat some of these concerns, many participants particularly younger parents establish rules, such as requiring children to remain physically close during periods of play, and not communicate with strangers. As a further precaution, participants would also regularly check their children's friends list to make sure there were not names that they did not recognise. Beyond these rules, participants also touched on the interface itself and how the decision not to include a chat feature meant they were comfortable with their children playing on a secondary device tethered to their data-enabled smartphone. Likewise, and as Sobel et al. (2017) note, this tethering did not just provide children with the freedom to play the game, more importantly, it limited their freedom, as children were implicitly nudged to stay close to their parents or risk being disconnected from the game.

In conclusion, Pokémon Go represents a nuanced form of intergenerational play that can advance the understanding of JME. By blending the kind of rich game mechanics commonly associated with more traditional video games, amidst the physical and social flows of ordinary life, families enjoyed a wider range of benefits. Yet, these benefits also brought a wider range of concerns in their wake. Nonetheless, these concerns were ultimately not insurmountable (Sobel et al., 2017), and could be overcome with the establishment of rules and compromises.

References

Aarsand, P. A. (2007). Computer and video games in family life: The digital divide as a resource in intergenerational interactions. *Childhood, 14*(2), 235–256.

Agate, J. R., Agate, S. T., Liechty, T., & Cochran, L. J. (2018). 'Roots and wings': An exploration of intergenerational play. *Journal of Intergenerational Relationships, 16*(4), 395–421.

Al Mahmud, A., Mubin, O., Shahid, S., & Martens, J. B. (2010). Designing social games for children and older adults: Two related case studies. *Entertainment Computing, 1*(3), 147–156. doi:10.1016/j.entcom.2010.09.001

Ali, A., Aziz, Z., & Majzub, R. (2011). Teaching and learning reading through play. *World Applied Sciences Journal, 14*(4), 15–20.

Barros, R. M., Silver, E. J., & Stein, R. E. K. (2009). School recess and group classroom behavior. *Pediatrics, 123*, 431–436. doi:10.1542/peds.2007-2825

Bartlett, S. (2002). Building better cities with children and youth. *Environment and Urbanization, 14*(2), 3–10.

Baym, N. K. (2015). *Personal connections in the digital age*. New York, NY: John Wiley & Sons.

Biggs, S., & Carr, A. (2015). Age-and child-friendly cities and the promise of intergenerational space. *Journal of Social Work Practice, 29*(1), 99–112.

Blurton Jones, N. (1972). Categories of child-child interaction. In N.Blurton Jones (Ed.), *Ethological studies of child behavior* (pp. 97–127). New York, NY: Cambridge University Press.

Boone, J. E., Gordon-Larsen, P., Adair, L. S., & Popkin, B. M. (2007). Screen time and physical activity during adolescence: Longitudinal effects on obesity in young adulthood. *International Journal of Behavioral Nutrition and Physical Activity, 4*(1), 26.

Bredekamp, S., & Copple, C. (1997). *Developmentally appropriate practice in early childhood programs* (Revised Ed.). Washington, DC: National Association for the Education of Young Children.

Bruner, J. S. (1976). *Play, its role in development and evolution*. New York, NY: Basic Books (AZ).

Bunz, U. (2012). Revisited: Communication media use in the grandparent/grandchild relationship. *Journal of Community Informatics, 8*(1).

Burdette, H. L., & Whitaker, R. C. (2005). A national study of neighborhood safety, outdoor play, television viewing, and obesity in preschool children. *Pediatrics, 116*, 657–662. doi:10.1542/peds.2004-2443

Burghardt, G. M. (2005). *The genesis of animal play: Testing the limits*. Cambridge, MA: MIT Press.

Chua, P. H., Jung, Y., Lwin, M. O., & Theng, Y. L. (2013). Let's play together: Effects of video- game play on intergenerational perceptions among youth and elderly participants. *Computers in Human Behavior, 29*(6), 2303–2311. doi:10.1016/j.chb.2013.04.037

Chudacoff, H. P. (2007). *Children at play: An American history*. New York, NY: NYU Press.

Clark, L. S. (2013). *The parent app: Understanding families in the digital age*. Oxford: Oxford University Press.

Clements, R. (2004). An investigation of the status of outdoor play. *Contemporary Issues in Early, 5*(1), 68–80.

Corsaro, W. A. (1979). Young children's conception of status and role. *Sociology of Education, 52*, 46–59.

Costa, L., & Veloso, A. (2016). Being (grand) players: Review of digital games and their potential to enhance intergenerational interactions. *Journal of Intergenerational Relationships, 14*(1), 43–59.

Crosnoe, R., & Trinitapoli, J. (2008). Shared family activities and the transition from childhood into adolescence. *Journal of Research on Adolescence, 18*(1), 23–48.

De Schutter, B., Brown, J. A., & Vanden Abeele, V. (2015). The domestication of digital games in the lives of older adults. *New Media & Society, 17*(7), 1170–1186.

De Schutter, B., & Vanden Abeele, V. (2008). Meaningful play in elderly life. In *Annual meeting of the international communication association*, Montreal, QC.

Derboven, J., Van Gils, M., & De Grooff, D. (2012). Designing for collaboration: A study in intergenerational social game design. *Universal Access in the Information Society, 11*(1), 57–65. doi:10.1007/s10209-011-0233-0

Drotner, K. (1999). *Unge, medier og modernitet: Pejlinger i et foranderligt landskab*. Valby: Borgen/Medier.

Duncan, P. A. (2015). Pigs, plans, and Play-Doh: Children's perspectives on play as revealed through their drawings. *American Journal of Play, 8*(1), 50–73.

Eberle, S. (2014). The elements of play: Toward a philosophy and a definition of play. *American Journal of Play, 6*(2), 214–233.

Eccles, J. S., Midgley, C., Wigfield, A., Buchanan, C. M., Reuman, D., Flanagan, C., & Mac Iver, D. (1993). Development during adolescence: The impact of stage-environment fit on young adolescents' experiences in schools and in families. *American Psychologist, 48*(2), 90–101.

Evans, L. (2015). *Locative social media: Place in the digital age*. Basingstoke: Springer.

Evans, L., & Saker, M. (2017). *Location-based social media: Space, time and identity*. Berlin: Springer.

Evans, L., & Saker, M. (2019). The playeur and Pokémon Go: Examining the effects of locative play on spatiality and sociability. *Mobile Media & Communication, 7*(2), 232–247.

Frith, J. (2013). Turning life into a game: Foursquare, gamification, and personal mobility. *Mobile Media & Communication, 1*(2), 248–262.

Frith, J., & Wilken, R. (2019). Social shaping of mobile geomedia services: An analysis of Yelp and Foursquare. *Communication and the Public, 4*(2), 133–149.

Fromme, J. (2003). Computer games as a part of children's culture. *Game Studies*, *3*(1), 49–62.

Frost, J. L. (2010). *A history of children's play and play environments: Toward a contemporary child-saving movement*. New York, NY: Routledge.

Fuchs, C. (2014). *Digital labour and Karl Marx*. New York, NY: Routledge.

Funk, J. B., Brouwer, J., Curtiss, K., & McBroom, E. (2009). Parents of preschoolers: Expert media recommendations and ratings knowledge, media-effects beliefs, and monitoring practices. *Pediatrics*, *123*(3), 981–988.

Garvey, C. (1984). *Children's talk*. London: Fontana.

Gee, J. P. (2003). What video games have to teach us about learning and literacy. *Computer Entertainment*, *1*(1), 20.

Genc, Z. (2014). Parents' perceptions about the mobile technology use of preschool aged children. *Procedia-Social and Behavioral Sciences*, *146*, 55–60.

Gergen, K. J. (2002). The challenge of absent presence. In J. E.Katz & M.Aakhus (Eds.), *Perpetual contact: Mobile communication, private talk, public performance* (pp. 227–241). Cambridge: Cambridge University Press. doi:10.1017/CBO9780 511489471.018

Gilmore, J. B. (1966). Play: A special behavior. In R. N. Haber (Ed.), *Current research in motivation* (pp. 343–355). New York, NY: Holt Rinehart & Winston.

Ginsburg, K. R. (2007). The importance of play in promoting healthy childhood development and maintaining strong parent-child bonds. *Pediatrics*, *119*, 182–191. doi:10.1542/peds.2006-2697

Graber, D. (2019). *Raising humans in a digital world: Helping kids build a healthy relationship with technology*. New York, NY: Amacom.

Gray, P. (2009). Play as a foundation for hunter-gatherer social existence. *American Journal of Play*, *1*, 476–522.

Gray, P. (2011). The decline of play and the rise of psychopathology in children and adolescents. *American Journal of Play*, *3*, 443–463.

Gray, P. (2013). *Free to learn: Why unleashing the instinct to play will make our children happier, more self-reliant, and better students for life*. New York, NY: Basic Books.

Hart, R. (2002). Containing children: Some lessons on planning for play from New York city. *Environment and Urbanization*, *14*(2), 135–148.

Harwood, J. (2007). *Understanding communication and aging: Developing knowledge and awareness*. Thousand Oaks, CA: Sage Publications Ltd.

Hausknecht, S., Neustaedter, C., & Kaufman, D. (2017). Blurring the lines of age: Intergenerational collaboration in alternate reality games. In M. Romero, K. Sawchuk, J. Blat, S. Sayago, & H. Ouellet (Eds.), *Game-based learning across the lifespan* (pp. 47–64). Cham: Springer.

Henricks, T. S. (2006). *Play reconsidered: Sociological perspectives on human expression*. Champaign, IL: University of Illinois Press.

Hiniker, A., Suh, H., Cao, S., & Kientz, J. A. (2016). Screen time tantrums: How families manage screen media experiences for toddlers and preschoolers. In *Proceedings of the 2016 CHI conference on human factors in computing systems* (pp. 648–660). New York, NY: ACM.

Holladay, S. J., & Seipke, H. L. (2007). Communication between grandparents and grand-children in geographically separated relationships. *Communication Studies*, *58*(3), 281–297. doi:10.1080/10510970701518371

Hutchinson, S. L., Yarnal, C. M., Stafford-Son, J., & Kerstetter, D. L. (2008). Beyond fun and friendship: The Red Hat Society as a coping resource for older women. *Ageing and Society, 28*(07), 979–999. doi:10.1017/S0144686X08007058

Jarrett, O. S., & US Play Coalition (2013). *A research-based case for recess*. Clemson, SC: US Play Coalition.

Kamenetz, A. (2018). *The art of screen time: How your family can balance digital media and real life*. New York, NY: Hachette.

Kardaras, N. (2016). *Glow kids: How screen addiction is hijacking our kids-and how to break the trance*. New York, NY: St. Martin's Press.

Kennedy, T. L., Smith, A., Wells, A. T., & Wellman, B. (2008). Networked families. *Pew Internet & American Life Project, 17*, 1–36.

Kenner, C., Ruby, M., Jessel, J., Gregory, E., & Arju, T. (2007). Intergenerational learning between children and grandparents in east London. *Journal of Early Childhood Research, 5*(3), 219–243.

Keogh, B. (2017). Pokémon Go, the novelty of nostalgia, and the ubiquity of the smartphone. *Mobile Media & Communication, 5*(1), 38–41.

Khosravi, P., Rezvani, A., & Wiewiora, A. (2016). The impact of technology on older adults' social isolation. *Computers in Human Behavior, 63*, 594–603.

Kuo, F. E., & Faber Taylor, A. (2004). A potential natural treatment for attention-deficit/hyperactivity disorder: Evidence from a national study. *American Journal of Public Health, 94*(9), 1580–1586.

Lanier, J. (2018). *Ten arguments for deleting your social media accounts right now*. New York, NY: Henry Holt.

Latour, B. (2005). *Reassembling the social: An introduction to actor-network-theory*. Oxford: Oxford University Press.

Lee, J. H., Windleharth, T., Yip, J., & Schmalz, M. (2017). Impact of location-based augmented reality games on people's information behavior: A case study of Pokemon GO. In *iConference 2017 Proceedings* (pp. 459–468), Wuhan.

Lenhart, A., Madden, M., & Hitlin, P. (2005). *Teens and Technology. Youth are leading the transition to a fully wired and mobile nation*. Washington, DC: Pew Internet and American Life Project.

Lewis, B. (2014). *Raising children in a digital age: Enjoying the best, avoiding the worst*. Oxford; London: Lion Books.

Livingstone, S. M. (2002). *Young people and new media: Childhood and the changing media environment*. London: Sage.

Livingstone, S., Mascheroni, G., Dreier, M., Chaudron, S., & Lagae, K. (2015). *How parents of young children manage digital devices at home: The role of income, education and parental style*. London: EU Kids Online, LSE.

Mainella, F. P., Agate, J. R., & Clark, B. S. (2011). Outdoor-based play and reconnection to nature: A neglected pathway to positive youth development. *New Directions for Youth Development, 2011*, 89–104. doi:10.1002/yd.v2011.130

Marx, M. S., Cohen-Mansfield, J., Renaudat, K., Libin, A., & Thein, K. (2005). Technology- mediated versus face-to-face intergenerational programming. *Journal of Intergenerational Relationships, 3*(3), 101–118. doi:10.1300/J194v03n03_07

Mäyrä, F. (2017). Pokémon GO: Entering the ludic society. *Mobile Media & Communication, 5*(1), 47–50.

Mesch, G. S. (2006). Family characteristics and intergenerational conflicts over the Internet. *Information, Communication & Society, 9*(4), 473–495. doi:10.1080/13691 180600858705

Meshel, D., & Mcglynn, R. (2004). Intergenerational contact, attitudes, and stereotypes of adolescents and older people. *EducGerontol, 30*(6), 457–479.

Mintz, S. (2004). *Huck's raft: A history of American childhood*. Cambridge, MA: Harvard University Press.

Mitas, O., Qian, X. L., Yarnal, C., & Kerstetter, D. (2011). "The fun begins now!": Broadening and building processes in Red Hat Society® participation. *Journal of Leisure Research, 43*(1), 30–55. doi:10.1080/00222216.2011.11950225

Negroponte, N. (1996). *Being digital*. New York, NY: Vintage.

Perry, F. (2016, July 22). Urban gamification: Can Pokémon GO transform our public spaces? *The Guardian*. Retrieved from https://www.theguardian.com/cities/2016/jul/22/urban-gamification-Pokémon-go-transform-public-spaces

Power, T. G. (2000). *Play and exploration in children and animals*. Mahwah, NJ: Lawrence Erlbaum Associates, Inc., Publishers.

Prensky, M. (2001). *Digital game-based learning*. New York, NY: McGraw-Hill.

Revell, T. (2017). Did *Pokémon Go* really kill 250 people in traffic accidents?. *NewScientist*. Retrieved from https://www.newscientist.com/article/2154881-did-pokemon-go-really-kill-250-people-in-traffic-accidents/

Ribble, M. (2009). *Raising a digital child* (p. 213). Eugene, OR: ISTE.

Rideout, V., Foehr, U., & Roberts, D. (2010). *Generation M²: Media in the lives of 8- to 18- year olds*. Menlo Park, CA: Kaiser Family Foundation.

Ruiz, S. A., & Silverstein, M. (2007). Relationships with grandparents and the emotional well-being of late adolescent and young adult grandchildren. *Journal of Social Issues, 63*(4), 793–808.

Saker, M., & Evans, L. (2016). Everyday life and locative play: An exploration of Foursquare and playful engagements with space and place. *Media, Culture & Society, 38*(8), 1169–1183.

Saker, M., & Frith, J. (2018). Locative media and sociability: Using location-based social networks to coordinate everyday life. *Architecture Minnesota, 14*(1).

Santosa, E. T. (2015). *Raising children in digital era*. Central Jakarta: Elex Media Komputindo.

Scott, D. (1995). The effect of video games on feelings of aggression. *The Journal of Psychology, 129*(2), 121–132.

Seo, H., & Lee, C. S. (2017). Emotion matters: What happens between young children and parents in a touch screen world. *International Journal of Communication, 11*, 20.

Siyahhan, S., Barab, S. A., & Downton, M. P. (2010). Using activity theory to understand intergenerational play: The case of Family Quest. *International Journal of Computer-Supported Collaborative Learning, 5*(4), 415–432.

Siyahhan, S., & Gee, E. (2018). *Families at play: Connecting and learning through video games*. Cambridge, MA: MIT Press.

Sobel, K., Bhattacharya, A., Hiniker, A., Lee, J. H., Kientz, J. A., & Yip, J. C. (2017, May). It wasn't really about the PokéMon: Parents' perspectives on a location-based mobile game. In *Proceedings of the 2017 CHI Conference on Human Factors in Computing Systems* (pp. 1483–1496).

Son, J. S., Kerstetter, D. L., Yarnal, C. M., & Baker, B. L. (2007). Promoting older women's health and well-being through social leisure environments: What we have learned from the Red Hat Society®. *Journal of Women & Aging, 19*(3–4), 89–104. doi:10.1300/J074v19n03_07

Stavrinos, D., Byington, K. W., & Schwebel, D. C. (2011). Distracted walking: Cell phones increase injury risk for college pedestrians. *Journal of Safety Research, 42*(2), 101–107.

Stegelin, D. A., Fite, K., Wisneski, D., & US Play Coalition (2015). *The critical place for play in education*. Clemson, SC: US Play Coalition.

Steiner-Adair, C., & Barker, T. H. (2013). *The big disconnect: Protecting childhood and family relationships in the digital age*. New York, NY: Harper Business.

Steyer, J. P. (2012). *Talking back to Facebook: The common sense guide to raising kids in the digital age*. New York, NY: Simon & Schuster.

Sutton-Smith, B. (1997). *The ambiguity of play*. Cambridge, MA: Harvard University Press.

Takeuchi, L. (2011). *Families matter: Designing media for a digital age*. New York: The Joan Ganz Cooney Center at Sesame Workshop.

Thai, A. M., Lowenstein, D., Ching, D., & Rejeski, D. (2009). *Game changer: Investing in digital play to advance children's learning and health*. New York, NY: Joan Ganz Cooney Center.

Tran, K. M. (2018). Families, resources, and learning around Pokémon Go. *E-learning and Digital Media, 15*(3), 113–127.

Turkle, S. (2017). *Alone together: Why we expect more from technology and less from each other*. New York, NY: Hachette.

Twenge, J. M., Joiner, T. E., Rogers, M. L., & Martin, G. N. (2018). Increases in depressive symptoms, suicide-related outcomes, and suicide rates among US adolescents after 2010 and links to increased new media screen time. *Clinical Psychological Science, 6*(1), 3–17.

Tyner, K. R. (1998). *Literacy in a digital world: Teaching and learning in the age of information*. London: Lawrence Erlbaum.

Uhlenberg, P. (2000). Integration of old and young. *The Gerontologist, 40*(3), 276–279. doi:10.1093/geront/40.3.276

Voida, A., & Greenberg, S. (2012). Console gaming across generations: Exploring interge- nerational interactions in collocated console gaming. *Universal Access in the Information Society, 11*(1), 45–56. doi:10.1007/s10209-011-0232-1

Weintraub, A. P. C., & Killian, T. S. (2007). Intergenerational programming: Older persons' perceptions of its impact. *Journal of Applied Gerontology, 26*(4), 370–384.

Whitlock, L. A., McLaughlin, A. C., & Allaire, J. C. (2012). Individual differences in response to cognitive training: Using a multi-modal, attentionally demanding game-based intervention for older adults. *Computers in Human Behavior, 28*(4), 1091–1096. doi:10.1016/j.chb.2012.01.012

Zelizer, V. A. (1985). *Pricing the priceless child: The changing social value of children*. New York, NY: Basic Books.

Zelizer, V. A. (1994). *Pricing the priceless child: The changing social value of children*. Princeton, NJ: Princeton University Press.

Chapter 4

Familial Locative Play: Social Relationships and Communities

4.1 Pokémon Go, Public Space and Community

During the first wave of Pokémon Go activity in 2016, one of the most visible sets of images of the emergence of the game was of massive crowds of players (see Wong, 2016). Masses of people playing the game in cities across the world led to a quickly formed discourse on the effects of Pokémon Go on sociality. For example, Kaczmarek, Misiak, Behnke, Dziekan, and Guzik (2017), in considering the benefits of Pokémon Go, highlighted socialisation and outdoor activity as significant benefits of the game. Hjorth and Richardson (2017, p. 10) noted that a positive effect of the game (and potentially subversive in effect) was that players can use such games to activate communities of interest in local contexts, organise urban events and public demonstrations of play.

This contextualisation of Pokémon Go play in public follows a well-established line of thinking with regards to mobile technologies and location-based applications. Humphreys (2017, pp. 16–17) argues that mobile technologies can act as social catalysts in three primary ways. First, mobile platforms are designed to facilitate engagement (Ling, 2008; Ling & Campbell, 2017). Calling, texting and messaging have long strengthened social ties (Ling, 2008), but newer platforms such as Grindr, Tinder, Swarm and Pokémon Go are examples of location-based mobile applications designed to allow people to find one another, chat and meet up. Humphreys notes that while Pokémon Go is not necessarily marketed as a social networking tool, its team features can facilitate in-group closeness and allow players to battle rival teams. There is a great deal of research on gaming that reveals that social interaction with other players is a common motivation for playing games (Hjorth & Richardson, 2014), which would fit with the social and 'mob' aspect of Pokémon Go observed in 2016. Second, mobile platforms can facilitate social interaction among people who play together. People may not tend to go out in public alone but may go out and play if they have friends to go with them while they use these mobile technologies (Humphreys, 2007). Third, social interactions emerge in response to mobile technology use (Ling, 2008). Bystanders or non-users can also interact with one another in response to witnessing or even reading about technology use (Humphreys, 2005), particularly with a phenomenon like the emergence of

Intergenerational Locative Play, 93–115
Copyright © 2021 Michael Saker and Leighton Evans
Published under an exclusive licence by Emerald Publishing Limited
doi:10.1108/978-1-83909-139-120211014

Pokémon Go. For example, Humphreys (2017, p. 17) notes that people complaining about Pokémon Go even if they don't use it is a form of social interaction that the game indirectly facilitates which can also contribute to a sense of commonality among strangers, a process called parochialisation (Humphreys, 2010; Humphreys & Liao, 2013). In 2016, as Pokémon Go players were hunting among others in public places, joining teams or battling for gyms, they were engaged in interactions with other players which contributed to this process of parochialisation. Critically, then, playing Pokémon Go has, from earlier on in the emergence of the game, been recognised as an activity that can facilitate new relationships and friendships through play.

The evidence for Pokémon Go being a facilitator of new relationships and friendships is fairly positive but does not necessarily illustrate what *kind* of relationships are formed. Bonus, Peebles, Mares, and Sarmiento (2018) conducted an online survey of 399 Pokémon Go–playing US adults aged 18–75 that indicated that playing the game was associated with various positive responses including nostalgic reverie, friendship formation and friendship intensification. Vella et al. (2019, p. 583) conducted a thematic analysis of qualitative data derived from players that revealed that playing Pokémon Go produced a sense of belonging, linked to a sense of place, as well as facilitating conversations with strangers and, importantly, strengthening social ties. This strengthening of social ties was attributed to shared passion for the game and the game mechanics that encouraged players out of their homes. Paasovaara, Jarusriboonchai, and Olsson (2017, p. 151) used a qualitative online survey to assess sociality through the game and found that the game design promotes encounters between players, the idle time during the game allows various forms of social interaction to take place, and the players gain various benefits from exchanging information with each other.

While these results are obviously encouraging in terms of the possibility and formation of new relationships and friendships, the granularity of such relationships is important. In particular, the nature of friendships in the age of social media indicates that close attention needs to be paid to the kind of friendships formed. In a time where 1,000 'friends' on Facebook gives no indication of the closeness of such ties, the efficacy of friendships created through Pokémon Go demands some attention with regards to what kinds of kinships are formed through play and in particular what kinds of relationships between players are formed through inter-generational play. In the following section, then, we pay critical attention to the kind of relationship forged with other players following Granovetter's (1973) distinction between weak and strong ties and Gerbaudo's (2012) concept of 'liquid sociality'. These theoretical frameworks are then used to examine the social relationships and communities that families engage with while playing Pokémon Go.

4.2 Strong Ties, Weak Ties, Latent Ties

The notion of different kinds of ties between people that come to characterise social relationships has been a feature of academic discourse for over 50 years, following Mark Granovetter's categorisation of three types of social ties among people in social networks: strong, weak and latent ties (Granovetter, 1973). According to Granovetter, strong ties exist between people who share close relationships, such as parents or families. In the case of this research, there are obviously already a very clear set of strong ties between parents and children, but there is the possibility of other strong ties forming between children that play together through co-ordinated play and adults that play the game. Weak ties are characterised as those between an individual and his/her 'acquaintances'. Granovetter argues that strong ties are vital in allowing people to share information and, therefore, this kind of tie has greater influence on motivation and mobilisation (Granovetter, 1973), which in the context of Pokémon Go is significant in terms of hunting, events, raids and battles. Raids are predicated on groups of players operating together, and these co-ordinated actions may be realised through a loose network of weak ties. While weak ties have less influence on mobilisation, this type of social tie offers potential opportunities for acquaintances to share movement information (Granovetter, 1973). In this way, 'weak ties provide people with access to information and resources…but strong ties have greater influence and motivation to be of assistance and are typically more easily available' (Granovetter, 1973, p. 1364). Acquaintances or weak ties, therefore, typically share fewer connections and resources between each other and may be of less utility in a game playing environment. However, a simple action between two people who become 'friends' through Pokémon Go but who have barely communicated previously (weak tie) could potentially help in the playing of the game (Gilbert & Karahalios, 2009) and could become a strong tie through play.

Granovetter describes a latent tie as a 'nodding' relationship between people who share a similar background, such as two people living on the same street (Granovetter, 1973). Latent ties can, in this way, be understood as an absent tie, in which the interaction between individuals is negligible (Granovetter, 1973; Orum, 1972). The latent tie is particularly interesting when considering Pokémon Go, as the game acts as a communal environment where the enrolment of players acts as a proxy latent tie. Following that enrolment, the player enters into an environment of gameplay where, given the mobility implicit in the game, the movement from latent ties to weak and potentially strong ties is a feature of the game itself. The ludic logic of the game, where players may come into close proximity and can develop the parochialisation identified by Humphreys (2017) as a feature of mobile sociality in Pokémon Go, can be seen as a mechanism for the formation of latent ties that may move into other kinds of social tie. While latent ties have been considered to only make small contributions towards social movements, Granovetter considers latent ties as holding a potential for creating interactions and dynamic movements (Granovetter, 1973). The latent tie acts as a connection that affords the possibility of increasing participation. Granovetter argues that social ties are linear, and the combination of emotional intensity, time, intimacy, mutuality and reciprocal services are indicators of the strength of social ties (Granovetter, 1973). Given this, the latent tie acts as a form of staging for the possibility of increasing social ties.

Social ties are clearly not static, just as social networks are not static structures. The evolution and dynamics of both ties and networks are continually influenced by spatial and temporal changes (Orum, 1972). However, there is a contradictory logic in how this operates. On the one hand, social ties, especially strong ties, can be seen as beneficial in expanding the membership of social organisations or groups. The contradictory argument suggests that strong ties actually bring impediments in the recruiting process to groups as participants will look to associate only with their close friends and family. In the context of this research, this is critically important. The participants in this research already have strong ties in their game playing group – that between parent and child. So, in this research, it is possible that the strong ties that already exist in the game playing group will actively inhibit the possibility of creating new strong ties with other players. This can be seen as a reaffirmation of the 'magic circle' (Huizinga, 1992/ 1938). As detailed in previous chapters, for Huizinga (1992/1938), this notion of the 'magic circle' insists that the play of any given game must occur within a spatially and temporally enclosed area, or playground, and is as such detached from 'ordinary' life. As Huizinga (1992/1938, p. 10) suggests, '[play] is distinct from "ordinary life" both as to locality and duration'. In this vein, when 'a player steps in and out of a game, he or she is crossing the boundary – or frame – that defines the game in time and space' (Salen & Zimmerman, 2004, p. 95). Should the existence of strong ties be inhibitory to new relationships, this could be understood as intergenerational play in Pokémon Go being akin to a new 'magic circle' where the play of the game is defined in space and time for family only or as an exclusion to making strong ties. The notion of strong ties being inhibitory has been noted in recent literature on social protest movements. For example, Deng and O'Brien (2013) note that strong ties can demobilise protesters when the collective action may cause punishment to participants. This causes families or close friends to be forbidden from attending collective events. In the context of Pokémon Go, this dynamic may mean that family members are inhibited in meeting other people and forming stronger ties through a sense of protection for their family.

Granovetter's theory of social ties has been critiqued and updated since the 1970s. Passy (2003) argued that it is critical to understand the function of social networks in order to understand the role of social tie in relationships in the context of social mobilisation. Passy argues that there are three functions of social networks: the socialisation function (shaping individuals' identities for building solidarity); the structural connection function (enhancing the identities that are built by the 'socialization function'); and decision-shaping function (which 'pushes' the prospective participants into an interactive network and 'pulling' them into groups) (Passy, 2003). Passy also suggested that co-ordinated action (such as Pokémon Go) should strengthen the function of social ties (Passy, 2003). Other social movement researchers have long recognised that mobilising individuals is heavily reliant on social ties (Diani & McAdam, 2003; Kitts, 2000; McAdam & Paulsen, 1993) while other social movement scholars have sought to make sense of the role, structures and dynamics when social ties are shaping collective actions. McAdam and Paulsen (1993) and Gould (2003) state the strength of ties is critical in collective actions; Marwell, Oliver, and Prahl (1988) argue that the density and frequency of social ties is critical to mobilisation, and salience and centrality of ties was argued to be critical in other research (Fernandez, 1989). What emerges from this research on social movements is that social ties are seen as critically important in collective action. In the context of Pokémon Go, it is necessary to understand how social ties play a role in collaborative play beyond the bubble of the family. In particular, the role of existing strong ties as a potential inhibitor to new strong ties may play a role in restricting co-ordinated movements of players in events and constraining the possibility of community – possibly inverting the research findings on strong ties from other mobility contexts.

The social aspect of Pokémon Go does not exist solely in the meeting of people while playing the game. Pokémon Go communities and groups have emerged on multiple digital platforms such as Facebook and Reddit. The contemporary social network is an essential part of the Pokémon Go milieu. Malcom Gladwell (2010) argues that social ties can be created online and migrate to an offline tie, and the expansion of social ties on social media brings about a new form of social organisation: 'liquid organising' (Gerbaudo, 2012). Gerbaudo argues that the function of weak ties has been enhanced via social media (Gerbaudo, 2012) and the formation of, and influence of, these ties has increased with the emergence of social media platforms. Gladwell (2010) goes as far as arguing that a network based on weak ties is the only social network that can be constructed on social media. However, Gerbaudo (2012) argues that strong ties can be formed from 'real' life meetings and extended on social media. In 'liquid organising', the 'Facebook Friendship' can be understood as a type of 'informal' relationship that has become a vital element that allows for a large and sustained mobilisation network in contemporary or 'liquid' social movements. In the context of Pokémon Go, the sharing of tactics, information, locations and routes across an informal network may, therefore, lead to co-ordinated play or opportunities for the creation of stronger ties that emerge from fleeting meetings while playing the game. Additionally, latent ties can also be activated by online social interaction. Online communication channels are an effective medium to create latent ties and transform these ties into weak ties through interactions across the platform (Haythornthwaite, 2001).

The role of social ties in the development of friendships and relationships through Pokémon Go in the context of intergenerational play does appear to be complex. The game, as a mobile application, should lend itself to increasing the possibility of transforming latent ties formed through being players into other ties. However, the pre-existence of strong ties in game playing families could act as a barrier to creating new ties through the formation of a new kind of 'magic circle' (Huizinga, 1992/1938) that may act to inhibit social interaction. Additionally, the mobile nature of the game and the use of online, rather than proximal, communities could lead to the formation of weak ties from latent ties rather than the strong ties that would usually characterise a friendship. While strong ties have been frequently identified as critical to increasing the mobility of social groups, in the case of Pokémon Go mobility is already an intrinsic factor in the game, and, therefore, strong ties are not necessary for mobility in the game. Moreover, there are other elements of the game that could bear on the type of ties formed during play. The parochialisation aspect of the game may lead to the development of strong ties through a sense of kinship among players. The nostalgic element of the game offers pre-existing knowledge which could be conducive to the formation of strong ties based on mutual interests. Many of the ludic features of Pokémon Go, such as raids, involve co-ordinated activities which, logically, should drive the strengthening of latent ties formed by the game into other kinds of ties. However, this is all mediated by the conditions of play for intergenerational players, a focus on the family, safety and strengthening pre-existing strong ties.

The focus of this chapter is to investigate what kinds of social ties are created by Pokémon Go for intergenerational players. This, of course, leads to two potential kinds of kinship: friendships between adults and friendships between children that play the game. In this sense, this chapter offers a very different view of the effects of Pokémon Go on relationships. The crucial factor in this research has been how the game has mediated the relationships between family members. In this chapter, that mediated relationship between family members becomes a condition of mediation itself in the possibility of using Pokémon Go as a vehicle for the formation of new relationships. While previous research has indicated that Pokémon Go has been a facilitator for new relationships, this chapter focuses on an understudied aspect of both the modes of playing the game itself and the kinds of relationships formed through the game. Critically, this chapter looks to understand what kind of social ties can be formed when the playing of Pokémon Go is itself performed in the context of the family unit. More precisely, the chapter is driven by the following research questions. First, what kinds of social relationships have developed for the families that play Pokémon Go together? This includes whether intergenerational players have made new friends, as well as strengthened current relationships. Second, has this hybrid reality game (HRG) facilitated friendships for the children that play Pokémon Go? In other words, is a community of players still a salient feature of playing this HRG, in the same way that it was shortly after its release in the Summer 2016?

4.3 New Relationships and Strong Tie Friendships

The survey that underpinned our empirical research provided results which indicate that playing Pokémon Go has led to new social relationships being developed through play. Initially, the Pokémon Go event remains an important staging for sociality though the game; 88% (145 from 165) respondents reported that they take part in Pokémon Go events, and, therefore, have some proximal contact with other players in the same activity. 91 (55%) respondents reported that children made new friends through play, while 74 (45%) reported that children did not make new friends during supervised play. However, the results for adults playing with their children were even more pronounced. 117 respondents (70%) reported making new friends through playing Pokémon Go with their children, indicating that the effect on forming new social relationships is far more salient for adults playing Pokémon Go compared to their children. This is especially true for male players; 88% (29 from 33 respondents) reported making new friends, while 66% (88 from 133) female players reported that they had made new friends while playing. While these results certainly indicate that intergenerational play through Pokémon Go has an effect on extending social circles and creating new social relationships, what is critical is the *kind* of friendship that has been made through playing the game.

Despite the evidence of players reporting that they have made new 'friends' through playing Pokémon Go with their children, in interviewing players very few identified that they had formed strong ties with other players which would be indicative of a friendship. One strong advocate for the role of Pokémon Go in creating new, strong tie friendships was Liza.

Interviewer:

So, for Pokémon Go and social connections, has playing Pokémon Go led to your children making any new friends?

Liza, 42, female, Indianapolis, Indiana, US:

They haven't. I mean, we have. But they haven't. They more try to find their own friends who are playing. We just don't really have any other families who are playing it like we are still. They did initially, but you know, they dropped off. Their friends and their friends' families dropped off. And so, you know, I've met two women in particular that I have their phone numbers and, you know, we maybe try to coordinate getting together in the evening with them to play. One has a nephew that she plays with, so you know, she has to coordinate getting the nephew. Ha-ha. And then the other one, as I said, is that mother. And I will say, there's a man that I'm friends with now that I play with, there's an Indianapolis group. I think you found me in the London group right, because we had gone to England last year, so I joined that group. Yeah. So, I'm in the Indianapolis group though. So, part of the reason that I'm so much further along in XP points than my family is that I'm really diligent about finding friends in the game. But then trying to keep track of who they are on social media so that when we're about to level up we can increase our XP by coordinating that effort. And so, I'd reached out to someone to coordinate dropping an egg so that we got more XP when we levelled up in our friendship. And so, then he friended me because we have a ton of friends in common, but he and I had never met. Ha-ha.

While children do not form new ties through playing in this scenario, Liza is confident that her playing Pokémon Go has led to the formation of new friendships. Liza emphasises that her concept of friendship and strong ties made through the game is contingent on elements of the game itself. Co-ordination of activity with friends met through the game, and ongoing communication to continue that co-ordination are characterised as the foundation of friendships for Liza. Also, the use of Facebook groups for making friends based on mutual gameplay is emphasised as a key mechanism in the formation of strong ties by Liza. Of extra significance is the notion of diligence raised as a critical factor in making friends and utilising friends for increasing experience points (XP) in the game. The diligent aspect of this implies a form of labour that is needed to move from the latent ties in the game (see the comment on 'levelled up in our friend-ship') to create stronger ties that can be characterised by friendships. The process of doing this is entwined with the dynamics of the game and social media com-munications channels but is driven by an instrumental need to improve and progress in the game itself. Liza reiterates the importance of social media with regards to the ties formed through Pokémon Go play.

Interviewer:

Oh no way! So, you had found out on Facebook that you had a ton of friends in common?

Liza, 42, female, Indianapolis, Indiana, US:

Yeah, yeah. So, I contacted one of my girlfriends who he clearly knew, and I said okay, this guy is friending me. And you know, I don't friend strangers on my Facebook page. So, I said who is this person and I'm ashamed to say this is how I met him, and he's asked me to friend him. And I just want to check. And she's like oh, yeah. He's harmless, he's great. So, it's kind of completed because I knew most of the other people in their friends' group. And so, he was just another person then that I met.

Interviewer:

That's crazy. It's a small world in certain regards but it has expanded your world in others. How interesting. Okay, so that's great. So, you've played Pokémon Go and have made friends it sounds like?

Liza, 42, female, Indianapolis, Indiana, US:

Yeah. Through Pokémon Go.

Liza illustrates how the use of social networks compliments the game itself in the formation of latent ties that can become strong ties through intentionality on the part of one or both of the parties involved. Here, Liza overcomes some of the suspicion and danger that could arise from befriending a person through a social network by confirming the status of the person through other ties in the network. However, there is some question as to whether these ties formed on social networks constitute a strong tie or friendship. Liza does, however, extend these links into meeting in person.

Interviewer:

Okay. And what's that interaction like? Is it where you physically see the people and you start talking? Can you tell me a little bit about that?

Liza, 42, female, Indianapolis, Indiana, US:

Yeah with the women, I see them. We see them. Like usually we'll meet up with them. With Jerry, I mean this only happened about a month ago. So, my interaction with him is usually just on Messenger sending photos of what we caught or where we are. He's on Team Valor as well and he's really into getting gold badges on gyms. I never cared about that. So, he's always asking me for help. So, he'll go and take over a gym and then send me a message that he's taken it over and that I need to throw Max and me in it too. Ha-ha.

Interviewer:

So, it becomes a larger group?

Liza, 42, female, Indianapolis, Indiana, US:

Right.

Liza meets with those people that she identifies as friends, going further than a latent or weak tie to form a relationship. It is also clear that communication via Facebook is not transitory; the communication is frequent and focused, and based on assisting one another's goals in the game. While this is an instrumental aim, it clearly has been one which has been beneficial to forming strong ties in Liza's view. However, Liza's experience of migrating from latent or loose ties formed in the game to friendships was almost unique in this research. Only one other participant expressed that they had formed something commensurate to a strong tie through the game.

Yes. Um the one and only I can think of is a specific example. My brother in law's brother, yeah, brother in law's brother, who I wouldn't have really had a reason to have much interaction with, him and his lad are into the game and because of that, we have done exchanges of gifts and things and have probably interacted more and probably realized that we got on better than we would have known each other outside of that. So yeah, that's the only one example I can think of. (Arthur, 38, male, Birmingham, UK).

Arthur's strong tie is also one which existed as a latent tie through family connection (rather than social networking) and the game. The common interest in Pokémon Go led to the development of a friendship and family relationship, as well as that friendship being developed through mutual intergenerational play. However, there is the possibility that this friendship may have developed in other ways thanks to the additional latent ties existing. What is most surprising is that across all interviews, only two participants expressed that they had formed strong ties with other players, despite the survey indicating that most players had made 'friends' through playing the game.

4.4 Communities of Play

The incongruence between the identification of strong ties being formed through play and the survey results of this research may be explained by assessing how players have categorised the kinds of kinship that has been formed through Pokémon Go. The term 'friend' appears to have been inflected by the milieu of the game (both in playing and communicating via social networks) to refer to a relationship more akin to what Granovetter (1973) described as a loose or latent tie. This is exemplified with some of the descriptions from participants as to what constitutes a community of Pokémon Go players.

Interviewer:

It sounds like playing Pokémon Go has led you to making new friends. Is that correct?

Wendy, 59, female, Orlando, Florida, US:

Oh, absolutely. I have a ball. Uh huh.

Interviewer:

Can you kind of describe these friendships that you've made?

Wendy, 59, female, Orlando, Florida, US:

Oh, like I come out, there's a lake. I don't know if you can see the background?

Interviewer:

Yeah, yeah.

Wendy, 59, female, Orlando, Florida, US:

This is, this is a place called Lake Eola. This is my normal weekend haunt. I come here on the weekends. I come here and do a couple of laps every lunch hour. So, I've gotten to know a lot of the same people and we catch up, we do some swaps, we do some raids. And we just have a good time. There's probably, on an event day, a community day or one of the Wednesday night raid nights, there's probably about a hundred to two hundred people here playing.

Interviewer:

Oh, wow!

Wendy, 59, female, Orlando, Florida, US:

Yeah, it's a big community.

Interviewer:

Yeah! And so, do you ever, outside of Pokémon Go, do you ever socialize with these new friends? Or is it primarily within Pokémon Go?

Wendy, 59, female, Orlando, Florida, US:

It's all just within Pokémon Go.

Wendy identifies that a new set of ties have been formed through playing Pokémon Go in a mutual environment constitutes a community based on temporal and spatial proximity and the shared activity of playing the game. This community remains bounded by those factors of forming the community though; once the gameplay stops in the same space and time, then the community dissolves and the ties that are in action during that time are dissolved with the lack of activity. The community as identified here is characterised by a set of very weak or latent ties. This can, if the circumstances dictate, lead to more substantial contact:

Interviewer:

And then you take part in these Pokémon Go events. Can you kind of describe what that's like?

Wendy, 59, female, Orlando, Florida, US:

Um. I just go out and have fun. I mean I'll catch up with people at lunch hour and say, are you guys doing the raid tonight? Like yeah okay, let's catch up at such and such a stop. And we just meander around. Maybe go in if it's like raining. We'll go in and find a place to catch a burger somewhere together. Or there's a couple of bars nearby. We'll go in and have a beer together. So, we just kind of wander and catch up with each other and talk about who caught the best 'shinies' … It's just fun.

The raid appears to be a key event in the formation of these loose communities. If the circumstances are right, the raid community can extend into other activities (if it is raining) and the social ties in the community will strengthen temporarily. This perception of the importance of the raid event is reiterated by Bill:

> Yeah, there's definitely people, people I talk to quite often now even if it's on Discord or Facebook. And I think, like I've gone out for a raid and I've said to my missus that I'll be out for like five minutes and I'll be out for forty minutes because we're all still hanging. And I've gone, I've met up with other to play Fifa. There's a large amount of them that all go to the pub and stuff together. I haven't done that yet. We've all gone, we've gone around a few people's houses. Jumped in people's cars. One of them like, I think we all walked to the raid and then it started hammering down and so then he gave everyone a lift home and stuff. (Bill, 28, male, Southend-on-Sea, UK).

Bill sits on the periphery of a community that meets and socialises, and through the raid, he temporarily moves from a latent to weak tie with this group. In addition, Bill maintains these ties through the social platforms used for coordinating action. However, these ties are still characterised as fleeting and cursory rather than strong, and contingent on the game rather than having moved away from the game. While there is nothing new in the development of this kind of virtual community (see Baym, 2015; Rheingold, 1993; Turkle, 1996, 2017), this community, for intergenerational players at least, is characterised by a weak form of participatory culture characterised by some shared social practices (Jenkins, Ito, & boyd, 2016) but without the strong ties formed through consistent and persistent social contact online that leads to strong ties outside the original milieu. In order for these community bonds to develop, there needs to be a further element of kinship, like already seen with family ties and, as Chloe illustrates, a set of other personal circumstances in key aspects of everyday life that can facilitate a move from the community to another set of ties:

> Chloe, 27, female, Newfoundland, Canada:
>
> So, when I started playing Pokémon Go, Devin got me on the Discord channels and everything for our area. Um, we started seeing this one name that kept popping up everywhere we went. And they had the same name on Discord. And then eventually we met up with them, with them and their partner. And it actually turned out to be a high-ranking official within our base.
>
> Interviewer:
>
> Oh no way!
>
> Chloe, 27, female, Newfoundland, Canada:
>
> Oh yeah. Like, like we had a captain and a lieutenant colonel playing Pokémon Go with us. And it's funny because you never would've thought it. But here we are and now we're best friends in Pokémon Go and we have each other on Discord. We don't chat

too much anymore. He got posted out. But yeah, so that's how I met him. Then there's another person across base who uh, is a supply tech like me. He's posted out at one of the other units. I met him downtown just near the base doing stuff. And friends on Pokémon Go will chat and we'll catch up whenever we see each other. Because not too often we'll run across paths when we work in different areas. But um, and yeah, even one of the guys that I work with. We've run into each other downtown and have hung out with him and his wife and his child, his little baby. Like, and it's not normally, I wouldn't normally go out of my way to talk to people like that. But when we all have kind of a mutual interest, a mutual goal, then it makes it easier.

Chloe's move from latent or weak tie through the online community and the game itself to stronger tie came through the profession of both her husband and her fellow player. Interestingly though, the tie with the lieutenant colonel ended as soon as the possibility of playing the game proximally ended, indicating that the tie itself was contingent on the game rather than having a developed strength beyond the game. Chloe does note that sociability does increase through playing the game, even if the strength of ties does not, thanks to the community aspect of play and parochialisation effect of the game. Chloe notes that the ephemeral and loose nature of these communities is, in itself, mobile:

Chloe, 27, female, Newfoundland, Canada:

So, like, I went to Newfoundland this summer for a course and uh, while I was there, I joined the Newfoundland Pokémon Go page. And I was only there for a week and it was the big Mewtwo raids, the big armouredMewtwo raids. And I was going to find somebody because I was staying on campus at MUN, trying to find somebody to help, help me in the Mewtwo raids. There was one other guy on the course that I was with who was also playing Pokémon Go but didn't want to go out in the evenings after class was done because it was exhausting. So, I'm up on the Pokémon Go page, met up with four or five people, I managed to get three raids done in one evening. And I don't normally like talking to new people, but when you see people standing around a Pokémon stop, you're just like, I know exactly what they're here for. So, all you do is you just be like, you uh, you here for the raid? Yeah! Oh, cool. Me too. So, I actually, from that one day that I got the three Mewtwo raids in, I made three friends on Facebook. I can't tell you what their names are because I can't remember. But I met like, there were four of us that night, but I had also met a couple of other people just going from stop to stop to stop. So, and I don't normally like meeting new people. Like my other sibling, I have anxiety, but I still get out of the house and do things. But I don't like meeting new people. But when it's Pokémon Go it's easier. I'm not, well, I say I'm not sure why. But it's likely because we all have common interests. We all have common goals.

Interviewer:

So, playing Pokémon Go allows you to approach people more easily because you know, you already know that there's an interest there.

Chloe, 27, female, Newfoundland, Canada:

Yeah.

Interviewer:

A shared interest.

The online community basis for Pokémon Go allowed Chloe to join another community in Canada and be part of their activities. Here, the idea of 'liquid sociality' (Gerbaudo, 2012) can be seen in practice; the 'Facebook Friendship' facilitated through groups is an informal relationship formed through the shared activity of play that facilitates the rapid joining of communities. The weak ties created through these groups can be leveraged to create further social interaction, but the temporary and fleeting nature of this interaction in particular shows that 'liquid sociality' in this context is characterised by the very rapid formation of groups for instrumental reasons in the game, without any development of strong ties.

While these communities may not foster strong social ties, there is other value that can emerge from the development of communities with weak ties. Tracy outlines the benefit of the Pokémon Go community for her daughter in Lansing, Michigan:

Um, downtown Lansing there's Washington Avenue. It basically runs, um, north to south and it's a couple of miles, I think. But every intersection has two pokéstops. One on each side and there's some in the middle of the blocks. So, there's like a shit ton for lack of a better word. And that ends up at the community college and there's a gym in there. So, most weekends, there are herds of people. And when I say herds, I mean herds, of people that go downtown and go start at the community college and work their way down Washington and then turn around and work their way back up. They do raids. So, it's a way to get out and be social and because of her autism, she's very outgoing. She wants to make friends really badly, but she doesn't understand ... socially appropriate behaviour. So, she has a hard time keeping friends. And she's very, very black and white. So, by going out and doing this big huge community thing where there's tons and tons of people around, it gives her a chance to work on those social skills. Like there's no stranger danger in my daughter's eyes. Everybody is a friend she has not yet met. Which can be a little terrifying. It at least is an opportunity where there's a common goal for her to participate but still maintain her individual, you know, safety bubble, so to speak. So, we do that a lot. (Tracy, 51, female, Lansing, Michigan, US).

The weak ties that characterise a community in Pokémon Go for intergenerational players in this situation provide a valuable and safe environment for socialisation. Additionally, the number of people involved in mutual activity around these pokéstops means that that there are ample opportunities for this activity to occur. At the same time, Tracy can maintain the weak strength of these ties for her daughter's safety. While the communities are not conducive to strong ties in this research, there are other benefits through the weak social ties which are not necessarily related to progress in the game. Overwhelmingly though community ties are linked, in this research, to progress through raids and events in the game and this activity is the foundation of the weak community ties formed.

4.5 Weak and Latent Ties

Just like with the ties identified in the Pokémon Go community, the overwhelming response from interviewees was that social ties formed through the game for intergenerational players are weak or latent ties.

Um, so people who I haven't known before. It only led to very kind of fleeting interactions. But nothing that is, you know, deeper than that. (Rhonda, 39, female, San Jose, California, US).

Yeah absolutely! Yeah, yeah. I don't know if they're necessarily, they're not like friends in that you know, you'd have them over for dinner. But you know, they're people that you talk to and you feel really comfortable with. I suppose, you know, it very rarely goes beyond Pokémon, like the conversation and stuff like that. And we generally tend not to hang around because we have, you know, we've got the kids and stuff like that. But um, yeah acquaintances, definitely. (Joe, 37, male, Southend-on-Sea, UK).

Not as much. But we, we know faces. We see faces around, you know, because we say hello and things like that. So yeah. (Ceri, 45, female, Essex, UK).

Interviewer:

Okay. So, would you consider them more acquaintances than friends?

Ceri, 45, female, Essex, UK:

Yeah. Just the Pokémon Go community I suppose, yeah.

The consensus from the interviews was that players develop a series of acquaintances when playing in an intergenerational context, rather than any strong ties with other players. This sits in contradiction with some of the research discussed at the beginning of this chapter. This can be attributed to the context in which these players play and experience the game; the parental tie with children constrains the possibility of building strong ties with other players as the need to protect the children takes precedence over developing nascent social connection.

> Um, acquaintances, yes. I wouldn't say close friends. We, our close friends already played. But there are people, especially like my son, because he's really good at memory, like knowing names, like usernames and stuff. He'll remember that so and so was this username and oh yeah, we played with him, you know, for these different raids. And he really remembers all of that. And he remembers the people who he liked playing with. And there are, like I mentioned, there's a dad, recently divorced with a little girl the same age as Lily. And it worked well because it's like, oh I have her on Wednesday nights, those are raid hours. Like I said, we go to the playground. We let the girls play for a half an hour and so she knows this little girl's name and she's gotten to know them. So, it's not something where we would probably say hey come over for a barbecue, because they are specifically Pokémon Go friends and we see them during that time but not necessarily outside of it. (Amelia, 45, female, Boise, Idaho, US).

Amelia's children clearly enjoy the social aspects of the game, but Amelia clearly delineates social contact made through the game and any social contact outside of the game. As mentioned earlier, this can be understood as a reaffirmation of the 'magic circle'. Huizinga's (1992/1938) idea of the 'magic circle' insists that the play of any given game must occur within a spatially and temporally enclosed area, or playground, and is as such detached from 'ordinary life'. In this context, play is distinct from 'ordinary life' and when 'a player steps in and out of a game, he or she is crossing the boundary – or frame – that defines the game in time and space' (Salen & Zimmerman, 2004, p. 95). In Amelia's example, the lack of development of strong ties with other players can be understood as intergenerational play in Pokémon Go being akin to a new 'magic circle' where the play of the game is defined as bounded in space and time, without the need or desire to develop the weak and latent ties created by the game into stronger ties through other sustained social contact. This kind of distanced, weak sociality was noted by a number of other interviewees in the context of playing alongside children.

Um. It's one of those things where, because I'm a stay at home mom and I always have my kids, I'm not generally available to go do the 'Pokémoning' things that other people want to do. And so, you know, even if we become in-game friends, the chances that I will be able to meet up with them again and actually play are kind of slim. Plus, it makes me feel anxious to attempt to do that kind of thing because I feel like my kids annoy people who don't have small children at the time. So, it's kind of a twofer there. (Liv, 27, female, Boise, Idaho, US).

Liv notes that she sees her children as a barrier to developing links with other players, although not in a negative manner. The game does facilitate links, but Liv does not pursue any further meetings or development of friendships with other players as the game is seen as an activity with her children – a 'magic circle' of intergenerational play. Stephanie illustrates the same kind of logic:

Interviewer:

I see okay. And when you're out, if you go to one of these raids, or even if you're out and about and looking for Pokémon, can you tell when others are looking for Pokémon as well? Is it something that you can kind of look over and go, oh I know what they're doing?

Stephanie, 42, female, Orlando, Florida, US:

Yes totally. And yes, we've met a few people that way. I mean not like lasting friendships, but you just talk. It's kind of nice, you get, you know you're outside and you kind of chat with people.

Interviewer:

And do you typically befriend or chat with people who also have children, or would you say that it's typically just anybody else who is playing?

Stephanie, 42, female, Orlando, Florida, US:

It's both but yeah, a lot of times they're adults that are playing and some of them have kids there too.

Interviewer:

Okay, but as you said, not lasting friendships necessarily.

Stephanie, 42, female, Orlando, Florida, US:

No.

Again, Stephanie's co-play with her children shapes the relationships she has with other players, and these are characterised as weak ties. Overwhelmingly, this kind of loose, cursory, fleeting connection was identified as the most common connection made between adult intergenerational players. In the context of the game itself, this is unexpected given the research previously on sociability and Pokémon Go, but when considering the need to care for children during play, provide a model for responsible sociability and attend to the needs of children during play the focus of intergenerational play is not on sociability but on the child or children. This then forms a new 'magic circle' that inhibits social contact and focuses on the game and child.

4.6 Children's Friends

While this chapter has focused on the kinds of social relationships developed by adult intergenerational players, the possibility of children developing strong ties with other children is also an important consideration. Just like with adult players though, the dynamic of intergenerational play and the formation of a 'magic circle' for intergenerational players mean that sociability is inhibited for children as well as adults. As the following exchange demonstrates:

> Bill, 28, male, Southend-on-Sea, UK:
>
> I think the main thing for my son is that he's way more confident in talking to other adults than I probably still am now. He'll go up and he will talk like, when we first started, you know, when you go and talk to people and you, he'd generally just stand by my leg and not do anything. Now, he'll talk their ear off all day and there's a load of other kids around Southend as well that play now.
>
> Interviewer:
>
> Okay, and so has he made any friends then?
>
> Bill, 28, male, Southend-on-Sea, UK:
>
> Um, I don't think I would say other kids through Pokémon Go. It's more because most of the people we see regularly don't have children or they have children, but they're grown up now. So, there's a few of them we see, and he has played with them a bit, but not I would say on a regular like friendship now.

For Bill, the sociability effect of the game for his son has been to improve his social skills with adults rather than make friends with other children. Playing as a father–child dyad leads to the child having more contact with adults or older children, limiting the possibility of developing friendships. This shows some congruence with the experience of adults in playing the game, and across the interviews very few respondents commented that their children made any friends through playing in an intergenerational manner. There was some evidence that the online communities of Pokémon Go can, for children enabled to access these communities, provide some of the latent and weak ties seen with adults:

> Um, well I know they've gotten new friends through the thing, but I think it's more or less people throwing their codes out there saying hey I want to be a friend because it's part of quests and stuff like that. And like our daughter Amanda, she's got friends overseas in, what is it, Poland and Germany and stuff like that. So, she likes getting presents from there and seeing the location. It's not so much being friends or communicating but she kind of likes that aspect. But it's similar with us. It's like hey, she's got friends that she's already got in school and she's friends with them as well. So, you know, they can like, like Josh down the road will show up and say hey, you guys doing this? And we'll run into him out in the field. (Alan, 50, male, Plymouth, Michigan, US).

Here, Alan's daughter Amanda leverages the online communities for instrumental reasons linked to progress in the game but does not develop (in Alan's opinion) the strong ties of a friendship. Conversely, existing friends seem to be more conducive to co-operational play for Alan and his family.

4.7 Existing Friends

The experience of Alan's family with regards to existing strong tie relationships was mirrored by other interviewees. The existing strong tie is a key part of the game for some intergenerational players, and these existing ties can reflect on how other ties players are viewed with regards to sociability.

> I also have a friend who plays with his two children occasionally as well. So, we'll occasionally meet up and with the kids together… [on other players] Um, not, I wouldn't call them friends as such. They're people I play a game with. I don't know much about their real lives or anything. I've obviously, I have real friends that do play it. So, we tend to play with them and then meet up with people or certain other families that may be there or certain events as well. We tend to hang with the families rather than just anyone. (Troy, 29, male, Norwich/East Anglia, UK).

Troy follows a theme that has already been identified, where existing strong ties developed outside of playing the game supersede any weak or latent ties developed through the game itself. Although it seems obvious, the migration of strong ties into the game acts as another inhibitory factor in developing the weak or latent ties of the game into a stronger relationship. Even when new people are met, other existing ties can easily dominate play, as Alan and Jo illustrate:

We've met new people and there's some old people we didn't know played Pokémon that Pokémon now. They're already friends of ours or even family. Like cousins of mine and their girlfriends are always playing and my brother. So, they'll go well we play, let's be friends. We're like okay that's cool. (Alan, 50, male, Plymouth, Michigan, US).

Interviewer:

Okay, but are you saying that both people that you didn't, or I guess what are you saying in that regard? In terms of people that had been playing and you realized oh my gosh, you both played together? Or were they people that you didn't really socialize with before and now you are socializing with them?

Jo, 50, female, Plymouth, Michigan, US:

I would say we socialize more with Beth now because she's on Pokémon.

I mean it's a little of both. I mean first people we were meeting were through this Discord group that you know we're getting to know. And you know, at these different raids or anything like that. But you know, it's just also other interested current friends and family that you didn't realize were into this game. And you're like oh, okay, this is kind of cool. Because you can still be even be more connected with your friends and family on top of meeting new people. (Alan, 50, male, Plymouth, Michigan, US).

The use of pre-existing strong social ties in game activities such as raids illustrates how such ties can exclude the possibility of creating new social ties. If pre-existing ties fulfil the need for progress in the game, then there is no need for the latent or weak ties created by the game and no desire to create new ties, even if in this case there are some new relationships that have been created – but in a more fleeting and cursory manner than pre-existing ties.

4.8 Conclusion

The research on individual players and players that do not play with children supports the notion that Pokémon Go, like other mobile applications, facilitates forming new relationships with other players, thanks to the shared temporal and spatial activity and other factors such as parochialisation. When playing in an intergenerational manner, the possibilities of forming new relationships still exist; the game itself creates a vast number of latent and weak ties and the online communities that have been formed through social media provide localised networks of players that can develop the possibility of strong social ties. In some cases, intergenerational players do create what they perceive as strong social ties based on their pursuit of progress within the game. This instrumental need to progress in the game, important to the majority of players, is a key driver in all the social interactions reported in this research. However, only in very few examples did this result in the development of new relationships characterised by strong social ties.

Overwhelmingly, the reflections of interviewees were that playing Pokémon Go in an intergenerational context leads to players developing a series of fleeting or cursory acquaintances with other players. This is in spite of the obvious factors that would promote sociability: shared spatial and temporal activity, shared interest in the game itself and progress in the game, parochialisation based on the game community and the existence of extensive social network–based localised game communities. Engagement with the game in an intergenerational context, therefore, has an effect on the transfer of social ties from latent or weak to strong. While intergenerational players are engaged with the same gameplay and activity in the game as other players, parental play with children clearly brings a new dynamic to the fore which inhibits, rather than promotes, the formation of new relationships. In essence, intergenerational play seems to form a new 'magic circle' of play. While Pokémon Go can remove the spatial bounding of Huizinga's (1992/ 1938) original 'magic circle', in intergenerational play the spatial and temporal barrier becomes a bubble in the manner of Peter Sloterdijk's spheres (Sloterdijk, 2011) where the parent–child dyad is effectively separated from other players. Other players are, of course, acknowledged and remembered by the dyad, but other players remain distanced and only considered as acquaintances characterised as a weak social tie or latent tie that could become more but rarely is in this mode of play.

While intergenerational play has demonstrable effects on family interaction, family movement, exercise and positives for child sociability and familial relationships, forming wider relationships and utilising the positive features of Pokémon Go for increasing sociability appear to be something inhibited by intergenerational play. This is not necessarily a negative effect of intergenerational play; the positive aspects of this mode of play may negate the need for wider social relationships, and in the context of intergenerational play, new relationships may not be an explicit aim of using the application. The reversal of many findings on the positive social effects of Pokémon Go play does mark intergenerational play as a different mode of play which challenges assumptions and previous research on Pokémon Go as a social phenomenon.

References

Baym, N. (2015). *Personal connections in the digital age*. Cambridge: Polity.

Bonus, J. A., Peebles, A., Mares, M. L., & Sarmiento, I. G. (2018). Look on the bright side (of media effects): Pokémon Go as a catalyst for positive life experiences. *Media Psychology*, *21*(2), 263–287.

Deng, Y., & O'Brien, K. (2013). Relational repression in China: Using social ties to demobilize protesters. *The China Quarterly*, *215*, 533–552. doi:10.1017/S03057 41013000714

Diani, M., & McAdam, D. (2003). *Social movements and networks*. New York, NY: Oxford University Press.

Fernandez, R. A. (1989). Multiorganizational fields and recruitment to social. *International Social Movement Research*, *2*, 315–343.

Gerbaudo, P. (2012). *Tweets and the streets: Social media and contemporary activism*. Lodon: Pluto Press.

Gilbert, E., & Karahalios, K. (2009, April). Predicting tie strength with social media. In *Proceedings of the SIGCHI conference on human factors in computing systems*, CHI 2009, April 4–9, 2009, Boston, Massachusetts, USA (pp. 211–220).

Gladwell, M. (2010). Small Change: Why the revolution will not be tweeted. *The New Yorker*, October 4, 2010, pp. 42–49. doi:10.5210/fm.v18i11.4966

Gould, R. (2003). Why do networks matter? In M. Diani & D. McAdam (Eds.), *Social movements and networks: Relational approaches to collective action* (pp. 234–257). Oxford; New York, NY: Oxford University Press.

Granovetter, M. S. (1973). The strength of weak ties. *American Journal of Sociology*, *78*(6), 1360–1380.

Haythornthwaite, C. (2001). Strong, weak, and latent ties and the impact of new media. *The Information Society*, *18*, 385–401.

Hjorth, L., & Richardson, I. (2014). *Gaming in social, locative and mobile media*. NewYork, NY: Springer.

Hjorth, L., & Richardson, I. (2017). Pokémon GO: Mobile media play, place-making, and the digital wayfarer. *Mobile Media and Communication*, *5*(1), 3–14. doi: 10.1177/2050157916680015

Huizinga, J. H. (1992). *Homo Ludens: A study of the play-element in culture*. London: Beacon Press. Original work published 1938.

Humphreys, L. (2005). Cellphones in public: Social interactions in a wireless era. *New Media & Society*, *7*(6), 810–833.

Humphreys, L. (2007). Mobile social networks and social practice: A case study of Dodgeball. *Journal of Computer-Mediated Communication*, *13*(1), 341–360. doi: 10.1111/j.1083-6101.2007.00399.x

Humphreys, L. (2010). Mobile social networks and urban public space. *New Media & Society*, *12*(5), 763–778.

Humphreys, L. (2017). Involvement shield or social catalyst: Thoughts on sociospatial practice of Pokémon GO. *Mobile Media & Communication*, *5*(1), 15–19. doi: 10.1177/2050157916677864

Humphreys, L., & Liao, T. (2013). Foursquare and the parochialization of public space. *First Monday*, *18*(11).

Jenkins, H., Ito, M., & boyd, D. (2016). *Participatory culture in a networked era: A conversation on youth, learning, commerce, and politics*. New York, NY: John Wiley & Sons.

Kaczmarek, L. D., Misiak, M., Behnke, M., Dziekan, M., & Guzik, P. (2017). The Pikachu effect: Social and health gaming motivations lead to greater benefits of Pokémon GO use. *Computers in Human Behavior*, *75*, 356–363.

Kitts, J. (2000). Mobilizing in black boxes: Social movements and social movement organization participation. *The social psychology of protest*, *5*(2), 241–257.

Ling, R. S. (2008). *New tech, new ties*. Cambridge, MA: MIT press.

Ling, R., & Campbell, S. W. (2017). Mobile communication: Bringing us together and tearing us apart. In R. Ling & S. W. Campbell (Eds.), *Mobile communication* (pp. 11–26). Abingdon: Routledge.

Marwell, G., Oliver, P., & Prahl, R. (1988). A theory of the critical mass. III. Social networks and collective action. *American Journal of Sociology, 94*, 502–534.

McAdam, D., & Paulsen, R. (1993). Specifying the relationship between social ties and activism. *American Journal of Sociology, 99*, 640–667.

Orum, A. M. (1972). *Black students in protest*. Washington, DC: American Socio-logical Association.

Paasovaara, S., Jarusriboonchai, P., & Olsson, T. (2017, November). Understanding collocated social interaction between Pokémon GO players. In *Proceedings of the 16th International Conference on Mobile and Ubiquitous Multimedia* (pp. 151–163). New York, NY: ACM.

Passy, F. (2003). Social networks matter. But how? In M. D. Mcadam (Ed.), *Social movements and networks relational approaches to collective action* (pp. 21–48). New York, NY: Oxford University Press.

Rheingold, H. (1993). *The virtual community: Homesteading on the electronic frontier. Reading*. MA: Addison-Wesley.

Salen, K., & Zimmerman, E. (2004). *Rules of play: Game design fundamentals*. Cambridge, MA: MIT Press.

Sloterdijk, P. (2011). *Bubbles: Spheres: Microspherology* (Vol. I). Cambridge, MA: MIT Press.

Turkle, S. (1996). Virtuality and its discontents: Searching for community in cyber-space. In J. Turow & A. L. Kavanaugh (Eds.), *The wired homestead: An MIT Press sourcebook on the internet and the family* (pp. 385–397), Cambridge: MIT Press.

Turkle, S. (2017). *Alone together: Why we expect more from technology and less from each other*. London: Hachette UK.

Vella, K., Johnson, D., Cheng, V. W. S., Davenport, T., Mitchell, J., Klarkowski, M., & Phillips, C. (2019). A sense of belonging: Pokemon GO and social connected-ness. *Games and Culture, 14*(6), 583–603.

Wong, J. C. (2016). The world's largest Pokémon Go gathering hits the streets of San Francisco. *The Guardian*, July 21, 2016. Retrieved from https://www.the-guardian.com/technology/2016/jul/21/pokemon-go-gathering-san-francisco

Chapter 5

Familial Locative Play: Digital Economy and Surveillance Capitalism

5.1 Pokémon Go as a Form of Surveillance Capitalism

As an application running on a mobile device, Pokémon Go has several unsurprising features with regards to surveillance of users, data production and harvesting, data processing and using that data for advertising and profiling of users. The logic of mobile media applications in this context has been a concern for many years as surveillant practices and technologies that produce, process, disseminate and utilise data from users. Bauman and Lyon (2013) use the term 'liquid surveillance' to describe how these technologies have altered the mode of contemporary surveillance. Liquid surveillance is when'the focused, systematic and routine attention to personal details for the purposes of influence, management, protection or direction' (Lyon, 2007, p. 14) surveillance aspect of these technologies is married to the form of modernity 'that does not stand still' that Bauman defines as liquid (Lyon, 2007, p. 3). The surveillant position remains unchanged, but the mode of that surveillance is in constant change as technologies develop, alter and emerge. This notion of an underlying surveillant logic in digital media and the applications used through digital media underpins Shoshana Zuboff's concept of surveillance capitalism (Zuboff, 2019a).

> Surveillance capitalism is not the same as digital technology. It is an economic logic that has hijacked the digital for its own purposes. The logic of surveillance capitalism begins with unilaterally claiming private human experience as free raw material for production and sales. It wants your walk in the park, online browsing and communications, hunt for a parking space, voice at the breakfast table … (Zuboff, 2019b).

Zuboff's concept has parallels with Martin Heidegger's (1977) notion that the essence of modern technology is nothing technological, but instead is a way of revealing the world as resource to be used. Zuboff conceptualises surveillance capitalism as a drive to quantify or extract the phenomenal experience of being

Intergenerational Locative Play, 117–141
Copyright © 2021 Michael Saker and Leighton Evans
Published under an exclusive licence by Emerald Publishing Limited
doi:10.1108/978-1-83909-139-120211017

human, transform that experience into data and then sell that data as part of a constructed image of the user, a data subject made from the endless streams of data produced by digitally enabled everyday activity. This logic is not limited by company or application but applies across the digital as a field of activity; anything that can produce data on the user can be enrolled into surveillance capitalism. Zuboff's contribution above that of liquid surveillance is the central position of capital in digital surveillance. Surveillance is not used in surveillance capitalism in the pursuit of safety or the punishment of wrongdoing – although the disciplinary or control modes of digital technology are not incompatible with the logic of surveillance capitalism. Instead, the continual surveillance of the user is part of a new logic of capitalism itself, where value is extracted from not only the surplus labour of the user as audience (Smythe, 1976) but also from all interactions with digital media, no matter how every day or mundane. The capitalisation of everyday experience, therefore, encompasses not only all use of digital media but also the aspect of everyday life that is being mediated by digital media at that time.

Unsurprisingly, Zuboff uses the development and use of Pokémon Go as an example of the pervasiveness of surveillance capitalism. In this analysis, the game itself acts as a form of concealment of the logic of surveillance capitalism. The aim of Pokémon Go is not, therefore, to capture Pokémon, but for the movement and activity of the user to be captured as data for processing to be sold. As befits a product of surveillance capitalism, Pokémon Go itself was born out of Google. John Hanke (Google Maps and Street View VC) launched Niantic Labs (Zuboff, 2019a, p. 311), and following the formation of Alphabet as a parent company for Google in 2015, Niantic was established as a separate company with $30 million in seed funding from Google. The relationship between Google and Niantic is not surprising when Google's model of operation is considered. Google's model of operation can be argued to be constant real-time biopolitical exploitation. Hardt and Negri (2000, p. 24) have argued that the contemporary capitalism of which Google is a foundational part is based on a form of Foucauldian biopower. Google's vision is one where the world is made completely knowable, controllable and predictable. Google is, therefore, a proponent of an ideology that Evgeny Morozov (2013, p. 5) calls 'technological solutionism'. Solutionism is a recasting of all complex social situations either as neatly defined problems with definite, computable solutions or as transparent and self-evident processes that can be easily optimised – if only the right algorithms are in place. Morozov argues that solutionism is a typical ideology of Silicon Valley entrepreneurs and intellectuals who glorify digital media as being the solution to societal problems. Morozov explicitly criticises the likes of Eric Schmidt (Google) and Mark Zuckerberg (Facebook) as technological solutionists that 'impoverish and infantilize our public debate' (Morozov, 2013, p. 43). Technological solutionism reimagines the individual and the social as part of the algorithms or systems of digital media, and, therefore, any problems arising at an individual or social level can be solved by these digital media. This notion clearly has roots in cybernetic theory and imagination, as well as exerting a form of biopower where individuals are subjugated under these systems in order to create new data subjects. In this view,

Google is ostensibly a control machine that aims at controlling people's perception of reality and transforming these perceptions into profits (Fuchs, 2015, p. 162).

Galloway (2017) uses an analogy of God to describe the kind of power relationship that Google has to the mere mortal users of its services. The power desired by Google is the knowledge not only of what we do but also of what we want to do. Google's aim is to stockpile information and use that information to build artificial models of mind that can be used to predict action (Foer, 2017). As Galloway (2017, p. 110) pictures it, Google 'knows that as we walk through the mall, we lust for a pair of Tory Burch Jolie Pumps or Bose QuietComfort Headphones. He knows you have a thing for girls with tattoos'. The objective of the harvesting of personal information is not an individualised tracking of the whole population. If Google insinuates itself into the intimate lives of each and every person, then massive databases that make numerical sense can be assembled (The Invisible Committee, 2015) to create a kind of cybernetic governmentality. While such governmentality operates in terms of a completely new logic, its subjects continue to think of themselves according to the old paradigm in a cultural lag. We may continue to believe that our 'personal' data belong to us and that we're only exercising our 'individual freedom' by deciding to let Google and Facebook or the police have access to them. The result of this accommodation is that the mass surveillance of individuals in this model is mass self-surveillance (Fuchs, 2011), a by-product of mass self-communication (Castells, 2009) that requires users' permanent input and activity to work. The specific characteristics of social media and the use of ubiquitous search engines, operating systems, email clients, the uploading of user-generated content and permanent communicative flows enable this form of surveillance.

In effect, Pokémon Go represents a dream application for a surveillance capitalist organisation. Pokémon Go fuses scale, scope and actuation for a continual source of context-rich data on users (Zuboff, 2019a, p. 312). Pokémon Go represents a kind of 'living lab' for the testing and simulation at scale of not only real-time contextual data but also the use of that data in nudging and controlling the movement of the user. By scale, here we refer to the automatic conditioning of collective behaviour rather than behaviour at the individual level; the summer of 2016 where Pokémon Go 'flash mobs' congregated in public spaces across the globe to capture rare Pokémon and train at gyms represented not only a new form of co-ordinated play but also co-ordinated and controlled movement. Moreover, this directing towards real-time constellations of behaviour occurs beyond the 'rim of individual awareness' (Zuboff, 2019a, p. 312). Essentially, Zuboff argues that the game itself nudges players towards interactions with both other users and most critically specific places in a form of gamification as behavioural modification. Indeed, for Zuboff, the critical aspect of Pokémon Go as an instance of surveillance capitalism is that while the game runs players through the real world as part of the game experience, this is done not for the sake of the game *that players think they are playing*. The shaping of behaviour and spatial experience is part of a larger game of surveillance capitalism. This is exemplified through Pokémon Go promotions, how playing Pokémon Go drives footfall and how physical places are surfaced through the interface to draw the attention of the player (Zuboff, 2019a, p. 314). Since 2017, Niantic has offered businesses the possibility of being 'sponsored locations' that pay for exposure (i.e. hosting a gym) on a cost-per-visit model. Organisations such as McDonald's have extensively used this system, sponsoring more than 3,000 locations in the game in Japan and in early 2020 entering a partnership with Niantic across Latin America and the Caribbean to promote their locations as locations within the game system (GoHub, 2020). The placement of critical ludic infrastructure in the game is co-ordinated with the business interests of advertisers, often without visibility to the gamer, and the playing of the game, therefore, becomes a series of controlled movements through a commercialised space. The game has two levels: the ludic experience and the commercial level that shapes that ludic experience.

Further to this, the application itself exhibits all the classic symptoms of a fully operational surveillance capitalism operation. The application collects vast amounts of data from both gameplay and the phones of users. The long list of permissions that the application demands users cede to before playing allows Niantic to create a location-based social graph through both game activity and activity using other services, allowing for a lucrative product for both data processing and brokering. Niantic has followed the classic Google model of operation to provide a highly sophisticated set of prediction services for Niantic's customers – advertisers (Zuboff, 2019a, p. 318). This hidden game is, in the context of surveillance capitalism, far more consequential than the game itself for players. Every time a player plays Pokémon Go, the player has a role in the larger game of cybernetic governmentality. Movement, behaviour and attention are translated into data to be used not only in the vulgar selling of advertising but also in the construction of vast databases being used to make the world 'more knowable' by making behaviour more predictable and controllable. Pokémon Go is, therefore, an ideal application because not only does playing generate data but also the game effectively nudges the user towards ideal forms of commercialised mobility and behaviour while the user remains distracted from this thanks to the ludic element of the game. Evading awareness of this is as neat a trick as a Pokémon popping up in front of us on the screen.

Against this backdrop of surveillance capitalism, it is worth considering the kind of labour that Pokémon Go feeds from to sate the demand for data from this economic logic. Pokémon Go is a location-based game; to play the game is to move, to be mobile. Movement through space is the critical dynamic in the successful playing of the game for users (Hjorth & Richardson, 2017). As this is the case, it is both the movement of the user and the encoding of physical spaces that the player moves though in play that become salient aspects of the overall Pokémon Go data rush. The labour of the player is not only realised through their mobility but also through a particular mode of mobility that is fashioned by the game itself. Biggs and Carr (2015, p. 99) note,

> ...it is possible to see a city as a concretion of certain channels of social relationship. It is a complex set of arrangements, set in

wood, brick, concrete and stone, which reflect and continue to shape the way people behave and interact over time and in space.

Pokémon Go adds another dimension to this concretion of the urban environment by shaping the way people behave in time and space for the provision of data – but this labour is disguised as leisure and social practice with others. In the context of the research of this book, this labour involves the enrolment of new actors into spatial labour practices. Space and place are commonly geared towards those who are old enough to work, and not so old or so young that they cannot work. Consequently, childhood and old age are marked by a sense of purposelessness. For Debord (1967), the spectacle of the city revolves around the various ways in which space and place are constructed as sites of production that limit social fluidity. In contrast, the 'playful' approaches to space that is encouraged in Pokémon Go inscribe a purpose in place of purposelessness.

It is this sense of purpose and playfulness that is the critical factor in concealing the laborious aspect of Pokémon Go. As Biggs and Carr (2015) point out, if play can emancipate people from work-based roles and pre-determined identities, it can also 'give meaning to the peripheral' (p. 107). Likewise, the fact that childhood and old age are not explicitly woven into urban environments, in a general sense, means these categories implicitly provide a 'creative drift' outside of the spectacle and its penchant for production (Biggs & Carr, 2015). 'Recognising "drift" as meaningful activity beyond the constraints of work and production significantly enhances the possibilities for generationally constituted space and empathic engagement between generational groups' (Biggs & Carr, 2015). Pokémon Go is a prime example of this, as playing the game allows users to step outside of their common roles and experience space and place in a playful manner that decontextualises the everyday. This playful mobility does entail Pokémon Go nudging families to move through and explore their surroundings in a manner that differs from a mindset dominated by destination. At the same time, this deconstruction of pre-determined spatial practices is embroiled in the production of data that makes our movements increasingly knowable and exacerbates asymmetries of power. From a Heideggerian perspective (Heidegger, 1977) vantage point, this situation constitutes the revealing of a concealing of a revealing. On the one hand, Pokémon Go provides the illusion of meaningful activity that resists the logic of capitalism. On the other hand, the meaning of this activity is twofold, with one side of this division veiled from players. While the practice of Pokémon Go might appear to deconstruct space and place, as well as pre-determined identities, it simultaneously ratifies the deconstruction of spatial practice as productive. Accordingly, players are not simply playing the game but working within the confines of system that presents a gamic veneer. Pokémon Go, therefore, does more than allow the appropriation of play spaces, which are understood as being so important to the personal development of children (Hart, 2002); Pokémon Go signifies the implicit appropriation of appropriated play spaces as work spaces geared toward the unspoken indoctrination of players into a culture predicated on surveillance capitalism. The game being played is hidden by another game being played – but it is the player that is ultimately played.

The majority of participants in this research, as we go on to elucidate, did not care about the use of data or data production as a product of their activity on Pokémon Go, but understood it as a necessary compromise in playing the game for 'free'. This is ultimately the key marker of the success of surveillance capitalism. These players were resigned to the situation as a benign backdrop to their activity, either seeing it as unimportant or a normalised part of contemporary life. The hegemony of surveillance capitalism seen in many responses is a testament to the power of the economic logic that has successfully ingratiated itself into everyday practices. This concealment of the economic prerogative of Niantic is important in understanding what has become of locative games as they have developed from Foursquare and Gowalla in 2010 to Pokémon Go in 2016 and beyond. While Niantic has created an experience that is clearly more compulsive than any other location-based game, the compulsion to play has gone hand in hand with a more efficient and comprehensive data harvesting architecture to create a more lucrative surveillance capitalism product. Likewise, the fact that it is a locative game alleviates parent concern about screen time for children and concerns about mobile media use on the part of adult users. These factors have created a 'sticky' game that brings together a confluence of motivations to play it – and continue playing it. At the same time though, there is far more going on than just collecting Pokémon in Pokémon Go. The deconstruction of pre-determined spatial practices through playing Pokémon Go is embroiled in the production of data that makes our movements increasingly knowable, exacerbating asymmetries of power and the exploitation of players (including children).

In sum, then, one of the aims of this chapter is to understand how issues of surveillance are perceived by the parents who play this HRG with their children. Consequently, the chapter is driven by the following research questions. First, are families cognisant of the data they produce by playing this HRG, and how this data might be used? Second, do families think critically about the gamic mechanics of this HRG, such as the spawning locations of Pokémon and the reasoning behind these decisions? Third, are participants concerned about the potential application of their gamic data, and if so, how are these concerns reconciled? Fourth, do participants use the familial playing of Pokémon Go as an opportunity to discuss the production of data and its multifaced uses with their children?

5.2 Data are Unimportant

The survey that underpinned our empirical research provided results which indicate that the everyday use of applications embroiled in surveillance capitalism is not viewed with the same problematic lens by users as it is by academics. Only 52 out of the 165 respondents (32%) had thought about how the locative data produced through playing Pokémon Go might be used. The underlying theme of the research on this topic is one where the idea of data surfaces only as an afterthought in the use of Pokémon Go, and whatever might be done with that data is relatively benign. Many participants simply felt that the data produced by the application could not be used in a meaningful way because of their socio-economic circumstances. As Bill explains:

> When asked about how the locative data that you produce while playing Pokémon Go with your kids might be used?] No. I don't have enough money to fall for any of that stuff. So, it's very different if I had a load of spare income that I could waste on it then I probably would. But I don't so it doesn't matter, ha-ha. (Bill, 28, male, Southend-on-Sea, UK).

The idea that the data can only be used to market high-end goods shows some understanding of how data could be used. This is not by any means a complete understanding of how the application itself can manipulate everyday movements through play or how that data are used to create a profile of the user commensurate with their socio-economic status through the use of other data. Other players were more understanding of the possibilities of the data created through using Pokémon Go, but no less accepting of that data trail as a payoff for use of the data.

> Yeah. As a former marketing director, I could see how exceptionally valuable that is to know where high-traffic areas are, how people continue to repeat those patterns, when and what times a day does it happen, what actually motivates them. Yeah, as a marketing director, it'd be really easy to get in good with Niantic and get some of that information. There's no question about it. I'm one of those people though that, you know, there's all this concern about like if, you know, Billa is listening to you. I don't care. I'm not doing anything wrong, so I don't care. Let them listen. My life is really boring, you know. So yeah, yeah, like I said. As a marketing director, there's a lot of really valuable information. There are a lot of different companies. But I don't see what the problem is with that. I think that that's actually a good thing. It means that they're spending their dollars wisely if they're able to get that information. So, I don't have a problem with it. Track away, Pokémon! Track away! Go ahead! (Amelia, 45, female, Boise, Idaho, US).

The reconceptualisation of the data as a personal privacy issue, rather than commercial and economic issue, shows that discourses on the nature of privacy around Pokémon Go (and any other number of applications) still concern a Foucauldian notion of governmentality and disciplinary force as the critical factor in surveillance. Surveillance is the big 'other' spying on the little person, and if we are all good and proper there is nothing to worry about. However, Zuboff's (2019a) argument about the nature of surveillance capitalism is far more like Deleuze's (1992) concept of the society of control, where there is no panoptical force that might be watching for wrongdoing.

Instead, control is diffused across the apparatus of everyday life to effectively make coercion by power a feature of everyday activity. The aim of surveillance capitalism is not surveillance of wrongdoing (indeed, wrongdoing might well be a lucrative area depending on the nature of the deviance). The aim of surveillance capitalism is to quantify or extract the phenomenal experience of being human, transform that experience into data and then sell that data as part of a constructed image of the user. In understanding the danger of surveillance as a purely a personal privacy issue, the true nature of surveillance capitalism is not considered. While there is some allusion to the value of the data in Amelia's answer, that is buried by the discourse on liberty – a discourse which in itself contends that personal liberty is affected but only for deviants. A success of surveillance capitalism is that it itself is not a discourse for users of applications; the greatest trick the devil ever pulled was convincing the world he didn't exist.

This notion of the kind of data surveillance being performed through Pokémon Go (and applications in general) being relatively benign was shared by other participants. This can be observed in the following extracts:

> Right. So, I guess like any big company, they could sell data. I mean, like you say, they don't have anything personal of ours per se. They couldn't really, you know, market it to, so we don't have any concerns with that. (Alan, 50, male, Plymouth, Michigan, US).

> Oh, everybody's trying to catch data one way or another. Whether it's to track your location, monitoring your calls, what not. Or if some black hat is attempting to do a phishing scam or there are types of trojan on your computer or what not. At the end everybody is out for your data and what not. The only real response that I've got for that. Hey, if you want to look through my camera and see stuff that you probably shouldn't see involving my nude self, then you know what, go ahead? Go right ahead. [...] Because I mean, you can't really do too much in terms of privacy unless you like go completely dark or you set up multiple perimeters like virtual private network to either your own connection or to a third party. But um. Can't really do too much about what people collect or what not. (Victor, 26, male, Muncie, Indiana, US).

> I mean no. I'm not going to not be online haha. You know? I'm not going to cut myself off. So no, I mean it just is what it is. I'm far more concerned about climate change and plastics in the oceans than I am about companies targeting me with, you know, yes it's creepy when, you know, you're about to maybe turn another decade and they start...or even when, I think when we started having babies, I don't know if I had gotten pregnant yet

> or you know, they figure out when you just got married so then you start seeing ads targeted to you about having babies. And it is creepy, but it is what it is. I mean when you've got, um, your health insurance companies, the breach of privacy or identity with companies is a lot more concerning to me than companies just tracking my movements. From what I understand, usually it's pretty anonymous, you know. Often times these trackings aren't linked specifically to you. I suppose an IP address and all that stuff it is. But my understanding is a lot of the data that is collected is not necessarily tied to an address or anything. It's just data that's collected on people without them knowing. (Liza, 42, female, Indianapolis, Indiana, US).

The key idea expressed here is that the data itself is anonymous (a form of detail-weak metadata) without the sophistication to actually create a data subject with any degree of accuracy. While Liza draws on the well-known example of expectant mothers being targeted with pre-natal products by supermarkets (a trick first identified through supermarket loyalty cards in the 1990s), this is presented as an outlier rather than the norm. Again, the actual aims, practices and successes of surveillance capitalism are obscured by a folk psychology notion of data harvesting and processing being imprecise, general and underdeveloped. This idea that the data produced by Pokémon Go is incomplete, partial and harmless sits in an uneasy tension with Zuboff's analysis of the application, but is in itself revealing of one particular, important understanding of surveillance capitalism in lay epistemology: it's not about me.

Other responses to this question did not doubt the power or efficiency of surveillance capitalism but considered it a normalised part of life in contemporary society. The hegemony of surveillance capitalism may be more problematic than misunderstanding the phenomena. While Pokémon Go players acknowledged that tracking and data profiling exists, it exists only as part of life itself – and hence is not something to worry about:

> Um, I don't worry about it. If someone's going to track me, there's a bajillion ways they could do that. And I don't care. I'm not going anywhere. (Jane, 28, female, Tacoma, Washington, US).

> Uh, not I don't really worry about that. Because so many other apps do it. It's not a worry. (Ceri, 45, female, Essex, UK).

> Well everyone's doing it aren't they? Google's doing it. And I think if you own a smart device you've got to accept that that's happening. [...] It bothers me but it's a compromise you'll have to make if you've got a smartphone, isn't it? If I play Pokémon Go or not, someone's going to be gathering that data. (Troy, 29, male, Norwich/East Anglia, UK).

This positioning of surveillance capitalism as something that happens and cannot be stopped indicates the acceptance of the logic of surveillance capitalism as a normalised aspect of everyday life. It happens; it cannot be avoided; I don't care. The attitude towards the collection and processing of data is one that indicates that this is not only accepted, but that the benign nature of the activity has also been accepted.

> Well, I feel like we live in an environment where that happens anyway, you know? Like, I don't, haha. How should I say it? I don't feel smart enough to be concerned about it. Like, it is happening, they're doing it. I'm like, whatever. You know, I'm not going to prevent fun from happening just because, you know. I use everything else. (Rhonda, 39, female, San Jose, California, US).

There are two critical notions in this response that are repeated throughout the interviews with our Pokémon Go playing participants. Firstly, data surveillance should not 'get in the way' of doing what you want to do in the digitally infused world. This idea positions surveillance capitalism not as at the centre of the digital but as a peripheral aspect that may intrude on 'fun' if it were to be taken too seriously. Secondly, that position is justified by the ubiquity of surveillance capitalism applications. If Pokémon Go is doing this, then it is ok because everything else is doing this too. Such a view does not 'join the dots' between applications. By viewing applications as discreet, this viewpoint sees surveillance capitalism as a series of independent operators that collect a little about you for their own purposes. The role of data brokerage, consolidation of applications by companies and the trading of data for consolidation are not part of this viewpoint. This is illustrated below:

> Um. I'm not. Because, you know, we are at this information and technology age where everything is 'spying' on you. I mean I have Billa in my house and people said, you know, they spy on your conversations and stuff. I mean you just have to be aware of what's happening with those data. Um, with my location, you know, cell phone companies have my location anyways. Um yeah. It's not a big concern to me. (Qui, 38, female, Plymouth, Michigan, US).

> Nah, I don't care. [...] Well you know my life is so unexciting. If Big Brother wants to check out what I'm doing, have at it. You know, there's a meme on Facebook I've seen with this, this you know, a housewife from the fifties sitting there. And in it she's talking to a Billa. It says Billa, can you give me a pancake, or a recipe for pancakes? You know, I mean if people are going to monitor me, so what, I don't care. (Wendy, 59, female, Orlando, Florida, US).

The unobtrusive nature of surveillance capitalism – the frictionless practice of collection and analysis – means that even with knowledge of surveillance it is interpreted as harmless because of the lack of impact and immediacy in the surveillant act. There is no 'Big Brother' there to wave a fist, just seamless data and convenience across applications.

> But I am an avid Google user and avid Facebook user and I just assumed that Google and Facebook are following me at all times and that they are watching every move because they will pop up with these little ads that I have no idea I even said that word out loud let alone in my head. And so, I just assume it's just one of those, there is so much data out there, it's being inundated, and I'm not doing anything wrong, so. If they want to follow me, they can, but if it's some benefit to making their maps more effective, making their gameplay more fun so that as long as it's benign it really doesn't bother me. (Mia, 39, female, Sonoma, California, US).

Again, Mia shows an awareness of the ubiquity of the practices of surveillance capitalism but in a deeply embedded position with regards to using applications in everyday life this knowledge needs to be accommodated in a schema of surveillance capitalism as benign and in the background. The drive to understand the practices of companies and applications as peripheral and a side effect of the efficiency that is brought to everyday life is again indicative of the hegemony of a particular discourse on surveillance capitalism that hides the discourse and argument of scholars on the phenomena. This hegemony is often expressed through the lack of circumspection on the issue by players:

> Um, it's not something I've really thought about to be honest. I don't know whether they do sell data. They most probably do I suppose. But I don't know. I'm not really overly bothered like by that sort of thing. Like I'm always being bombarded with ads on Facebook and that sort of thing anyway. That's something that I've kind of accepted now anyway. And so, I'm not worried about, you know, anyone monitoring my movements. I suppose I could be with Ethan [son] but he doesn't have like an online profile yet. He just has my wife's account on the spare phone. (Joe, 37, male, Southend-on-Sea, UK).

The acceptance of the visible aspect of surveillance capitalism and the accommodation of bombardment with advertising as a speed bump in the use of applications are another justifications in the acceptance of surveillance capitalist practices as benign. These minor irritants can be accepted by users, as their ubiquity has led to an acceptance of such practices as a part of life rather than an abnormality or an indication of both the transformation of everyday life and the shaping of everyday life through surveillance capitalism. Each example here shows an acceptance of the practices of surveillance capitalism as something that occurs without any real consequence or effect on everyday life, mobility or freedom of choice with regards to movement, consumer behaviour or political choices (even post-Cambridge Analytica). When consumer choice is considered, it is only considered in terms of overt, visible marketing rather than 'nudging' towards particular choices through the control of movement, motion and visibility of the environment in Pokémon Go.

> I never really thought about it to be honest. I know I should. It's partly because we live in such a society now where nothing is private between social media and just having your telephone on. Like, I know that when you play and the GPS pulls where you are, so you might be presented ads for nearby restaurants or whatever. It doesn't really bother me. Does that make sense? (Carol, 34, female, San Antonio, Texas, US).

> So, yes. At the same time, I don't see it as a problem as long as you know that it's being used. So, for example, they're going to market a new restaurant to me that's going to be right down the road from where I usually play. Now just because they market it doesn't mean I have to go down there and spend money there. And so, it doesn't bother me just because I am aware of that and I don't see a problem with it necessarily. (Liv, 27, female, Boise, Idaho, US).

The knowledge of how data are being used in Liv's response is one where knowledge is partial and framed by a discourse of data surveillance as being used in a mass-media era broadcast advertising model. A restaurant near to a play area is advertised; what is missing is why the area of play has been selected by the application. The direction of causality in the lay epistemology view of Pokémon Go practices is that the game is matching up what is nearby to the random allocation of play areas in the interface between user, application and physical world. Zuboff's analysis emphasises that the proximity and presence of businesses and advertisers in the physical world dictates the location of play areas and Pokémon, gyms and other features of the game. Awareness is, therefore, framed by a discourse of benign push, rather than shaped and controlled mobility for the purpose of economic gain.

5.3 Misunderstanding the Game within the Game

This pervasive discourse on the nature of surveillance through the application serves to conceal the economic logic of surveillance capitalism. This concealment is not limited to the explicit economic logic. Not one reply framed or conceptualised the game or playing the game as a form of unpaid labour, with the product of the labour being data to be used in the production of capital. Remember that Zuboff argues that the game itself nudges players towards interactions with both other users and most critically specific places in a form of gamification as behavioural modification. For Zuboff, the critical aspect of Pokémon Go as an instance of surveillance capitalism is that while the game runs players through the real world as part of the game experience, this is done not for the sake of the game *that players think they are playing*. The shaping of behaviour and spatial experience is part of a larger game of surveillance capitalism. The game in essence is to provoke, use and process game-player labour to feed the economic logic of surveillance capitalism while disguising that labour as play. As players go around playing the game, they are engaged in the wider game that Zuboff identifies. This is most salient in Pokémon Go in the location of Pokémon spawning. These locations are chosen, not random. Data from players, revenue from advertisers and their needs and predictions made on the data profiles of users are just some of the variables that combine to inform the location of spawning Pokémon. The game as understood by players is to catch these Pokémon; the game for Niantic is to drive mobile consumers to locations based on the spawning of Pokémon. Unsurprisingly, the lay epistemology of Pokémon Go works to conceal the underlying game being played.

> Interviewer:
>
> And do you ever think about why Pokémon Go might spawn in certain locations?
>
> Jane, 28, female, Tacoma, Washington, US:
>
> Yeah, we do. Ha-ha.
>
> Interviewer:
>
> Ha-ha, and why do you think about that? Or what are your thoughts on it?
>
> Jane, 28, female, Tacoma, Washington, US:
>
> Well we're nerds so we want to get to, uh, where the most Pokémon are spawning without having to do too much driving. So we can park and walk around one spot rather than drive to six different places. Because it's madness.

This response shows a partial, yet very distanced, understanding of the ludic mechanism underpinning the game. By parking in one spot, the player is anticipating that in that spot there will be many Pokémon to catch. However, what is missing is why there are many Pokémon there. The disconnection between the phenomena and the logic for that phenomena was a common theme in considering the game itself and misunderstanding the game.

> Um, not really. I mean there's um, it seems relatively random. On service stations and stuff, they tend to spawn in higher numbers.

> But yeah, it doesn't seem like certain things spawn in the same spot all the time. It seems to be pretty random. (Troy, 29, male, Norwich/East Anglia, UK).

Again, there is a logic to understanding that Pokémon spawn in higher numbers in commercial areas, but this is dismissed as an outlier to the randomness of spawn locations. This skirting around spawn locations in these responses is an extension of the discourse of inefficient and inexact data processing and targeting in surveillance capitalism in general. 'These things could be strategically placed, but I'm not sure so it is better to position them as random' seems to be the accepted version of events.

> Um. It just generally seems to be where there are more likely to be more people, then there are more likely to be more Pokémon. Which just kind of makes sense really. I never, you know, thought about it too much, but you know. I bet in fact, you know, we've got a member of our group who sort of plays the sister game called Ingress. And he purposefully tries to, you know, make more Pokémon appear so it kind of, it kind of seems you can manipulate it anyway. But I've never really thought about it. About why they've put anything there. It doesn't really concern me. (Joe, 37, male, Southend-on-Sea, UK).

> Um, yeah. The reason why, um, there's giant spawns is there's giant cell phones, you know, amount of cell phones. With community day, you know, there's a whole bunch of people. And I think I read somewhere that the amount of spawns depends on the amount of people there. And you know, with cell phones and data, you know, it can track that. (Qui, 38, female, Plymouth, Michigan, US).

The idea of a mass of people is again an interesting skirting around the instrumentality of the application. The correlation between density of users and location is, of course, sensible. What is missing is the causal connection between the density of users and locations. The notion expressed in the examples above is that it is the activity of the user that drives the location of spawns – but under the logic of surveillance capitalism, it is the location of spawns that drives the behaviour and movement of users. Frith (2017) outlines how the 'lure' of the game is important in driving footfall to businesses, and the spawning locations are critical for this. The element missing from the explanation from players is the logic of surveillance capitalism which is so well disguised by the game itself. Within this ludic discourse, other folk tales of the game itself begin to emerge. Not only is the game itself straightforward but can be gamed by others that have experience of using location-based games. The notion of control over the game, or at least the possibility of control by those that understand the game through experience, is indicative again of the randomness of the game in the conventional belief system of players. However, the randomness being brought to order by another player is a stronger statement in terms of how the game within the game is not only misunderstood but also actively rejected as anecdotal evidence suggests that the game can be brought to heel by players, rather than following a logic dictated by Niantic. The idea that players, or the community itself, have some role or oversight of spawn locations was expressed in other ways:

> The why? No. I mean we do kind of track where they're spawning. Like, you know, I'm on some of those forums it'll say hey, there's this Pokémon spawning at this spot. And we might go there to try to see it or just be aware of it. But um, I've never thought of it... well you know what, I take that back. I have noticed that like water Pokémons spawn nearer to the lake. Other than that though. (Stephanie, 42, female, Orlando, Florida, US).

The tracking and sharing of locations of spawning sites is an interesting dynamic of control in Pokémon Go. While the players are sharing this information and acting upon it, there is the possibility of establishing or regaining a sense of control over the game environment through a communal sharing of resources. This kind of community behaviour still is not rooted in an understanding of why there are Pokémon spawning in these locations and for what purpose.

Amelia came closest of our respondents to unpicking the logic of the game behind the game in Pokémon Go.

> Um, yeah. Actually, I've always been curious. Because all of a sudden, a new PokéStop will come up on a street that we've driven, like you know, ten times a day kind of thing. Like why, why here all of a sudden? And I'm curious how they pick that particular corner or what it happens to be. It's never been something that again, I can see how I probably have a little better understanding as a former marketing director. You know, well of course there's sponsored stops like Starbucks and Sprint and stuff. You know, that makes complete sense. But other than that, to me, it's like well yeah, there's you know, a whole bunch of people traveling down this road so of course they're going to put a couple of Pokémon stops there. So, I think about it and I understand it and I don't understand that sometimes. But I've never had a concern about it. Until they put a Pokémon stop in my front yard. And then we might have a concern with it. And I know that was a huge issue in the beginning. You know somebody all of a sudden had a random PokéStops, but the thing is though that, and that's one of the things that I was fine with my son playing Pokémon Go, was that they handled it well. You know, when there was a problem and there was all of a sudden the Pokémon stop where it shouldn't have been in somebody's front yard, they got rid of it. It's not like they said, oh well sorry, we put one there. Good luck with it.

> They handled it very socially responsibly and so for me, as long
> as the company continues to do that, spawn away. You know?
> Anywhere that they want to put them. (Amelia, 45, female, Boise,
> Idaho, US).

The inclusion of sponsored stops here shows an understanding of the game that underlies the game, allied to an understanding of footfall and mobility which other participants identified but did not link to commercial relationships. Again though, there is no concern about this and more concern with private property and personal space than behaviour modification and control on the basis of data accumulation and commercial gain. In all these responses, the game within the game is partially understood but that partial understanding is again successfully masked by the constructed discourse of surveillance capitalism as inexact, unspecifying and anonymous in nature.

5.4 Understanding the Game

As the survey results discussed earlier implied, there were a number of respondents that were concerned about the nature of surveillance capitalism and did show a clear understanding of the underlying logic of Pokémon Go:

> Ha-ha. Well I mean it's quite obvious. Starbucks does ad
> placement in the game, so my thought is a lot of it is about,
> because if you go out into a rural area, there's like nothing out
> there. And so, I assume that it's tied to population density. And
> I'm again, I'm sure that people, organizations, stores, restaurants,
> like if they wanted to have a stop that they could probably pay
> Niantic to have a stop or a gym put in their location. (Liza, 42,
> female, Indianapolis, Indiana, US).

In this instance, the understanding is still partial as population density is seen as a key metric rather than commercial gain. However, Liza does identify that sponsors such as Starbucks have advertising placements and this affects spawning locations, and that companies can enter into commercial arrangements with Niantic to have their locations promoted. Of course, this does not fully comprehend the all-encompassing nature of surveillance capitalism and the co-construction of data subjects with other applications that Niantic (Google) is involved in through their activities. Even for those players that do have an appreciation of that level of coordination and subject construction, the overall effect can be explained away and justified by the payoff that one receives from the use of applications:

> I don't really think about that because the phone itself as a,
> because I develop apps too and I've seen, the phone itself is just
> a huge beacon for tracking in general and Pokémon Go is

probably the least of my concerns as it relates to that. Google itself, because I use Google products. Google Maps and some other Google products, Google itself and Apple as well, their tracking is so much more extensive than what Pokémon is doing. And as you know, they're sharing that now with the adventure sync. If you have the adventure sync feature turned on, then they're sharing, they're tracking data with Apple. I have an iPhone. Yeah, so it's tracking my every step, it knows how many flights of stairs I climb. So, the reason I said no as an answer is that I just know that I'm being tracked. I know it. And in fact, I use it to my advantage because I use it as a way to force me, the other reason I'm still playing is it forces me to do just a little in terms of the physical fitness every day. I work on the ninth floor in my building and it's two flights for every floor. So, I take the stairs every morning. So that's like eighteen flights of steps and I get credit for that on the adventure sync. And you know, when I get to the top, I'm winded but I'm getting credit for it. It's almost like the equivalent of a half a mile, a half a kilometre of walking. So no, I guess my point is that I don't, I don't care that they track it because I know that the tracking is so extensive that this is just a drop in the bucket compared to what it is. If you're going to use a smartphone, you need to know that you're basically always being tracked. (Faizan, 49, male, Denver, Colorado, US).

The extent of surveillance and the sharing, trading and consolidation of data are appreciated in Faizan's response, but this is combined with a justification based on one product of that surveillance for the commodity (the user or player) – enhanced data on one's own activity to be used for one's own perceived benefit. Other participants had more specific concerns based on Niantic's behaviour, but this did not curtail the desire to play for long:

Yeah, for them tracking my location, yeah it will tell them hey, these are the areas that I go to for the most part. Let's go ahead and put more interesting items here, just try to draw people into that area. In terms of knowing how that is or what not, that might be a little bit of a different concern. Because during the beginnings of it, Niantic didn't have their settings set up and collected just about any data that we had on our phones, not just GPS, which at that point it was a little bit concerning because there's some parts I do want to keep private. So, I stopped playing the game just for that week period of time. But what they just did, it just got changed, it was pretty much fine for the most part. Just continued playing. (Victor, 26, male, Muncie, Indiana, US).

The cessation of play entirely because of the data practices of Niantic is an extreme in this research and does indicate a very keen and precise understanding of the nature of the surveillance capitalist game played by Niantic. However, the acceptance of the changes made by Niantic in response to claims made in 2016 about data privacy is problematic. Niantic's own privacy policy from 2016 makes it clear that their data collection practices remain vast:

> We collect and store information about your (or your authorized child's) location when you (or your authorized child) use our App and take game actions that use the location services made available through your (or your authorized child's) device's mobile operating system, which makes use of cell/mobile tower triangulation, wifi triangulation, and/or GPS. You understand and agree that by using our App you (or your authorized child) will be transmitting your (or your authorized child's) device location to us and some of that location information, along with your (or your authorized child's) user name, may be shared through the App...

> We collect certain information that your (or your authorized child's) mobile device sends when you (or your authorized child) use our Services, like a device identifier, user settings, and the operating system of your (or your authorized child's) device, as well as information about your use of our Services while using the mobile device. (Niantic, 2020).

In this policy, Niantic reserved the rights to location information, usernames, device identifiers, user settings, operating systems and use of services as a right through the terms and conditions agreed to by users – including those derived from children. While Victor was satisfied with Niantic's policy changes, it is fairly clear that the data accumulation through Pokémon Go remained vast. Even armed with this kind of understanding, players were not deterred from playing the game:

> Yeah. Not even just with Pokémon Go but in general with maps and GPS locating, yeah it does, I have some concerns about that. My husband has a lot of concerns about that. I tend to just be like, try not to think about it. But I mean I kind of worry just in general about how our phones track our location. Not specifically necessarily to Pokémon Go but that's a big part of it because I'm walking around with Pokémon Go a lot and just in general, how my phone is when tracking me where I'm going. [...] Just a feeling in general. It's kind of scary that yeah, Google knows where we are all the time. That Facebook can suggest advertisements based on where we've been and you know, what we've looked at. We just don't have privacy the same way we used to ten years ago. Some of it's good, some of it, like it's kind of cool if Facebook knows I like these kinds of jeans and now it's suggesting it. But

> you get a little like wow. But yeah, not specific to Emerson and Pokémon Go. Just in general with society. Pokémon Go is part of that because it's tracking. (Stephanie, 42, female, Orlando, Florida, US).

Again, the data practices are considered but contextualised in granular advertising practices rather than behavioural modification and profiling. Even when the player is a computer scientist, the understanding of surveillance capitalism is compromised by the familiar discourses on inexact profiling and a lack of relevance.

> Because I'm not very interesting from the point of view of mass data. So, any data I produce is just part of a dilution of data. It doesn't individually reflect me or my family or our lives. Mainly too targeted advertising or even targeting developments in the future, I would have thought, you know, people going well that's a good spot for a cafe because there's that level of movement. But I don't see any of those things as negative. Again, it's not something that concerns…I think there is a hysteria around personal data. It's not something that I feel like I need to instil in my children because I don't think it's anything to worry about really. […] because there are seven billion people on the planet and we're not that interesting. So, and I'm a big fan of big data. I think that the progressions that are on the horizon for our society for what we can do with big data, bear in mind I'm a computer scientist haha… (Arthur, 38, male, Birmingham, UK).

Again, the great victory of Niantic in this case and surveillance capitalism in general is the concealment of the economic logic of data accumulation. The overlaying of a popular discourse of benign intent, inept or inexact data provision and analysis and a 'hysteria' over personal data facilitate the continued use of applications like Pokémon Go (and any number of other applications). Most interestingly in Arthur's response is the explicit *support* for the big data practice of surveillance capitalist companies in terms of how they will allow society to progress. This kind of solutionism (Morozov, 2013) – the idea that given the right code, algorithms and robots, technology can solve all of mankind's problems, effectively making life 'frictionless' and trouble-free – would be music to the ears of every surveillance capitalist.

5.5 Tracking Children

As detailed above, Niantic's own privacy policy explicitly allows for the tracking and use of data from children. In this research on intergenerational play, the surveillance of children was expected to be a key identified issue prior to the research. However, the actual research showed that this is not the key issue it was expected to be. The survey of users in this research again illustrated a general lack of concern around the potential tracking of children by the application. Only 32 of 165 users (19%) had broached the subject of personal data with their children in the context of playing Pokémon Go. From the interviews, most participants had not broached the subject with their children because it was perceived that children would not understand the issue. This can be observed in the following exchange.

Interviewer:

Have you talked about personal data with your kids?

Bill, 28, male, Southend-on-Sea, UK:

Not really. I don't think they'd understand. I mean there are stuff where, because I'm really, my missus wants to get Billa and stuff. And I'm like nah, dude's always listening. But my friend wouldn't use WhatsApp. Because he'd only use Signal because of the fact that Facebook can ready every WhatsApp. And I'm like, I just use WhatsApp. I don't really care.

Bill's reason for not talking about personal data with his children is contextualised in a general lack of concern for the implications of personal data in general, consistent with the findings throughout this research. Bill is far from alone in this view.

No, no. I think because of his age it's just, it doesn't really seem like something that we sort of, you know need to mention. He's just too young. (Joe, 37, male, Southend-on-Sea, UK).

The idea of children being too young to understand the operations and implications of surveillance capitalism (predicated on an accurate understanding from parents, which this research does not wholly support) usually goes hand in hand with parents controlling the devices children use to play. This is not always the case though, but even with their own devices, children are not explicitly educated on data practices.

Interviewer: And as your daughter gets older and kind of where she is right now at what, six and a half, does that ever concern you in terms of the locative data that's tracking her now that she has her own device?

Um. No, not really. The location tracking is just kind of like where we're going with our society. People are talking about microchips in our hand so we can pay for shit. So, I'm not really that concerned. It's just part of modern society. (Mia, 39, female, Sonoma, California, US).

The justification for location tracking in a post-humanist future of implantation is a particularly bleak way of conceptualising the tracking of a six-year old (that has a device of their own). The idea of hegemony or normalisation of surveillance capitalism has already been discussed in this chapter, but it reappears both in Mia's response and Victor's below:

> ...[talking about daughter] To the extent, I'll probably be like. But at the same time, she's going to be starting new in the upgrade digital era. So, more people will try to get more information about everything and anything. So the only things I'll be able to do with her in terms of that when she actually goes out on her own and plays games like this, is to let her know the importance of keeping your information safe and not letting it go to anybody that you don't trust or what not. Because Facebook take that as an example for the most part, they've been getting a lot of attention recently, supposedly taking all of our data, what not, and selling it to people. When what people don't realize is that it's a cliché thing that we're the customers for the most part. They're going to advertise anything that we search on our browser history via cookies and do what they can to keep the website afloat. But for the most part, just let her know the importance of your information, what it can do to you in the wrong hands, and just anything I can think of. (Victor, 26, male, Muncie, Indiana, US).

Victor does raise the point that when his daughter is old enough and ready for her own device; then an important part of deleveraging from intergenerational co-play will be to educate on the implications of data privacy and personal data. This shielding of children by parents on this issue – in that parents bear the brunt of personal data production and use when playing with their children – was raised several times. As a form of protection, this positions the parent at the data subject until children pass an age where their agency is perceived as sufficient to pass into a data subject position themselves. The perception of a particular passing into data subjectivity was best captured by Christine:

> Um. Well one, because of their ages, I have all passwords and I sign into everything. So, they're not really signing into a whole lot of stuff. Like they're not, you know, signing into their stuff on someone else's phone or something like that. Um, but that being said, I mean I have kind of had that talk with them about, because they have Snapchat and TikTok which may not be the best thing. But it's fun and it's something that I closely monitor so they can't like friend people, or you know, unless I know them. Unless I know who, they are, you know, that kind of thing. And so, we've kind of had that talk but not in like great depth. So, you know, I think, you know Sam's turning twelve this year. I think maybe next year we should have that, you know, talk with he just because

of where she's at maturity wise. You know? I just don't quite thing that they're ready for all of that information quite yet. But I think definitely if you have older kids, fourteen, fifteen, sixteen, you know, eighteen, it's definitely something you should talk about. (Christine, 27, female, Denver, Colorado, US).

Such views still position surveillance capitalism as an inevitable consequence of a life in contemporary society, with parental responsibility one of delaying and monitoring until an age and maturity is reached when it is safe for children to be fully enrolled into surveillance capitalism on their own. Pokémon Go in the context of intergenerational play, therefore, acts as a bridge between a partial exposure to the logic of surveillance capitalism and a full enrolment sometime in adolescence where the necessity to use digital infrastructure outweighs the consequences of tracking and harvesting personal data.

5.6 Conclusion

The following exchange between two parents who both play Pokémon Go with their children is an exemplary summary of the findings on voluntary surveillance and locative play:

Mick, 26, male, Newfoundland, Canada:

Not really. We don't put much thought into it.

Chloe, 27, female, Newfoundland, Canada:

It's actually not a lot of information. I mean, I guess, because I log in through my Facebook and link my Facebook. So, I guess they would have access. But I mean you can always choose to remove the access to your Facebook contacts. Because I set mine up. Do you want to add your friends from Facebook? No.

Mick, 26, male, Newfoundland, Canada:

Yeah, it would be able to like, track an individual depending on what settings you have turned on in the app.

Chloe, 27, female, Newfoundland, Canada:

Yeah. And really the big thing is you have to be aware of your privacy settings on your phone itself because that's going to give away more data than Pokémon Go will.

Chloe, 27, female, Newfoundland, Canada:

It's never really a concern for me because um, my game only uses location data, so GPS, when it's open. And all my apps are that way. They only give out my location or only use the GPS when I'm using that app. I have a friend who, they go to the gym, and their gym is across the street from a KFC, and because they have all their location data on, they got a notification through Facebook saying hey, you've visited KFC on this street recently. Can you tell us about your visit? They didn't go to KFC! They went to the gym! But because their location is on for everything all the time. So if you're mindful of the location sharing that you're doing already, then it's not really that big of an issue. It's only when you're' allowing the game to be using the data.

Mick, 26, male, Newfoundland, Canada:

Even then, like, I haven't really seen anything concerning come out. Like, unless they're just putting it into a massive, massive database and then come out with this crazy algorithm that tracks everybody. Because like, there's a lot of things where it's a lot more clear that uh, that there's stuff going on. Like when you do a Google search with how to, how to change oil in your car or something like that and then you go on Facebook and you're getting a whole bunch of ads for oil filters or oil companies or something like that. It's like, huh, I wonder why they're targeting me with something like that now.

The fact is that Niantic is putting all the data collected by its games into a massive database and using algorithms to profile, predict and shape user behaviour in order to create data subjects that will follow the suggestions, nudges and commercial imperatives of companies. Mick understands that this is a possibility, rather than the actuality, of using Pokémon Go. While parents are clearly concerned for their children and exposing them to personal data practices, their own labour in playing with their children is generally considered as a relatively harmless pastime, a part of being in a digitally infused world. The concept of what that digitally infused world of experience entails is the key finding from this segment of the research on intergenerational play. The general awareness of an issue with data, of something problematic, is generally superseded by a discursive explaining away of the seriousness of Niantic's use of data in this research. The idea that the data profiling is imprecise, unimportant or benign effectively twists the causality of surveillance capitalism itself. In such a view, the player retains some sense of agency over their activity as the game itself is random, not aligned with commercial aims or not involved in behavioural changes through the control of mobility and movement of players through urban landscapes. The game on the surface remains the only game; the physical environment is made into a game scape to be played. Zubof's (2019a) analysis of Pokémon Go (and surveillance capitalism in general) invites us to invert this understanding of the game. The physical environment is not transformed into a game space; instead, the players themselves run through a maze like Skinner's rats, collecting Pokémon in a giant operant conditioning experiment designed to push and nudge players to particular outcomes and choices in line with the commercial agreements signed by Niantic and its partners. The great success of the game interface is to keep this logic hidden under the activity of collecting Pokémon, battling at gyms and visiting PokéStops. Location sharing and targeted advertising are indicative of a background hum of data activity that is characterised by its generality.

This discourse on how data work as part of Pokémon Go is as interesting as the lack of acknowledgement of unpaid labour on the part of players. The lay epistemology of personal data works as a justification for play and as a concealment of the practices of Niantic (and indeed many other companies). It is tempting to describe such a discourse as a form of cognitive dissonance, but that would be to misunderstand the nature of understanding of the application itself. Players are not confronted with the results of personal data surveillance and processing in an overt manner; this occurs at the margins of experience of play, rather than overtly centre-front on the screen as one flicks a Poké Ball at a Pokémon. Recall that Zuboff claims that the directing towards real-time constellations of behaviour by Pokémon Go occurs beyond the 'rim of individual awareness' (Zuboff, 2019a, p. 312). In explaining playing Pokémon Go as a means of provision of useless metadata to unseen, benign algorithms, the success of surveillance capitalism is seen in disguising the intention of the application. The success here also plays a considerable role in informing parents on how to broach the subject with their children. The opacity of process, the uncertainty of the folk discourse itself means that apart from controlling accounts under their own name and password (and therefore contributing to their own data subjectivity) parents are left with little to offer children in terms of avoidance of the system of control, especially as that element of control is missing from many understandings of how this very system works.

References

Bauman, Z., & Lyon, D. (2013). *Liquid surveillance: A conversation*. Hoboken, NJ: John Wiley & Sons.

Biggs, S., & Carr, A. (2015). Age- and child-friendly cities and the promise of inter-generational space. *Journal of Social Work Practice*, *29*(1), 99–112. doi:10.1080/02650533.2014.993942

Castells, M. (2009). *Communication power*. Oxford: Oxford University Press.

Debord, G. (1967/1977). *Society of the spectacle*. Detroit, MI: Black & Red.

Deleuze, G. (1992). Postscript on the societies of control. *October*, *59*, 3–7.

Foer, F. (2017). *World without mind: The existential threat of big tech*. New York, NY: Penguin Books.

Frith, J. (2017). The digital "lure": Small businesses and Pokémon Go. *Mobile Media & Communication*, *5*(1), 51–54. doi:10.1177/2050157916677861

Fuchs, C. (2011). Critique of the political economy of web 2.0 surveillance. In C. Fuchs, K. Boersma, A. Albrechtslund, & M. Sandoval (Eds.), *Internet and surveillance: The challenges of web 2.0 and social media* (pp. 31–70). New York, NY: Routledge.

Fuchs, C. (2015). *Social media: A critical introduction* (1st ed.). Los Angeles, CA: SAGE Publications.

Galloway, S. (2017). *The four: The hidden DNA of Amazon, Apple, Facebook, and Google*. New York, NY: Penguin.

GoHub. (2020). Pokémon GO announces new sponsored locations with McDonalds. Retrieved from https://pokemongohub.net/post/news/pokemon-go-announces-new-sponsored-locations-with-mcdonalds/. Accessed on March 03, 2020.

Hardt, M., & Negri, A. (2000). *Empire*. Cambridge, MA: Harvard University Press.

Hart, R. (2002). Containing children: Some lessons on planning for play from New York city. *Environment and Urbanization, 14*(2), 135–148.

Heidegger, M. (1977). *The question concerning technology, and other essays*. New York, NY: Harper Perennial.

Hjorth, L., & Richardson, I. (2017). Pokémon GO: Mobile media play, place-making, and the digital wayfarer. *Mobile Media & Communication, 5*(1), 3–14. doi:10.1177/2050157916680015

Lyon, D. (2007). *Surveillance studies: An overview*. Malden, MA: Polity Press.

Morozov, E. (2013). *To save everything, click here: Smart machines, dumb humans, and the myth of technological perfectionism*. New York, NY: Perseus Books.

Niantic. (2020). *Niantic Terms of Service*. Retrieved from https://nianticlabs.com/terms/en/. Accessed on February 09, 2020.

Smythe, D. (1976/2001). On the audience commodity and its work. In M. G. Durham & D. Kellner (Eds.), *Media and cultural studies: Keyworks*(pp. 230–256). Malden, MA: Blackwell.

The Invisible Committee. (2015). *To our friends*. Los Angeles, CA: Semiotext(e).

Zuboff, S. (2019a). *The age of surveillance capitalism*. New York, NY: Profile.

Zuboff. (2019b). It's not that we've failed to rein in Facebook and Google. We've not even tried. The Guardian. Retrieved from https://www.theguardian.com/commentisfree/2019/jul/02/facebook-google-data-change-our-behaviour-democracy. Accessed on February 9, 2020.

Chapter 6

Familial Locative Play: Looking to the Future

6.1 The Impetus for This Book

The impetus for this book began with a conversation one of the authors had with a Pokémon Go player soon after its release back in 2017. Though the conversation was ostensibly about the impact Pokémon Go was having on his experience of space and place and how he moved through his environment, it quickly became apparent that the decision to play this hybrid reality game (HRG) was not a choice he had made alone. In fact, the reason he began playing Pokémon Go was because his son wanted to but was neither old enough nor had the necessary technology to play alone. Consequently, our interviewee soon found himself spending considerable chunks of his weekends wandering around nearby parks in pursuit of Pokémon with his son. Likewise, he also found himself frequently playing as he travelled to and from work, and oftentimes at his son's request. While his reason, then, for playing the game did not begin with a personal interest in Pokémon or a hidden penchant for locative media, the co-playing of this game had unforeseen benefits that extended beyond the application. More precisely, this joint-media engagement (JME) provided a space for him and his son to bond over a shared activity that was more dynamic than, say, playing a traditional video game at home. This early conversation, then, as well as the discovery that this situation was far from unique (Evans & Saker, 2019; Sobel et al., 2017) serves as a point of departure for the research underpinning our book. Equally, it marks a development from the previous studies we have undertaken on locative games, which have predominantly revolved around issues pertaining to spatiality and mobility (Evans & Saker, 2017).

Over the course of this book, we have examined how an assortment of families incorporate, integrate and utilise Pokémon Go in their lives and on a daily basis. In doing so, we have brought together two important areas of study: research on the physical, spatial and social impact of Pokémon Go, as outlined in chapter 2, alongside studies on video games from the vantage point of interventional play or JME, as outlined in chapter 3. This bringing together of these separate but related

Intergenerational Locative Play, 143–154
Copyright © 2021 Michael Saker and Leighton Evans
Published under an exclusive licence by Emerald Publishing Limited
doi:10.1108/978-1-83909-139-120211019

areas of study is important for two reasons. First, research in the context of JME has commonly involved families playing more traditional video games within the domestic sphere (Siyahhan & Gee, 2018). Second – and as should be apparent at this point – locative games, such as Pokémon Go, implicate a very different experience that explicitly involves players physically interacting and traversing their concrete surroundings (Evans & Saker, 2019; Sobel et al., 2017; Tran, 2018), offering a meaningful counterpoint to the suggestion many adolescents have now moved out of the streets (Zelizer, 1994) and into their bedrooms (Livingstone, 2002). Equally, the digital economy underpinning this Pokémon Go, and with it the gathering of personal data, similarly presents a new range of challenges for parents to work through that exceeds the kind of concerns commonly associated with video games that are played at home.

In the next section, then, we thread our key findings around the following themes: (1) spatial activity and cognisance, (2) familial rhythms and digital labour, (3) playful bonding and 'non-confrontational spaces', (4) personal development and cursory connections, (5) familial challenges and concerns, (6) surveillance and the game beneath the game, before considering the meaning of these findings in the context of the broader canons of locative media and intergenerational play. Following this, we briefly reflect on locative games in light of COVID-19 and what a COVID-19 and post-COVID-19 world might look like through the lens of intergenerational locative play. In doing so, we also reflect on the adaptivity of Pokémon Go and what this might suggest about further research in this field.

6.2 Spatial Activity and Cognisance

In line with extant research on locative media, and indeed, pervasive games (Saker & Evans, 2016a), for the most part our research found that the familial playing of Pokémon Go led to families being more physically active than they perhaps would have been were it not for this HRG. Equally, and again, echoing extant literature (Saker & Evans, 2016a), this HRG had a marked effect on the ways in which families approached and moved through their surroundings. Here, families would often – counterintuitively – choose to take longer routes, so as to extend locative play, just as they would regularly frequent new environments as a by-product of the game (de Lange, 2009; Evans & Saker, 2019; Lemos, 2010; McGarrigle, 2010; Papangelis et al., 2017; Saker & Evans, 2020). In other words, the impact of Pokémon Go on our participants is congruent with the spatial tendencies of the player (Evans & Saker, 2019). Yet, there were also notable differences. While previous research has shown that the playing of this HRG can lead to players inhabiting 'odd' or 'strange' places that are not suited to play or playfulness (Evans & Saker, 2019), our research suggests that families are more cognisant of the environments that they play in, and this cognisance is symptomatic of the familial relationships underpinning their experience. That is, the main focus of parents is, understandably, keeping their children safe, and this, of course, supersedes any desire to capture Pokémon. Accordingly, families would usually choose to play this HRG in large, open spaces, such as parks (Perry, 2016), for the following reasons. First, open spaces meant children were easier to keep an eye on. Second, these environments reduced the likelihood of children playing near motor vehicles. At the same time, the impact of concomitant spatial practices also extended beyond the confines of the games, in a manner that, again, differs from older locative games (Evans & Saker, 2017). For some families, playing Pokémon Go not only meant they inhabited new environments but also equally led to them spending time in these surroundings once the gameplay had finished. In other words, the spatial impact of the familial playing of Pokémon Go appears to be more intensive that the spatial impact associated with older forms of locative games and location-based social networks (LBSNs) (Saker & Evans, 2016a, 2016b).

6.3 Familial Rhythms and Digital Labour

An important aspect of the familial playing of Pokémon Go is the extent to which this HRG fits into the lives of the families that play this game together. For many of our participants, Pokémon Go effectively blended with the rhythms of family life. And this blending was particularly pronounced during the working week. Here, families would frequently play Pokémon Go as they travelled, for example, to and from school. Equally, this practice had the potential to do more than just turn ordinary life 'into a game' (Frith, 2013). For some parents, the game was used as a bargaining tool to entice children to complete this or that task, in the interest of expediency. Equally, the affordances of this HRG meant that parents could play the game on their own, while commuting, for instance, to and from work, as well as during their lunch break. In these instances, parents would commonly focus on smaller gamic tasks that could be performed quickly and in a relaxed manner, but which had meaningful consequences for their general progression in the game. Interestingly, the decision to perform this 'maintenance', as it was repeatedly referred, was not always made by the parent or parents alone but was at the behest of children. As a corollary to this, then, familial locative play presents an interesting form of 'playbor' (Kücklich, 2005), one that is predicated on the locative aspect of the game. Importantly, for these parents, playing Pokémon Go for their children was not experienced as labour *per se*, but something they did precisely because it made their children happy. Likewise, we would also suggest this presents an interesting take on the kind of 'absent presence' (Gergen, 2002) commonly associated with mobile media usage. Though children were not physically nearby while parents played alone, they were nonetheless cognitively woven into the process through the motivation to play. At the same time, this weekly 'maintenance' meant there were more gamic opportunities for families to take advantage of when it came to the weekend. In contrast to older locative games, then, where the playing of these applications did not really shift in relation to what day they were played (Evans & Saker, 2017), our research found that families approached Pokémon Go very differently when it came to weekends. While weekdays were predominately about fitting the game into the flows of daily life, weekends routinely involved extended periods of familial locative play (e.g. raids or community days) that specifically implicated certain locations for a specified period of time. In other words, the gamic experience of this HRG was commensurate with the implicit mood of either the working week or weekends, with the playing of this game either implicating 'maintenance' or facilitating extended periods of play. Likewise, this also suggests that Pokémon Go can be approached as a game in its own right, which, again, differs from earlier locative games and LBSNs. This is a point we will return to later in the chapter.

6.4 Playful Bonding and Non-confrontational Space

As other studies of JME have shown, the playing of video games can have a positive effect on familial relationships (Siyahhan & Gee, 2018; Sobel et al., 2017; Takeuchi, 2011). And the same is true of Pokémon Go. Importantly, the gamic experience was deemed compelling enough for children to want to play – and continue playing – alongside their parents. Yet, the co-playing of this game was not simply seen as 'time' together. More specifically, and resonating with Sobel et al. (2017), the familial playing of this HRG facilitated 'quality time' for our participants, which then provided a talking point that could be leveraged in situations outside of the game. Equally, and perhaps more significantly, the familial playing of Pokémon Go allowed parents to engage their children in conversations that they felt were noticeably more personal than they perhaps would have been were it not for the game. Here, we would suggest that the concomitant strengthening of familial bonds through this HRG was specifically enhanced by the locative affordances of this HRG. While intergenerational play through the lens of more traditional video games can improve communication (Aarsand, 2007), it is unlikely that these games will involve the same volume of communal periods in-between play. Contrastingly, the affordances of Pokémon Go means player necessarily do not only spent time together playing the game but also spent time together moving between spaces of play. And for many of the families we spoke to, this aspect of locative play was considered important. By taking the focus away from communication, the game allowed these families to forge a 'non-confrontation space' that helped children to feel more comfortable about conversing. In other words, by playing the game with their parents and because of the ambulation implicated in this pastime, children were more able to open up and discuss aspects of their lives that they might have otherwise concealed. Again, the locative aspect is significant. As one of our participants tellingly commented, 'I think we get stuck in our roles when we're in certain places'. Accordingly, the playing of Pokémon Go is not just as about the provision of 'non-confrontational' spaces *per se* – although this is unquestionably important – but equally about family members sharing aspects of themselves that often get lost in the roles they adopt within the domestic sphere.

6.5 Personal Development and Cursory Connections

Another noteworthy aspect of familial locative play is the effect parents felt it had on the personal development of their children. While video games can, of course, involve large communities of players (Kelly, 2004), for the most part, these communities play in digital space of the gamic world. In contrast, the playing of Pokémon Go not only encompasses a large community of players that play together – certainly in the context of gaming applications (Iqbal, 2020) – but it is also common for these players to share the same physical environment as a result of the hybrid space of the game (de Souza e Silva, 2006). For the families that we spoke to, then, when their children played Pokémon Go, they were not just learning how to play the game *per se*, more importantly, by playing in concrete settings beyond the home, their children were also learning how to behave and interact with other people in ordinary live. As one of our participants astutely observed, 'here is a game … that uses the environment in a way that I don't know of any other games doing'. In other words, the locative aspect of the game was understood as opening up learning opportunities that would not be – perhaps – possible in the context of more traditional video games. In much the same way that children were seemingly able to open up about themselves during periods of play because the focus was not on the conversation, many participants commented that the familial playing of this game allowed their children to become more confident when it came to communicating with other adults. At the same time, this is not to imply families were necessarily developing strong relationships with other players during periods of locative play, as, for the most part, this was not the case. Though Pokémon Go does involve a wide community of players, as we have touched on above, and families do often play with families they have a previous relationship with, as well as those they do not, the ensuing relationships are predominately ephemeral, implicating cursory connections that are briefly forged to assist gamic advancement. Here, the most important relationship for families was, understandably, the relationship between parent and child. While families did play with other players, then, relationships were utilised to progress in the game, not to progress in the community.

6.6 Familial Challenges and Concerns

In line with Sobel et al. (2017), our research also found that the familial playing of Pokémon Go led to various challenges and concerns. For the majority of our participants, their concerns included physical safety, strangers and the pernicious effects of screen time (Sobel et al, 2017). Of course, these apprehensions are indicative of the locative aspect of the game. Though concerns about strangers persist in the context of traditional video games (Internet Matters, 2019), we would suggest they take on a different hue when the game is locative and interactions with other players have a higher likelihood of taking place in the physical realm. Yet, these concerns were ultimately not insurmountable. And in many ways the reason for this was equally wrapped up in the locative aspects of this HRG. Again, resonating with Sobel et al. (2017), our participants established congruent rules surrounding play that effectively reduced the fears they may have originally had. Here, parents would only let their children speak to other players if they were with them. Likewise, parents would keep track of who their children were friends with. At the same time, some of the concerns parents initially had were themselves pre-empted through the design of the interface. The fact the application does not have a 'chat' function, for instance, was repeatedly brought up as a feature – or rather lack thereof – that made parents feel more comfortable about their children using this application. Likewise, parents also touched on the tethering of their children to their data plan. In doing so, children were unable to physically wander too far away from their parents or they would risk losing connection (Sobel et al., 2017).

6.7 Surveillance and the Game Beneath the Game

In the main, our research suggests that familial concerns about locative play did not explicitly include fears about the digital economy and surveillance capitalism (Zuboff, 2019). While some participants were aware of the data, they may produce by playing Pokémon Go, this was something they neither fixated on nor were overly worried about. Consequently, this was not something that was discussed with their children. Instead, families believed that their data were neither important nor personalised. Following this, the majority of participants did not question why Pokémon might appear in certain locations. Instead, the appearance of Pokémon was understood as being as a random aspect of the game, rather than a 'lure' (Frith, 2017) to facilitate consumption. And we would suggest the general stance families took on surveillance capitalism is indicative of two things: First, a lack of knowledge about locative data and its usage. Second, the familial dynamic underpinning this pastime. First, then, while parents had a clear sense of what physical dangers locative play might lead to, the use of locative data did not evoke the same kind of vivid apprehensions. Instead, the implications for locative data were reconciled as a contingent element of play that could not be avoided. Equally, a recurring belief in gamic randomness meant participants did not think critically about their physical positioning as it pertains to the gamic experience. Second, for many parents, the playing of this game was framed as facilitating 'quality' time together. Consequently, the labour of this practice was explicitly related to the happiness of their children, which further concealed questions concerning surveillance capitalism, rather than revealing them.

6.8 Mobile Magic Circles and the Next Generation of Locative Games

In many ways, then, what our findings, as summarised above, point toward is a developing relationship between the 'magic circle' (Huizinga, 1992/1938) and ordinary life. While the locative games that emerged in the early 2010s, during the halcyon days of locative media, effectively blurred the suggested border between play and ordinary life (Frith, 2013; Saker & Evans, 2016a) – which was precisely part of their initial appeal – it seems unlikely that families would approach the playing of say, Foursquare, with the same vigour that families now approach the playing of Pokémon Go (Sobel et al., 2017). For the most part, this is because older locative games struggled to sustain themselves beyond the initial novelty of 'hybrid space' (de Souza e Silva, 2006). And this novelty was ultimately not enough to compensate for gamic mechanics that were, if we are being brutally honest, not dynamic nor exiting enough to be enduring. Consequently, the clear majority of locative media from around 2013 onwards either developed new applications for its data or fell by the wayside (Evans & Saker, 2017; Frith & Wilken, 2019). Still, and as we underlined in our opening chapter, locative applications, and more specifically, locative games did not simply die out. Instead, the lessons learned from earlier locative media culminated in the development of Pokémon Go, which has been the focus of this book.

Importantly, we would argue that Pokémon Go provides a gamic experience that is compelling enough to transcend its locative status – a point we will come back to in the next section. While Pokémon Go can, of course, blend with daily life á la Foursquare, it can equally be approached as a game in its own right. This can clearly be seen by the familial use of this HRG in the context of weekends, as outlined above. In these instances, the gamic experience often involved a specific space, lasted for a particular period of time, and was markedly more intense than the 'maintenance' families undertook during the week. In other words, this kind of locative play was not about blurring the boundaries between play and ordinary life but instead about forging a mobile magic circle of sorts that ambulated with families as they traversed their physical surroundings. And it is precisely the ability of this HRG to either complement or supplant ordinary life – alongside its richer gamic mechanisms – that we would suggest makes this game more compelling, and indeed more lasting, than earlier forms of locative play.

With Niantic apparently, on the cusp of developing a range of new locative games (Niantic, 2020), it would seem the next generation of locative games will continue to develop in various ways that will warrant further circumspection. At the same time of course, the research presented through this book stems from a very different world; a world just prior to COVID-19. Of course, the magnitude of his global pandemic has implications that far exceed the scope of locative games. Nonetheless, given the focus of our book and the roles sociability and mobility play in the experience of Pokémon Go, it would be remiss of us not to reflect on these changing circumstances in light of locative games. In the following section, then, we turn to the playing of Pokémon Go in a COVID-19 world, and how this HRG is adapting to an environment suddenly predicated on immobility and social distancing. In particular, then, we use this final section to reflect on the future of familial locative at a time when location is increasingly critical.

6.9 The End of Mobility: COVID-19 and Pokémon Go

For a game as contingent on mobility and motion as Pokémon Go, 2020 has been little short of a disaster. The enforced lockdowns of populations across the globe to try and halt the spread of COVID-19 has meant that the key mechanism of play in the game – to move around spaces and collect Pokémon, visit gyms and attend events and raids – has been stopped along with much else of the daily activity of people across the globe. In this book, we have outlined how Pokémon Go has become a vital part of the everyday family activity and fundamental to the rhythms of family life for those that play the game. We have also argued that the business model for the game is fundamentally tied to the motion and movement of play which allows Niantic to harness player data for its surveillance capitalism business model. These critical aspects of Pokémon Go activity essentially ground to a halt from March 2020 as the world shielded from COVID-19. Ironically, this cessation of Pokémon Go activity came hand in hand with the surfacing of location-based applications as a potential saviour in the fight against the virus. Just as the long tail of location-based media and the 'zombie' of LBSN animating and haunting contemporary applications (Evans & Saker, 2017, p. 88) finally reached the minds of the public, Pokémon Go went into a forced hiatus. There has been considerable debate in with regards to the surveillance technologies are being used for contact tracing, quarantine enforcement, movement permission, social distancing/movement monitoring, and symptom tracking and how civil liberties have to be sacrificed for public health (Kitchen, 2020, p. 1). Indeed, the efficacy of this kind of technological intervention has also been questioned (Rosenberg, 2020; Stanley & Granick, 2020). Nevertheless, the moment for these applications arrived – and Pokémon Go, the most visible and popular of these applications outside of Google Maps, was rendered obsolete.

Niantic moved quickly to at least keep the game playable during lockdown. Niantic improved the Adventure Sync connection, which allows the mobile device the game is installed on to track steps to earn in-game rewards even while the game is not being played. The impetus behind this move was to allow the game to work with indoor movement and activities so 'activities like cleaning your house and running on a treadmill count toward game achievements' (Orland, 2020). Remote raids were added, allowing players to join raids that appear on the application map or 'nearby' page without having to go to the physical location of the raid (Byford, 2020a). In game, social activities and features were enhanced to allow players to keep in touch when not in physical proximity (Takahashi, 2020) and the *Pokémon Go Fest* became an online-only event that allowed for greater attendance with proceeds going to Black Lives Matter (Byford, 2020b). The necessary changes for self-isolation and social distancing also included reducing in-game barriers and pay walls to extras being relaxed or lifted entirely.

These changes to the game have provoked some debate around the intentionality of such change. While Marissa Martinelli praised the changes for making the game more playable than before, Sam Adams noted that a game predicated on 'Go' is not really the same in the age of stay and questioned whether the changes made by Niantic were simply a form of profiteering (revenue jumped by 67% in the week of March 16th) (Martinelli & Adams, 2020). This replacement revenue would, of course, become very useful as location-specific data used for targeted advertising decreased thanks to a lack of movement of players. This does raise a significant point about the game in lockdown. While play might be maintained, mobility has been sacrificed, and as such Niantic will need to monetise the game in new ways that go beyond the established surveillance capitalism model. While in-game revenue replaces some of this, bringing in the intense lens of surveillance capitalism into the home and closely surveilling the activities and daily rhythms of the family in the home may raise far more questions than those raised earlier in this book.

On the other hand, there are positives that the game can provide during the unprecedented lockdown. Lincoln Geraghty highlighted the positive impact that existing Pokémon Go communities and new communities established during the pandemic had as a supportive fan-based community for players (Geraghty, 2020). The existence of these communities as a social aid during self-isolation will be of great benefit to many players. For the intergenerational player, there could be opportunities to perhaps amend the new magic circle of play identified in chapter 4 and extend the latent social ties that the community and the game provide. Indeed, the continuation of the game itself could be an aide to continuing regular patterns of family life that the game has established, as other rhythms of everyday life, including the rhythms of work and education, have been interrupted. On the other hand, though, this enforced confinement is more likely to strengthen the 'magic circle' of play (Huizinga, 1992/1938) for intergenerational players as families spend all their time together and any time playing Pokémon Go without spatial and temporal proximity to other players.

For this research, what is more critical is what happens to Pokémon Go in the post-pandemic world. By post-pandemic, we do not refer to a world free of COVID-19 but instead one where the social distancing principles that have become a part of everyday life during the pandemic are maintained and evolved as the world adjusts to the presence of COVID-19 past lockdowns and isolation. This poses significant questions both about the game itself and the playing of the game. Pokémon Go has been forced to change during the pandemic; it is likely that it will not be the same game when the measures to control the pandemic start to recede. Will players want to be involved with large social events in public spaces, with limited social distancing from others? Assuming a robust and real-time COVID-19 tracking system being in place, then maybe players will be happy. However, such systems will be highly contingent on which country and area the game is being played in and, as noted above, bring issues with surveillance and civil liberties which may mean they are not the panacea that some assume for the virus. Frequently in this research, interviewees have identified busy locations for Pokémon spawning that attract many players. It could be that these popular spots become less attractive to players that wish to distance from others or that at least have become wearier of physical contact as the virus still has a presence in the world. In which case, the sociability aspect of the game may change entirely. Niantic may need to consider a more granular approach to the spawning of Pokémon that keeps players apart rather than bringing them together, calling into question the further existence of raids and gyms as a fundamental part of the game architecture.

It is these potential changes which call into question the future of Pokémon Go, not only for intergenerational players. As James Poniewozik (2020) argues, the 'go' of Pokémon Go has been replaced with 'stay'. Walking 50 km a week in pursuit of Pokémon has been replaced with pacing at home. Pokémon Go can, in the time of lockdown at least, no longer deliver the world to players. The game is no longer *the* game in these circumstances. Thanks to this, the way that the game has fitted into the rhythms of family life has fundamentally been altered. The value of exercise, time spent in the mediated environment and co-ordination of activity between family members have been completely disrupted in the pandemic lockdown. The critical question is whether this enforced change to the game can be reversed when the conditions in society allow for Pokémon Go to go back to the 'old' game – if that ever happens.

Due to these changes, many of the insights on intergenerational play we have outlined here will now be in a state of alteration, and post-pandemic we can expect to see new practices of play and new manners of play for intergenerational players. Moreover, the game itself will have to change; the economic model for the game has become compromised by lockdown, and Niantic will have to realign the game itself if it wants to continue to realise the profits and data it harvested from the game pre-COVID-19. In light of that, the game is clearly going to undergo further changes which will reshape the practices of the intergenerational players that still see a value in playing the game together in the post-pandemic landscape.

Yet, the fact Pokémon Go has managed to adapt to this situation is in and of itself is telling of how far the next generation of HRGs have come. One might have assumed COVID-19 would have finally brought about the death of locative games. Such an assumption, however, would be to overlook the inherent adapt-ability of locative media (Evans & Saker, 2017) and the extent to which new applications are more than just the locations they implicate. Moving forward, then, while the future of the player is perhaps more uncertain than it has ever been, it nonetheless provides a valuable lens through which to continue exploring the phenomenology and sociability of place in the context of emerging technol-ogies and ludology. How the player responds to this new environment, then, will not only reveal how the contours of locatives games have changed but also more importantly reveal how we are learning to adapt to a world that no longer feels as suited to play.

References

Aarsand, P. A. (2007). Computer and video games in family life: The digital divide as a resource in intergenerational interactions. *Childhood*, *14*(2), 235–256.

Byford, S. (2020a). Pokémon Go adds remote raids so you don't have to go outside. *The Verge*. Retrieved from https://www.theverge.com/2020/4/15/21221659/poke-mon-go-remote-raid-passes-coronavirus. Accessed on June 24, 2020.

Byford, S. (2020b). Tickets for the online-only Pokémon Go Fest 2020 go on sale today. *The Verge*. Retrieved from https://www.theverge.com/2020/6/15/21291244/pokemon-go-fest-2020-events-details-ticket-price. Accessed on June 24, 2020.

Evans, L., & Saker, M. (2017). *Location-based social media: Space, time and identity*. Berlin: Springer.

Evans, L., & Saker, M. (2019). The playeur and Pokémon Go: Examining the effects of locative play on spatiality and sociability. *Mobile Media & Communication*, *7*(2), 232–247. doi:org/10.1177/2050157918798866

Frith, J. (2013). Turning life into a game: Foursquare, gamification, and personal mobility. *Mobile Media & Communication, 1*(2), 248–262.

Frith, J. (2017). The digital "lure": Small businesses and Pokémon Go. *Mobile Media & Communication, 5*(1), 51–54. doi:10.1177/2050157916677861

Frith, J., & Wilken, R. (2019). Social shaping of mobile geomedia services: An analysis of Yelp and Foursquare. *Communication and the Public, 4*(2), 133–149.

Geraghty, L. (2020). What 'Pokemon Go' and its online community during the coronavirus lockdown show us about fandom. Retrieved from https://www.port.ac.uk/news-events-and-blogs/blogs/popular-culture/what-pokemon-go-and-its-online-community-during-the-coronavirus-lockdown-show-us-about-fandom. Accessed on June 24, 2020.

Gergen, K. J. (2002). The challenge of absent presence. In J. E. Katz & M. Aakhus (Eds.), *Perpetual contact: Mobile communication, private talk, public performance* (pp. 227–241). Cambridge, MA: Cambridge University Press.

Huizinga, J. H. (1992/1938). *Homo Ludens: A study of the play-element in culture*. London: Beacon Press.

Internet Matters. (2019). Parent generation game. Retrieved from https://www.internetmatters.org/hub/research/parenting-generation-game-report/

Iqbal, M. (2020). Pokémon GO revenue and usage statistics. *Business of Apps*. Retrieved from https://www.businessofapps.com/data/Pokémon-go-statistics/

Kelly, R. V. (2004). *Massively multiplayer online role-playing games: The people, the addiction and the playing experience*. Jefferson, NC: McFarland.

Kitchin, R. (2020). Civil liberties or public health, or civil liberties and public health? Using surveillance technologies to tackle the spread of COVID-19. *Space and Polity*. Retrieved from https://www.tandfonline.com/doi/full/10.1080/13562576.2020.1770587

Kücklich, J. (2005). Precarious playbour: Modders and the digital games industry. Retrieved from http://five.fibreculturejournal.org/fcj-025-precarious-playbour-modders-and-the-digital-games-industry/

de Lange, M. (2009). From always on to always there: Locative media as Playful Technologies. In A. de Souza e Silva & D. M. Soto (Eds.), *Digital cityscapes: Merging digital and urban playspaces* (pp. 55–70). New York, NY: Peter Lang.

Lemos, A. (2010). Post—mass media functions, locative media, and informational territories: New ways of thinking about territory, place, and mobility in contemporary society. *Space and Culture, 13*(4), 403–420.

Livingstone, S. (2002). *Young people and new media: Childhood and the changing media environment*. London; Thousand Oaks, CA: Sage.

Martinelli, M., & Adams, S. (2020). Pokémon go is thriving even though everyone's at home. *Slate*. Retrieved from https://slate.com/culture/2020/04/pokemon-go-coronavirus-profiteering.html. Accessed on June 24, 2020.

McGarrigle, C. (2010). The construction of locative situations: Locative media and the situationist international, recuperation or redux?. *Digital Creativity, 21*(1), 55–62.

Niantic. (2020). New real-world adventures coming to the niantic platform. *Niantic*. Retrieved from https://nianticlabs.com/en/blog/new-real-world-adventures/

Orland, K. (2020). How to play Pokémon Go when everyone's stuck inside. *Arstechnica*. Retrieved from https://arstechnica.com/gaming/2020/03/pokemon-go-adjusts-to-the-quarantine-era/. Accessed on June 24, 2020.

Papangelis, K., Metzger, M., Sheng, Y., Liang, H. N., Chamberlain, A., & Khan, V. J. (2017). "Get off my lawn!": Starting to understand territoriality in location based mobile games. In *Proceedings of the 2017 CHI conference extended abstracts on human factors in computing systems*, Denver, CO (pp. 1955–1961).

Perry, F. (2016, July 22). Urban gamification: Can PokéMon GO transform our public spaces?. *The Guardian*. Retrieved from https://www.theguardian.com/cities/2016/jul/22/urban-gamification -Pokémon-go-transform-public-spaces

Poniewozik, J. (2020). Pokémon, Stay. *New York Times*. Retrieved from https://www.nytimes.com/2020/04/01/arts/pokemon-go-coronavirus.html. Accessed on June 24, 2020.

Rosenberg, S. (2020). Location data likely to play limited role in fighting coronavirus. *Axios*. Retrieved from https://www.axios.com/location-data-likely-to-play-limited-role-in-fighting-coronavirus-9cb140a9-3e63-4142-8879-41370dd3002e.html. Accessed on June 24, 2020.

Saker, M., & Evans, L. (2016a). Everyday life and locative play: An exploration of Foursquare and playful engagements with space and place. *Media, Culture & Society*, *38*(8), 1169–1183.

Saker, M., & Evans, L. (2016b). Locative mobile media and time: Foursquare and technological memory. *First Monday*, *21*(2).

Saker, M., & Evans, L. (2020). Personalising the urban: A critical account of locative media and the digital inscription of place. In L. Rajendran & N. Odeleye (Eds), *Mediated identities in the futures of place: Emerging practices and spatial cultures* (pp. 39–55). Cham: Springer.

Siyahhan, S., & Gee, E. (2018). *Families at play: Connecting and learning through video games*. Cambridge, MA: MIT Press.

Sobel, K., Bhattacharya, A., Hiniker, A., Lee, J. H., Kientz, J. A., & Yip, J. C. (2017). It wasn't really about the Pokémon: Parents' perspectives on a location-based mobile game. In *Proceedings of the 2017 CHI conference on human factors in computing systems*, Denver, CO (pp. 1483–1496).

de Souza e Silva, A. (2006). From cyber to hybrid: Mobile technologies as interfaces of hybrid spaces. *Space and Culture*, *9*(3), 261–278.

Stanley, J., & Granick, J. (2020). ACLU white paper: The limits of location tracking in an epidemic. Retrieved from https://www.aclu.org/report/aclu-white-paper-limits-location-tracking-epidemic?redirect=aclu-white-paper-limits-location-tracking-epidemic. Accessed on June 24, 2020.

Takahashi, D. (2020). Niantic is updating Pokémon Go and other games as coronavirus keeps us inside. *VentureBeat*. Retrieved from https://venturebeat.com/2020/03/30/niantic-is-updating-pokemon-go-and-other-games-as-coronavirus-keeps-us-inside/. Accessed on June 24, 2020.

Takeuchi, L. (2011). *Families matter: Designing media for a digital age*. New York, NY: The Joan Ganz Cooney Center at Sesame Workshop.

Tran, K. M. (2018). Families, resources, and learning around Pokémon Go. *E-learning and Digital Media*, *15*(3), 113–127.

Zelizer, V. A. (1994). *Pricing the priceless child: The changing social value of children*. Princeton, NJ: Princeton University Press.

Zuboff, S. (2019). *The age of surveillance capitalism*. New York, NY: Profile.

Index

Printed in the United States
By Bookmasters